S0-AYC-631

Galveston Community College Library

Galveston, Texas

Presented by

Dr. James O. Ross

DAVID GLENN HUNT
MEMORIAL LIBRARY
GALVESTON COLLEGE

PN   Irwin   Ft. Crockett
4121   Modern speech
.I 7

Copy 1

          Irwin   Ft. Crockett
PN   Modern speech
4121
.I 7

Copy 1
     OCT   8   6046

THE DAVID GLENN HUNT
MEMORIAL LIBRARY
GALVESTON COMMUNITY COLLEGE
GALVESTON, TEXAS

AFFECTIVE DISORDERS

DIRECTIONS IN PSYCHIATRY
MONOGRAPH SERIES

1. Diagnostics and Psychopathology, 1987

2. Psychobiology and Psychopharmacology, 1988

3. Affective Disorders, 1988

A NORTON PROFESSIONAL BOOK

DIRECTIONS IN PSYCHIATRY
MONOGRAPH SERIES

AFFECTIVE DISORDERS

NUMBER 3

EDITED BY

Frederic Flach, M.D.

W.W. Norton & Company • New York • London

616.8527
A 256

Copyright © 1988 by The Hatherleigh Co., Ltd.

Portions of this work copyright © 1981, 1982, 1983, 1984, 1985, 1986 by

The Hatherleigh Co., Ltd.

All rights reserved.

Published simultaneously in Canada by Penguin Books Canada Ltd.,
2801 John Street, Markham, Ontario L3R 1B4.

Printed in the United States of America.

First Edition

Library of Congress Cataloging-in-Publication Data

Affective disorders.

   (Directions in psychiatry monograph series ; no. 3)
    1. Affective disorders. 2. Depression, Mental.
I. Flach, Frederic F. II. Series.
RC537.A3153   1988   616.85'27   88-1310

ISBN 0-393-70055-0

W. W. Norton & Company, Inc., 500 Fifth Avenue, New York, N. Y. 10110
W. W. Norton & Company Ltd., 37 Great Russell Street, London WC1B 3NU

1 2 3 4 5 6 7 8 9 0

Editor

FREDERIC FLACH, M.D., Adjunct Associate Professor of Psychiatry, Cornell University Medical College, and Attending Psychiatrist, Payne Whitney Clinic of New York Hospital and St. Vincent's Hospital and Medical Center, New York.

Editorial Board

E. JAMES ANTHONY, M.D., F.R.C.PSY., Director of Child and Adolescent Psychotherapy, Chestnut Lodge, Rockville, MD.

ROSS J. BALDESSARINI, M.D., Professor of Psychiatry and Neuroscience, Harvard Medical School; Interim Director, Mailman Laboratories for Psychiatric Research, McLean Hospital, Belmont, MA.

JOEL ELKES, M.D., Professor of Psychiatry, University of Louisville; Distinguished Service Professor Emeritus, Johns Hopkins University, Baltimore, MD.

JOSEPH T. ENGLISH, M.D., Director of Psychiatry, St. Vincent's Hospital and Medical Center, New York; Professor of Psychiatry, New York Medical College; Adjunct Professor of Psychiatry, Cornell University Medical College, New York.

SHERVERT H. FRAZIER, M.D., Professor of Psychiatry, Harvard Medical School; Psychiatrist-in-Chief, McLean Hospital, Belmont, MA.

CARL P. MALMQUIST, M.D., Professor of Psychiatry, Institute of Child Development; Professor of Law and Professor of Criminal Justice, University of Minnesota, Minneapolis, MN.

TIMOTHY B. MORITZ, M.D., Staff Psychiatrist, Charter Hospital of Las Vegas, Las Vegas, NV.

HOWARD P. ROME, M.D., Professor of Psychiatry Emeritus, Mayo Graduate School of Medicine, Rochester, MN.

MICHAEL A. SCHWARTZ, M.D., Associate Clinical Professor of Psychiatry, New York Medical College; Chief, Psychiatric Research Training, St. Vincent's Hospital and Medical Center, New York; Adjunct Professor of Medical Anthropology, The New School for Social Research, New York.

LOUIS JOLYON WEST, M.D., Professor and Chairman, Department of Psychiatry and Biobehavioral Sciences; Director, The Neuropsychiatric Institute, University of California, Los Angeles.

PETER C. WHYBROW, M.D., Professor and Chairman, Department of Psychiatry, University of Pennsylvania, Philadelphia.

ROBERT L. WILLIAMS, M.D., D.C. and Irene Ellwood Professor and Chairman of Psychiatry, Chief of Psychiatry Service, Baylor College of Medicine, Houston.

Contributors

Thomas A. Ban, M.D.
Professor of Psychiatry, Vanderbilt University Medical Center, Nashville, Tenn.

Joseph E. Comaty, M.S.
Associate Unit Research Chief, Illinois State Psychiatric Institute, Chicago, Ill.

John M. Davis, M.D.
Director, Central Research Program, Illinois State Psychiatric Institute, Chicago, Ill.

Florence L. Denmark, Ph.D.
Thomas Hunter Professor of Psychology at Hunter College and the City University of New York.

Michael H. Ebert, M.D.
Professor and Chairman, Department of Psychiatry, Vanderbilt University Medical Center, Nashville, Tenn.

Barbara Friedman, M.A.
Fiscal Officer for Wellman Research Laboratory, Massachusetts General Hospital.

Mark S. Gold, M.D.
Director of Research, Fair Oaks Hospital, Summit, NJ and Delray Beach, Fla.

Peter Herridge, M.D.
Director, Neuropsychiatric Evaluation Services, Fair Oaks Hospital, Summit, NJ.

Frederick M. Jacobsen, M.D.
Medical Officer, Laboratory of Clinical Science, Section on Neuropharmacology and Clinical Psychobiology Branch, National Institute of Mental Health, Bethesda, Md.

Philip G. Janicak, M.D.
  Unit and Research Chief, Illinois State Psychiatric Institute, Chicago, Ill.
Robin B. Jarrett, Ph.D.
  Assistant Professor of Psychiatry, Department of Psychiatry and Mental Health Clinical Research Center, University of Texas Southwestern Medical Center, Dallas.
Ronna M. Kabatznick, Ph.D.
  Psychological consultant and journalist.
Martin B. Keller, M.D.
  Director of Outpatient Research, Department of Psychiatry; Associate Professor of Psychiatry, Massachusetts General Hospital, Boston.
Richard Krueger, M.D.
  Clinical Instructor in Psychiatry, Boston University School of Medicine, Boston, Mass.
Philip W. Lavori, Ph.D.
  Lecturer on Psychiatry (Mathematical Statistics), Harvard Medical School, and Chief of Biostatistics, Massachusetts General Hospital.
Elinor M. Levy, Ph.D.
  Associate Professor of Microbiology, Boston University School of Medicine, Boston, Mass.
Peter T. Loosen, M.D.
  Professor of Psychiatry and Medicine, and Chief, Psychiatry Service, VA Medical Center, Durham, NC.
Steven M. Mirin, M.D.
  Associate Clinical Professor of Psychiatry, Harvard Medical School; Research Psychiatrist, Alcohol and Drug Abuse Research Center, McLean Hospital, Belmont, Mass.; Medical Director, Westwood Lodge Hospital, Westwood, Mass.
Timothy H. Monk, Ph.D.
  Associate Professor of Psychiatry, University of Pittsburgh School of Medicine, PA.
Ralph A. O'Connell, M.D.
  Associate Director and Clinical Director, Department of Psychiatry, St. Vincent's Hospital and Medical Center of New York; Clinical Professor of Psychiatry, New York Medical College.
Burkhard Pflug, Prof. Dr. med.
  Head of the Department of Psychiatry, University of Frankfurt (Main), West Germany.
Norman E. Rosenthal, M.D.
  Director of Outpatient Services of the Clinical Psychobiology Branch, National Institute of Mental Health, Bethesda, Md.

Alec Roy, M.D.
Visiting Associate, National Institute on Alcohol Abuse and Alcoholism, Bethesda, Md.

A. John Rush, M.D.
Betty Jo Hay Professor of Psychiatry, Department of Psychiatry and Mental Health Clinical Research Center, University of Texas Southwestern Medical Center, Dallas.

Henry I. Spitz, M.D.
Clinical Professor of Psychiatry, Columbia University College of Physicians and Surgeons; Director, Training Programs in Marital Therapy and Group Psychotherapy, New York State Psychiatric Institute, New York.

Anthony Storr, F.R.C.P., F.R.C.Psych.
Emeritus Fellow of Green College, Oxford University, England; Honorary Consulting Psychiatrist to the Oxfordshire Health Authority.

Peter C. Whybrow, M.D.
Professor and Chairman, Department of Psychiatry, University of Pennsylvania, Philadelphia.

Burns Woodward, M.D.
Clinical Instructor in Psychiatry, Boston University School of Medicine; Assistant Medical Director, Westwood Lodge Hospital, Westwood, Mass.

Contents

Introduction

Much of my own research has focused on the topic of depression. In some ways, this was a result of coincidence. In my first year of psychiatric residency at the Payne Whitney Clinic in New York, one of the patients assigned to me was a very successful businessman in his late forties who was profoundly depressed. I was quite puzzled by his predicament. On the surface at least, he seemed to have achieved what many ambitious young people hoped to some day, if they were lucky — wealth, an attractive wife, several healthy children, respect in his community. Why, then, was he so seriously depressed?

As it happened, his episode of depression had been preceded by a brief spurt of intense mania. Thus, he fitted into the diagnostic category we then called manic-depressive illness, which is now referred to as bipolar disorder. My supervisor guided me carefully as I investigated the psychodynamics. Apparently this man had had profound conflicts with his own father, such that his own success activated a serious sense of guilt for having surpassed him. We talked of this. As a novice in psychotherapy, I found it hard to grasp why the analysis of this point did not rapidly relieve his distress. But it did not. Over the ensuing months of therapy I slowly discovered that intentionally diverting his attention from his morbid preoccupations rather than belaboring them induced some degree of improvement. I later called this tactic decentralization; it became the subject of my first scientific paper, in which I also suggested that in treating depressed patients one should not assume the traditional psychoanalytic stance of silence; rather, one should be more active, minimizing the patient's tendency to assume that a therapist's reticence implies agreement with his or her self-accusations and low esteem.

In the end, with neither antidepressants nor lithium available to us then, it was only through the administration of a series of electric convulsive treatments that we were able to induce sufficient clearing of his depressed mood to permit his discharge and return home.

Shortly thereafter, I was offered the opportunity to become director of the newly established metabolic research unit at the hospital. During the years that followed, we studied thyroid and calcium metabolism in patients with affective disorders. We discovered that 1-triiodothyronine seemed to have some kind of antidepressant property and that depressed patients excreted substantial amounts of calcium during episodes of depression, only to shift to calcium retention as they recovered, a phenomenon that could not be accounted for simply by an increase in physical activity.

This research convinced me, however, that a simple, direct physical explanation for the mood of depression was quite unlikely. In fact, I began to question whether depression itself was even an illness. Too many of my patients seemed to have perfectly good reasons to be disturbed. Some had experienced financial reverses. Some were going through divorce. Some were still reeling from the death of a child. Others had just been informed that they were suffering with physical illnesses that might prove fatal.

But if depression itself were not the illness, what might be?

I found an answer in another set of questions. It seemed that it was not so much being depressed that was the problem, but rather how one experienced depression. How much ability did one have to recover from such a mood on one's own and in a reasonable period of time (whatever reasonable might be)? In this context, depression per se could be viewed as a natural human experience occurring in response to profound change, particularly loss. It was a necessary condition, required as a catalyst to promote movement toward the next phase of a person's life.

For me, this new way of conceptualizing depression put the complex psychobiological elements of the condition into a much more workable framework. I no longer felt compelled to choose among psychological, biological, or environmental factors in considering the etiology of affective disorders. Early parental loss might set up a sensitivity to loss later on in life. A man or woman with a strong need for control might be propelled into a panic by the slightest twinge of helplessness. Either option might make it difficult for an individual to experience depression in a healthy way. The dexamethasone test and the TRH test were not really measuring sadness and melancholy as such. Antidepressant drugs and electric convulsive treatments were not attacking mood. Even genetic studies that indicated a tendency for affective disorders to run in families were not necessarily tracking biological patterns that predetermined mood. Rather, the evidence for a biological component to affective disorders might be pointing to something else, to another factor, one I have defined as psychobiological resilience.

I began to view many patients suffering with affective disorders as really subject to a lack of resilience. That is, once they had become depressed, they found it difficult if not impossible to pull themselves out of their disabling moods. Moreover, the consequences of being depressed only served to compound their already compromised state. This lack of resilience can be psychological, for example rooted in shame; then psychotherapy would be of primary importance in mobilizing recovery. Or it might be biological in nature; then resilience-enhancing drugs, otherwise known as antidepressants, might be called for. Or the patients might be enmeshed in family environments that impeded or even crushed their resilience, in which case family therapy would become an essential part of their rehabilitation. Or all three dimensions might be operative, in varying proportions.

There is a subtle, but very real, difference between viewing a patient with a mood disorder as suffering from an unwarranted depression and viewing him as experiencing what may be a valid alteration of mood, but one from which he cannot recover on his own. Again and again I have found that acknowledging a patient's right to be depressed and identifying his real problem as being his inability to bring himself out of his mood does not merely enable him to accept his condition more readily. It promotes rapport. It encourages compliance. It frequently accelerates recovery.

Of course, despite what we clinicians believe to be our best efforts, we are all faced at one time or another with the depressed patient who fails to recover. In practice most of us depend primarily on our face-to-face observations to make a diagnosis. Much of the time these are sufficient, but sometimes they are just not enough. While various psychological tests, the dexamethasone suppression test, measurements of plasma levels of antidepressants, and the like have not become routine evaluation procedures, each certainly has its place in the reevaluation of patients who are not responding in the way in which we expect them to.

For example, I recently requested a full psychological test evaluation for a young man whom I had been treating for a serious depression for nearly eight months. He was a graduate of a fine college. He had earned a Masters in Business Administration at an excellent business school. At 30, he was promoted to senior marketing executive with a growing electronics company. In spite of regular psychotherapy sessions, a trial of tricyclic antidepressant drug treatment monitored with plasma levels, and the addition of small doses of thyroid hormone and lithium to facilitate the response to these drugs, he showed little improvement.

The results of the psychological testing surprised me. Depression proved to be minimal finding, although suicidal risk was apparent. The structure of his personality was replete with hysterical and obsessive-compulsive characterological features. Even more amazing, his Intelligence Quotient was 109, making me wonder how he had been able to achieve as much as he had, or whether his psychopathology had compromised a previously much more effective level of intelligence. I had to question whether his persistent depression was in no small part signaling a message that, as his responsibilities had mounted, he had indeed begun to find himself overwhelmed by them. In the light of this information, I referred him to colleague who specializes in characterological disorders and whose approach to this patient's problems I believed to be more suitable than my own.

In this volume of the Directions in Psychiatry Monograph Series, we have tried to give appropriate balance to the numerous variables that enter into the evaluation and treatment of patients suffering with affective disorders. If the reader gains nothing more than increased alertness to the growing danger of missing the diagnosis of physical disease in patients who appear to be depressed, that alone seems worth our effort. We have sought to include some of the more innovative approaches to understanding these disorders, such as their link to immunology, their intimate relationships to circadian rhythms, and the way in which sunlight seems to alleviate dysphoric moods.

Recently, specific short-term psychotherapeutic techniques such as cognitive therapy and interpersonal therapy have received considerable attention. One study in particular suggests that either of these approaches is as effective as antidepressant medication in treating depression. I find this conclusion quite perplexing. It runs counter to my own theoretical bias and clinical experience. I have always noted a number of patients who resiliently recover from depression with brief psychotherapy alone; I have regularly contrasted them with others who, regardless of one's psychotherapeutic strategy, seem to lack sufficient biological resilience and, sooner rather than later, require drug therapy.

I believe that Anthony Storr's review of the principles of psychotherapy in depression helps put some of this controversy into perspective. It is one of the finest discussions of the subject I have read anywhere. Not only did I find it extremely informative in spite of my own years of experience, but I actually felt a lifting in my own spirits for having read what he had to say and the clarity with which it was expressed.

—Frederic Flach, M.D.

AFFECTIVE DISORDERS

1

Adaptive Styles in the Etiology of Depression
Peter C. Whybrow

EDITOR'S NOTE

Understanding the origins of any patient's experience of depression and selecting therapeutic strategies to deal appropriately with the various ways in which his need to cope with change and loss has evolved over years are essential elements in successful clinical management. Here, the author reviews the salient aspects of attachment and separation from a developmental perspective, stressing the importance of a childhood environment that permits the individual to gradually learn how to tolerate separation, eventually supplement with others the exclusive caring originally provided by parents, and provide one's own needed supports as an adult. The nature of the bonds formed and subsequently modified during childhood is a substructure that supports self-esteem and autonomy in adult life. Self-reliance is not isolation, but rather depends on being able to rely trustingly on others, to know on whom to rely and when, and to permit oneself to be relied upon.

Three common maladaptive personality styles that stem from a failure to master the attachment-separation experience early in life are described: dependence on a dominant person, excessive control, and pseudoindependence. Each in its own way is an attempt to avoid the pain of loss or rejection and, although initially it can represent a successful form of coping, eventually it creates a special vulnerability to depression. In psychotherapy, due attention must be paid to dealing with these unhealthy adjustment patterns.

Introduction

Psychological mechanisms play a significant role in both the genesis and resolution of depression. Although psychodynamic factors are more apparent in so-called reactive depressions — those in which events of a specific and identifiable nature appear related to the onset of the episode of dysphoric mood—they cannot be ignored even in the treatment of patients whose symptoms are primarily of the melancholic type and in whom clear-cut precipitating causes may not be obvious. Whether the goals of psychotherapy are limited and supportive or intensive and aimed at fundamental characterological changes, the psychological management of the depressed patient requires a careful understanding of maladaptive behavior patterns which have set the stage for the patient's illness and may retard recovery.

It is generally accepted that a significant loss, frequently highly personalized, is commonly a cause for depression, particularly when such a trauma involves a diminution in self-esteem. However, the manner in which a particular patient has tended to cope with various losses over the years—his mode of adaptation—can take a number of different forms, each of which calls for an appropriate therapeutic strategy. To understand these styles, it seems logical to review, briefly, the close relationship between the quality of human attachments on the one hand and vulnerability to depression and loss of self-esteem on the other.

Normal Adaptation and the Development of Autonomy

All living creatures maintain a relative autonomy from their environment. This is implemented by adaptation. In this regard human beings do not differ from other organisms except that they are more complex.

Adaptation is essentially the appropriate response of the organism to an environmental challenge, whether it be an invading microorganism or a perceived psychic assault. When the individual can adapt with some degree of success, this phenomenon is called *coping.* From the perspective of practical psychobiology, we may view human depression as a temporary failure to adapt successfully—a state in which the individual is transiently overwhelmed by diverse challenge. This is not necessarily pathological. In fact, the disruptions and learned adaptations to various challenges early in life make later coping possible. Exposure to infectious agents builds immunity. The complex dendritic structure of the cerebellum grows more complex under the challenge of learning how to walk. Innate ability is no less important than the quality of environmental events in this process of growth. However, acquisition of coping ability is facilitated by consistency in environmental challenge. Thus an environment that is capricious, punitive, unpredictable, overprotective, or inadequate in its challenge will usually result in restricted styles of personality coping.

For the growing child, as for the adult, change is an everyday occurrence. One of the central issues in childhood involves the experience of separation and loss. As the child learns how to successfully master these, autonomy and an objective regard of self are also built. Feelings of helplessness and even hopelessness are integral parts of this development. Engel has called these "signal functions" — warnings to permit the anticipation of special traumas that have been experienced previously and now threaten to overwhelm the individual unless successful adaptation is achieved.

The Role of Attachment and Separation

The significance of attachments in the formation of self-esteem and autonomy is not unique to human beings. In primates, for example, the reaction to separation is clearly defined. Close attachment between parent and offspring and, later, between peers is the developmental mode in primates. Once such attachment is formed, disruption causes a stage of protest and, subsequently, withdrawal involving both a psychological detachment and a somatic withdrawal.

A similar syndrome in response to separation from the caring parent has been the object of considerable study in human infants. Attention was first specifically drawn to this phenomenon by Spitz, who focused largely on the withdrawal phase and termed it *anaclitic depression*. Later Bowlby's studies and those of others made it apparent that the reaction to separation follows a typical pattern, best understood in sequence and essentially as follows.

During the first year of life, the child begins to form specific attachment to the person who provides most of his or her care, as well as to the environment in which that care takes place. Most importantly, through the central nervous system an awareness develops of the special association between subjective comfort and events that occur. Thus, in a strange environment and particularly in the presence of a stranger, the infant at first protests, then becomes tense and cries out. If the preferred person does not return, the protest continues, but after a while it merges into what appears to be a despairing detachment. Engel called this *conservation-withdrawal*, citing the example of the infant Monica who had been fed through a gastric fistula with minimal nurturing because of her mother's depression. When her protest was exhausted, a phase of conservation-withdrawal became dominant — a passive, sleeplike state associated with virtually no motor activity and cessation of gastric secretion.

Such withdrawal appears to be an adaptive response to a depriving environment. It is an experience that is, to some degree, unavoidable in the life of any infant or child. In fact if not too severe, traumatic or prolonged, it is invaluable as a developmental challenge. As the child grows, the biological state becomes associated with subjective feelings of helplessness, to which feelings of hopelessness may be added later as the person consciously recognizes the inadequacy of his capacity to respond. This basic psychosomatic process stands in sharp contrast to the active-engaging posture that the growing infant adopts when secure in an environment perceived as nurturing.

In humans, the basic psychobiological process of attachment and separation is significantly modified by abstract conceptual thought. Our ability to adapt to and modify our environment in our own interest is a function of a particularly complex and vigilant nervous system that integrates and modulates every detail of our response. As we grow we learn to tolerate separation and to supplement with others the exclusive caring originally provided by parents. Eventually, we provide our own needed supports and set standards that are both internal and specific to ourselves.

Self-esteem and Competence

Self-esteem is a healthy respect for one's abilities and appreciation of one's limitations. Its regulation is perhaps one of the most complicated mechanisms in human psychology. There is no single road to a sense of mastery. Throughout life, we strive for autonomy and discover, in the process, ingenious ways to cope. Based on past experiences, we form ideals against which to measure achievement, and self-esteem becomes, in large part, a function of the extent to which a person believes he can and does live up to the goals he has set for himself. From a developmental point of view, it is critical to remember that the substructure that supports self-esteem, ego ideals and autonomy in adult life derives from the nature of the bonds that were developed and subsequently modified during the individual's childhood in relationships with members of his primary family.

As Bowlby (1983) has pointed out:

When an individual is confident that an attachment figure will be available to him when he deserves it, that person will be much less prone to either intense or chronic fear than will be an individual who for any reason has no such confidence.

Confidence in the accessibility and responsiveness to attachment figures, or lack of it, is built up slowly during all the years of immaturity; and once developed, these expectations tend to persist relatively unchanged throughout life.

Self-reliance is not, therefore, the cultural stereotype of needing no one. Rather it is the ability to rely trustingly on others, to know on whom to rely and when, and to permit oneself to be relied upon.

Grief

Over a period of years, one's sense of self and of reality evolves, as one builds an analogue of the perceived world and then embellishes it. This becomes a private template for adaptation and the maintenance of autonomy, serving to help us cope with the changes and losses that life inevitably provides, such as leaving home, illness, romantic and sexual attachment and loss, marriage, divorce, children and the death of those close to us. When we falter at times in these adaptations, it is natural to reexperience to some degree the helplessness and hopelessness that we experienced as children faced with situations that seemed to be more than we could cope with at the time. Such subjective feelings are reported as depression. The healthy person recognizes them, understands them, struggles with them and eventually recovers by means of his own adaptive modes.

Many of these features are seen in the normal experience of grief—the reaction that follows the death or loss of someone with whom one has enjoyed a close emotional bond. The stages in the process of grief resemble those seen in depression. The initial reaction is disbelief or protest. Somatic distress and a preoccupation with the image of the dead person go hand in hand. Subsequently there may be a transient loss of the usual patterns in which we conduct our lives, with some withdrawal and guilty speculation on what contribution we have made to the person's death or unhappiness during his or her lifetime. However, while these disturbances seem indistinguishable from depressive illness at times, most people accept the experience in themselves or in their friends and relatives as quite normal, providing the person recovers from the impact in a reasonable period of time and does not enter a serious psychiatric disorder.

Maladaptive Personality Styles and Depression

Vulnerability to depressive illness seems to be increased in persons who, for whatever reason, have never satisfactorily resolved the psychobiological issues surrounding attachment and separation. Such persons remain extremely sensitive to loss—or perceived loss—whether of people, animals, their own career goals, philosophical aspirations, friendships, material things. Frequently, in defending against this contingency and its associated feelings of helplessness and hopelessness, such persons have acquired adaptive styles that are meant to aid them in coping but are, in fact, often setting them up to exchange a more normal period of grief for a serious episode of illness.

The common denominator among these styles is rigidity. Some of the mechanisms — or rescue operations — may work quite well for years, but at some point, often in middle age, a special combination of events may disrupt the precarious equilibrium and with it, their self-esteem.

I have found it useful to cluster such adaptive types into three major, though somewhat overlapping, categories:

(1) *Dependence on a dominant person:* Here, the basic rescue strategy has been to transfer the unresolved issues surrounding attachment and separation from the parenting figures to others in the subject's life who appear competent and capable. Thus no true self-reliance develops during the maturing years and the person enters adult life with a constricted series of adaptive options.

Such persons find it difficult to enter the usual commerce of adult life, since their own self-esteem is tied too closely to the opinions of those around them. This does not mean that adaptation is impossible; in fact, it is sometimes quite successful for a long time. The key to their adequate psychosocial function, however, is dependence on some dominant figure who maintains a caretaker's role.

Traditionally, this form of working adaptation has been seen more commonly among women in our culture, possibly in part because it has been considered acceptable, perhaps even desirable, for women to be dependent on a dominant male figure. Often such women married early, moved away from the primary family, and spent considerable energy in the new relationship trying to please the person on whom they now depend for their self-worth. If the husband reciprocates with kindness and support, this kind of balance could continue for years, and was usually threatened when their role as mother diminished as their children grew up and left home. More recently, however, it has been recognized that men can just as readily form such dependent attachments on women, leaving their primary homes without adequate autonomy and looking to their lovers or wives for parental support.

Such an adaptation frequently serves well until the primary bond with the dominant figure is disrupted by desertion, cruelty, infidelity, death or some other intercurrent event. Unfortunately, such persons frequently form a liaison with those who are themselves struggling to ward off the pain of attachment-separation problems by means of pseudoindependence, a style described later on, and who themselves have a need for support but have, by one means or another, been able to rely exclusively on their own abilities early in their adult lives. Frequently, in such a marriage, as the man becomes increasingly engaged in a professional role he is no longer able or willing to nurture his dependent wife; as a woman devotes more of her time to children or her own pursuits, her dependent husband feels abandoned.

Under such circumstances, the adaptive style starts to crack. The dedication and investment in the affairs of the family or the other bring diminishing rewards. With one partner or the other becoming increasingly remote, the vulnerable person feels a sense of growing helplessness and hopelessness that is identified as depression and that may well progress to severe illness. Anger erupts—something that has been there for a long time and is basically driven by a person's sense of never having been truly provided for or cared about, either in the primary family or within the present relationship. Withdrawal and serious depression may ensue.

(2) *Excessive control:* When there is an inconsistency in the available caring figures during the maturational years, a potential adaptation in adolescence and early adult life is to reduce to a minimum the number of situations in which the difficult task of resolving separation anxiety is likely to occur. The need to control the day-to-day details of life becomes a primary mechanism of adaptation. Basic to this strategy is the restriction of novelty and the unexpected. Planning assumes great importance. Surprises are often greeted with a hostile response. In such a character structure there is little spontaneity; instead, meticulousness and reliability are developed to an extreme. Because these obsessive styles are highly marketable and well rewarded, such people do fairly well early in life.

This adaptation is usually seen as a psychological rescue attempt in an individual who has had little opportunity to develop a fundamental trust in others. It serves to compensate for an inadequate resolution of the attachment-separation paradigm. When the adaptive style is threatened by an increased number of events that the person can no longer keep under control, the underlying lack of trust rapidly appears. Overt suspiciousness and even paranoia may emerge, covering up the intense sense of helplessness that such persons usually feel. This, in turn, only isolates them even further from human contact.

Even when the strategy of control is working, such persons find difficulty in delegating authority to others. It is not uncommon for the very work habits that permit them to rise through organizational ranks or in professions to become serious handicaps when positions of real authority and leadership are reached. Gradually they fail as they become unable to control the steadily increasing number of variables with which they have to deal. Aging, illness, and other life problems that reduce the ability to remain in control shake the foundation of this defense against the pain of loss, leading to depression.

(3) *Pseudoindependence:* This method of adaptation is closely allied with that of maintaining excessive control. Again the individual avoids close contact with others and thereby reduces the opportunities for loss. To all

outward appearance, such persons appear independent, competent, with high aspirations for themselves and others. They may believe in a well-structured philosophy based on social or religious beliefs. They may enjoy serving others and usually do it well. Hence they are often valuable members of their communities.

However, they often have broken away from their primary family early in life, setting up, by effort and hard work, an independent life of their own. Instinctively, they make others dependent on them, perhaps thereby gaining vicarious gratification, clearly feeling safer under such circumstances.

On the other hand, not far beneath the surface and usually within their awareness, they often yearn for a close relationship with a caring person—someone who fits the very ego ideal for which they themselves reach. Not infrequently, such persons marry each other and create a life together characterized by remoteness on an emotional level. Here again, illness, aging, the departure of those who have been dependent on them—such as children growing up and leaving—represent special threats to their ability to cope. Because they are fearful of being dependent, they often resist seeking professional help until there is no choice left, and consulting a psychiatrist can represent an occasion of intense fear, even panic. In therapy, they are frequently resistant to complying with antidepressant medication if recommended, feeling further compromised in their effort to maintain independence.

Adaptive Styles and Therapy

The particular styles that the patient has assumed during his lifetime to deal with disturbed attachment-separation issues and protect against the impact of depression will reflect themselves in the relationship that is formed with the psychiatrist and in the attitude the patient has in approaching treatment. The practicing physician must carefully note the emergence of such factors as early as possible in his contact with the patient. Sometimes, as in the case of the individual who has sought the protection of depending on a dominant other, finding an understanding and empathetic therapist serves to restore a sense of security and worth, catalyzing recovery. There is, in such instances, a risk that the patient will become too dependent on the therapist and unable to maintain improvement when the end of the therapeutic relationship is in sight. It is the doctor's task to give the patient the support needed early on, but simultaneously to cultivate a greater degree of self-reliance as therapy progresses.

The distrustful, severely controlled patient can be particularly problematic. He is often reluctant to open up and communicate spontaneously with the psychiatrist for fear of losing further control. Compliance with medication regimens is commonly difficult to obtain. There will be times in the course of sessions when the psychiatrist's patience may be tried by what he may perceive to be a power struggle between the patient and himself but what actually represents the patient's attempt to regain control over every aspect of his own life. Symptomatic relief, with antidepressants, often permits the patient to function more efficiently again and thus alleviates the distress and heightened need for control that derives from the strong sense of helplessness. However, since the goals that such patients set for themselves are usually unattainable, one of the major tasks in treatment is to help them accept the impossibility of their obsessive style and learn how to feel comfortable with uncertainty, ambiguity, and risk and how to gradually place greater trust in others worthy of it.

For patients whose style has been one of pseudoindependence, one of the main challenges in treatment is to help them accept whatever limitations life has forced on them and to learn how to permit themselves to rely on others.

Issues around attachment and separation, loss and its resolution, are obviously not the only way in which depression emerges. Many other factors, both social and biological, conspire with intrapsychic mechanisms to precipitate the final common path to dysfunction. Such dysfunction itself, however, can represent for the depressed patient a unique pathway to growth and a singular opportunity to learn new and better adaptive styles. Once the immediate, disorganizing elements in depression have been relieved, the patient has an excellent opportunity to work with therapist to rethink some of the rescue mechanisms that he has developed automatically in earlier years. While many of these may have served him well, aspects of them have clearly done him disservice, and this is the time to acquire additional ones, particularly the flexibility that will allow him to cope more effectively with challenge in his present and future life.

Selected Reading

Bowlby J: *Attachment* (2nd ed.) Basic Books, New York, 1983.

Schmale A, Engel G: The role of conservation-withdrawal in depressive reactions. Jones A, Benedek T (eds): In, *Depression and Human Existence*, Little, Brown, Boston, 1975.

Spitz R, Wolf K: Anaclitic depression *Psychoanalytic Study of the Child*, Vol II, International Universities Press, New York, 1946, pp. 313–342.

2

Women and Suicide
Florence L. Denmark and Ronna M. Kabatznick

EDITOR'S NOTE

Studies into the epidemiology of suicide clearly indicate significant differences between men and women in this society with regard to attempted and completed suicide. Women make more attempts, and these are, by and large, usually by less violent means. Men, on the other hand, more often succeed and are far more likely to employ guns or other violent methods.

The authors explore some of these differences, stressing, from their point of view, the part which developmental influences and male-female stereotypes play in their creation. For example, if women are unduly conditioned to feel helpless, the use of suicidal gestures to express that mood or to influence their environment may result. Since, traditionally, home and interpersonal relationships have meant more to women, whereas career and financial success have meant more to men, disruption in the former seems more significant as a trigger for loss and suicidal attempts in women. However, it would appear that a change in marital status, from married to divorced or widowed, has more devastating effects on men when one reviews suicide statistics.

As the roles for men and women change in society, both motive and method of suicide in women may change as well.

Introduction

Emile Durkheim, in his classic treatise *Suicide*,[1] advanced the notion that social factors influence the incidence and prevalence of suicide. Earlier studies had concentrated on biological and cosmic factors, but Durkheim was the first to correlate certain social phenomena (e.g., family structure,

10

political and economic groups, and religious affiliation) with suicide rates. He suggested that there would be a relationship between the number of suicides in a given community and the degree to which individuals were integrated into its social structure. If one wanted to understand and ameliorate the conditions that determined suicide rates, one would have to conduct a thorough examination of the characteristics of the social structure. On the issue of women, he insightfully believed that greater freedom and economic equality would eventually reduce their suicide rates.

The purpose of this chapter is to examine the relationship between female suicide behaviors and some of the social forces Durkheim deemed so influential.

Environmental Influences and Female Development

Women commit suicide one-third as many times as men but attempt it three times more often.[2-4] The question is whether there is anything inherent to the collective developmental and socialization experiences of women that contributes to this pattern.

Researchers have documented the particular responses boys and girls learn because of their gender.[5] For example, at birth, female babies are wrapped in pink blankets and male babies in blue, although this practice has changed somewhat during recent years. Style of clothing is similarly affected, with the unchallenged assumption that the boy requires clothing that is sturdier than the feminine frock. In fact, stereotyped behavior expectancies for sons often begin prenatally, to the extent that the sex of the active fetus will often be inferred as male and a more quiescent fetus as female.[6] Mothers usually touch and talk more to their female babies and concomitantly are more tolerant of periods in which they are separated from their male babies. The fact that nursery schools receive far more applications for boys than girls[7] may suggest that mothers are more willing to separate from sons than from daughters or that they are less able or willing to tolerate the expectedly high level of physical activity boys seem to manifest.

Patterns of emotional dependency and passivity for the female child are established and reinforced throughout the school years. Chesler[8] reported that aggressive, highly competitive, and destructive boys are more likely to be referred to guidance counselors, while girls are referred for personality problems, such as shyness, feelings of inferiority, and extreme fears. Other evidence suggests that both children and adults who deviate from traditional sex-role norms (that is, behave in ways associated with those of the opposite sex) are labeled emotionally ill more often than those who behave in expected ways.[9,10] Thus, the socialization process offers a series of specific rewards and punishments to girls and boys for conforming or deviating from sex-role norms.

Denmark[5] described the usual female socialization process as one that negated the concept of mastery and self-confidence. Since women are typically discouraged from developing a sense of competence over things and events generally considered to be socially desirable, female self-esteem would presumably be less than that of males. While male exploratory and aggressive behaviors are supported and reinforced, acting passively and obediently may reap similar rewards for a female. Even in play, boys are encouraged to engage in competitive and active games and sports, while girls are often oriented towards dolls and other sedentary domestic activities.

Deaux and Emswiller[11] reported that women and men make different attributions to their experiences of success and failure. When a women succeeds at a task, she is more likely than a man to attribute the success to luck or to an arbitrary, random event. Men, on the other hand, are more likely to attribute their success to internal attributes, such as perseverance and skill. Failure for women is internalized or taken as a personal defeat, whereas failure for men is typically externalized or interpreted as the result of an unlucky or unfair situation.

Even linguistically, women tend to use passive speech that may be the verbal outcome of the internalization of powerlessness. Tag questions (It's a nice day, isn't it? The movie was great, don't you think?) and unassertive statements (Dinner's at six) characterize female rather than male conversational patterns.[12] Thus, women often seem to depend on the responses of others for the verification of their experience of satisfaction and competence.

Given the fact that women and men receive such different developmental treatment, is it not reasonable to assume that they would choose different methods for the suicide act?

Special Features of Suicide in Women

Women use less dangerous methods for suicide and thus have a better chance of surviving the experience. Violent methods—such as hanging, firearms, explosives, and cutting instruments—are more often used by men than by women. Poisoning, wrist slashing, and drug overdose are characteristic of methods most often used by women. However, sex differences emerge even when the same method is used. Lester[13] reported that more men shoot themselves in the head while more women shoot themselves in the body. Several explanations may be offered to account for these differences.

First, it appears that methods of suicide also depend, in part, on their availability and acceptance in the culture. In Great Britain, for instance, where possession of firearms without a permit is illegal, suicides with guns are uncommon. In contrast, suicides by shooting are frequent in the United States because these restrictions are either nonexistent or ignored. Since the possession and use of firearms are generally less sanctioned for women, it follows that women rarely use them to carry out the suicide act. Similarly, the promulgation of violence in our society has been promoted as an exclusively male privilege.

Second, physical attractiveness usually has more significance for women than for men. Most societies seem to give more explicit consideration to the physical beauty of the woman. Male attractiveness is usually dependent more on skill and physical strength than on physical appearance alone. In general, physically attractive people are found to be more popular; however, physically attractive women are reported to be happier and better adjusted and have more positive self-concepts than unattractive women.[14] Given the enormous emphasis we place on physical attributes of women, it is conceivable that women would be more likely to be concerned about how they will look when they are dead. In fact, women fear what might happen to their bodies after their death significantly more often than men do.[15] Women may therefore prefer methods of suicide that preserve the norm of physical attractiveness — even in death.

Third, it appears that women may select methods for suicide that are less lethal because they are uncertain whether they really want to die. Less violent and immediate means give the attempter time to go to an emergency room or to be rescued. Moreover, Lester[16] found that more men than women die from suicide with *each* method. For example, Lester[13] reported that fewer women than men actually die when jumping to their death.

The fact that women use less lethal means and attempt suicide considerably more often than they succeed can lead some to the erroneous conclusion that their gestures need not be taken seriously. However, it is the belief of most experts[17] that suicide attempters should be treated quite seriously. If someone — male or female — has tried to commit suicide once and fails, the chances are that such a person will try again and may well succeed the next time.

Research evidence suggests that completed suicides are perceived to be more "masculine" than attempted suicides. In addition, when the same subjects were asked to predict which types of people are most likely to kill themselves, females with traditionally feminine characteristics, such as passivity and emotionalism, were judged three times less likely to do so than males with traditionally masculine characteristics such as aggressiveness and self-containment.[18] In other words, men may be driven to succeed in their suicide attempts in order to prove their masculinity. Women, on the other hand, may feel less social stigma attached to attempting suicide without intending to succeed because they are less afraid to be perceived as feminine and are more accustomed to the concept of failure.

Manipulative Intent

One of the most common stereotypes regarding women's behavior is that they characteristically manipulate others as a means of gaining attention and power. In fact, one of the few ways women have been able to exert influence has been through indirect means.[19] Many women who try to use the more direct and forceful techniques indicative of those with status report suffering negative consequences. Stengel[20] proposed that women were more inclined to use suicidal behavior as a means of manipulating others because other means of exerting pressure were often not open to them.

Chesler[8] has also attributed the high proportion of attempted suicides among women to their powerlessness to change their environment, stating that, "like female tears, female suicide attempts constitute an act of resignation and helplessness to obtain secondary reward or temporary relief."

However, no sex differences were found in studies assessing motives in suicide notes.[21] Similarly, no differences were found in the degree to which women and men communicate their suicidal intent before their death. Therefore, the manipulative-intent hypothesis seems to be an overstated and unsupported one.

The Romanticization and Eroticization of Death

Our culture is saturated with images suggesting that suicide is a heroic and often romantic form of death. On the issue of women, McClelland[22] noted that death and sexuality often bear a particular association with each other and referred to this as the Harlequin complex because of the figure who was both lover and death. (Popular love stories actually use the Harlequin name as part of a series title.) Suicide for some women may be fantasized as a lover with the power of seduction and rescue. The concept embodies the traditional elements of the socialization process extolling the notion that events will magically occur and that the woman will "live happily ever after." Women brought up to believe that situations will magically work out often minimize their own ability to influence or control the outcomes of circumstances. Rather, they may unrealistically rely on some external force; if that fails, suicide may become a viable alternative.

The Changing Roles of Women and Men

Sex-role norms are in a flux. More women and men are entering nontraditional occupations. Marriage is no longer considered the safe enclave it once was. Nevertheless, recent studies suggest that motives for the suicidal actions of women tend to be interpersonal,[23,24] whereas motives for men tend to be intrapsychic and precipitated by such experiences as job loss or financial problems.[25] Whenever the most meaningful and socially significant aspect of a person's life is in danger or destroyed, suicide is likely to be considered.

As roles change, so may suicidal rates — and motives — for women. Some interesting trends have emerged as women have entered the professional community. Schaar[26] reported that women in psychology have a suicide rate about three times that of women in general. Similarly, the suicide rate of female doctors is three to five times higher than that expected for women over the age of 25, but this rate does not differ from that of male physicians. Female physicians, however, commit suicide at a younger age. Almost half of these suicides occur before the age of 40, and single women in residency programs are the most vulnerable group.[27]

Suicide and Marriage

Suicide rates vary with marital status, with the lowest rates occurring among the married, intermediate rates among the widowed and single, and the highest rate among the divorced.[2] While men have a higher rate of suicide than women in all these categories, the disparity for men across marital categories is much greater than for women.[28] For instance, for the ages of 25 to 64, single women are 47% more likely to commit suicide than married women, whereas single men are 97% more likely to commit suicide than married men. Likewise, the disparity for widowed and divorced persons compared with married persons is much greater for women. It seems that the change in marital status from married to divorced or widowed has a more devastating effect on men.

It is difficult to discern the meaning and extent of suicide statistics because they account only for those reported. They do not, for obvious reasons and difficulties, include indirectly suicidal deaths such as ones that result from alcoholism, drug abuse, reckless driving, or lack of attention to medical directives. Similarly, labeling a person's death as suicidal often entails considerations that are independent of the actual cause. Such factors as race, social class, and area of residence influence the classification process. In addition, the sex of the suicide completer may sometimes be a factor in a family's decision to label, discuss, or communicate the cause of death.

Suicide, Menstruation, Pregnancy, and Abortion

Several reviews,[21,29,30] on the relationship between suicidal behavior and menstruation have indicated that attempted suicide seems to occur at the highest rate during the premenstrual and menstrual phases. No association has been found between completed suicide and the menstrual cycle.

Suicide among pregnant women is rare. Rosenberg and Silver[31] estimated that the completed suicide rate of pregnant women was approximately one-sixth of that in the nonpregnant women. Other research[32] found that attempted suicide was more common than completed suicide among pregnant women. They estimated that during the first two trimesters it was about as common for a pregnant woman to attempt suicide as it was for women in general. For most the pregnancy was incidental to the attempt, which was related to the same kinds of emotional instabilities and problems that characterized the attempts of the nonpregnant women.

Reliable statistics on the relationship between suicide and abortion are confounded by the fact that women have sometimes had to threaten suicide in order to obtain medical and psychiatric permission for the procedure. Kenyon[33] concluded that the majority of reports find suicidal behavior to be more frequent in women requesting abortion than in general psychiatric referrals. The study, however, was conducted when abortion laws throughout the nation were particularly strict.

Conclusion

Suicide ranks as the ninth leading cause of death in the United States. Certified suicides constitute a rate of 11 deaths per 100,000. About 22,000 suicides are reported annually, but as noted above this figure represents only the lethal end of attempted suicide.

Durkheim[1] prophetically believed that as the social forces impinging on individuals changed, so would suicide rates. Hopefully, scientists will come closer to identifying forces which influence this form of death for women and for men. Durkheim's vision of greater freedom and economic equality will in part be achieved when completed and attempted suicide rates for women show a significant decline. This will happen as we alter the female socialization process in the direction which leads towards true independence and responsibility.

References

1. Durkheim E: *Suicide*, Free Press, New York, 1951.

2. Resnick HLP: Suicide. In Kaplan HI, Freedman AM, Sadock BJ (eds): *Comprehensive Textbook of Psychiatry*, Vol. II, Williams & Wilkins, Baltimore, 1980, pp. 2085-2098.

3. Paykel ES: Life stress, depression, and attempted suicide. *J. Hum. Stress* 1:3-12, 1976.

4. Weissman M: The epidemiology of suicide attempts, 1960-1971. *Arch. Gen. Psychiatry* 30:737-746, 1974.

5. Denmark F: Growing up male. In Zuckerman E (ed): *Women and Men: Roles, Attitudes and Power Relationships*. Radcliffe Club, New York, 1975.

6. Lewis M: Culture and gender roles: There's no unisex in the nursery. *Psychology Today*, May, 1972, pp. 54-57.

7. Sherman J: *On the Psychology of Women*, Charles C Thomas, Springfield, IL, 1971.

8. Chesler P: *Woman and Madness*, Doubleday, Garden City, NY, 1972.

9. Kelly K, Kiersky S: Psychotherapists and sexual stereotypes: A study of bias in diagnostic interviews employing videotape simulations. Unpublished research, Graduate School and University Center, City University of New York, 1978.

10. Broverman IK, Broverman DM, Clarkson FE, Rosencrantz P, Vogel SR: Sex-role stereotypes and clinical judgments of mental health. *J. Consult. Clin. Psychol.* 34:1-7, 1970.

11. Deaux K, Emswiller T: Explanation of successful performance on sexlinked tasks: What is skill for the male is luck for the female. *J. Pers. Soc. Psychol.* 29:80-85, 1974.

12. Adams K, Ware N: Sexism and the English language: The linguistic implications of being a woman. In Freeman J (ed): *Women: A Feminist Perspective*, Mayfield, Palo Alto, CA, 1979.

13. Lester D: Sex difference in suicidal behavior. In Gomberg ES, Franks V (eds): *Gender and Disordered Behavior*, Brunner/Mazel, New York, 1979.

14. Berscheid E, Walster EH: Physical attractiveness. In Berkowitz L (ed): *Advances in Experimental Social Psychology*, Vol. 7, Academic Press, New York, 1974.

15. Diggory J, Rothman D: Values destroyed by death. *J. Abnorm. Soc. Psychol.* 63:205-210, 1961.

16. Lester D: *Why People Kill Themselves*, Charles C Thomas, Springfield, IL, 1972.

17. Farberow N, Shneidman E: *The Cry for Help*, McGraw-Hill, New York, 1961.

18. Linehan M: Suicide and attempted suicide. *Percept. Mot. Skills* 37:31-34, 1973.

19. Johnson P: Social power and sex roles stereotypes. Paper presented at the meeting of the Western Psychological Association, San Francisco, May, 1974.

20. Stengel E: *Suicide and Attempted Suicide*, Penguin, Baltimore, 1964.

21. Lester D: Suicidal behavior in men and women. *Mental Hygiene* 53:340–345, 1969.

22. McClelland D: The Harlequin complex. In White R (ed): *The Study of Lives*, Atherton, New York, 1963, pp. 94–119.

23. Beck A, Lester D, Kovacs H: Attempted suicide by males and females. *Psychol. Rep.* 33:965–966, 1973.

24. Farberow N: Self-destruction and identity. *Humanitas* 6:45–68, 1970.

25. Lester D: Suicide, sex and mental disorder. *Psychol. Rep.* 27:61–62, 1970.

26. Schaar K: Suicide rate high among women psychologists. *A.P.A. Monitor* 5(1), 1974.

27. Roeske NCA: Women in psychiatry: A review. *Am. J. Psychiatry* 133:365–372, 1976.

28. Gove W: The relationship between sex roles, marital status and mental illness. *Social Forces* 51:34–44, 1972.

29. Wetzl R, McClure J: Suicide and the menstrual cycle. *Compr. Psychiatry* 13:369–374, 1972.

30. Parlee M: The premenstrual syndrome. *Psychol. Bull.* 80:454–465, 1973.

31. Rosenberg A, Silver E: Suicide, psychiatrists and therapeutic abortion. *Calif. Med.* 102:407–411, 1965.

32. Whittack F, Edwards J: Pregnancy and attempted suicide during pregnancy. *Compr. Psychiatry* 9:1–21, 1968.

33. Kenyon F: Termination of pregnancy on psychiatric ground. *Br. J. Med. Psychol.* 42:243–254, 1969.

3

Early Parental Loss and Depression
Alec Roy

EDITOR'S NOTE

In practice, most of us have long assumed that a definitive relationship exists between the early loss of a parent and the occurrence of depression in later life. That such an event is seriously stressful and meaningful is beyond dispute. However, as psychopathological and psychodynamic studies have evolved, many of our premises have come under scrutiny, with some being seriously questioned altogether and others being more carefully refined.

In this chapter the author explores existing studies of the role of early parental loss in psychiatric illness. The findings are controversial. It would seem that the reason for the loss — whether due to death, family disruption, or some environmental factor, such as wartime evacuation — assumes a critical dimension. Separation against the background of family instability appears much more traumatic than when it results from death. Some investigators have even concluded that early death of the mother may not significantly influence predisposition to mental illness or sensitize an individual to later stress. However, in one study, it was observed that psychotic-like depressive symptoms seemed more common when early loss was due to death, whereas neurotic depressive symptoms were more common when it resulted from separation.

There is a high incidence of early parental separation among patients who have attempted suicide; but here again this seems to occur against the background of poor family life prior to the loss.

On the whole, while early parental separation does appear more often in the histories of depressed patients than others, it is well to remember that it does not seem to be a factor in the vast majority of depressed individuals. Most importantly, intervention at the right time can make a great difference. In one study, for example, 75% of early-separated women with poor preseparation relationships and poor substitute care had psychiatric symptoms compared with only 27% of early-separated women with poor preseparation relationships but adequate substitute care.

In this culture, in which divorce and marital disruption seem to be increasingly widespread, the importance of providing counseling and support systems to children affected by such events is self-evident.

Introduction

It has long been thought that early parental loss may be a risk factor for developing depression as an adult. The papers of Karl Abraham and Freud's paper "Mourning and Melancholia" have been particularly influential. It thus comes as a surprise to read Brown and Harris' book *Social Origins of Depression*,[1] in which they report their own study and review the literature and conclude that "while in [the community studied] there is a large association between loss of mother and later depression, there is not much in the literature to support such a clear-cut result. Indeed the literature on loss of a parent and depression is one of the great puzzles in psychiatry." Further, they mention "the curious failure to establish that early loss of parents plays any role in the aetiology of depression." In the decade since the publication of Brown and Harris' book, there have been a number of studies that have contributed to this subject and that will be reviewed here.

Community Studies

Brown et al.[2] reported their own large community study of women, carried out in south London. A random sample of 458 women were interviewed in their homes by trained interviewers. Loss of mother before 11 years of age was found to be significantly associated with depression in these women. Brown et al. write: "The fact that 43% of the 40 women in Camberwell with a loss of a mother before 11 were considered to be psychiatric cases (almost all depressed), compared with 14% of the remaining 418 women, is impressive evidence of an aetiological effect." Some psychiatrists, however, were skeptical about whether the depressive disorders identified by Brown's group in the community were comparable with the depressive disorders seen in psychiatric patients in clinics and hospitals.

Two psychiatrists, Tennant and Bebbington, and their coworkers in Professor John Wing's social psychiatry unit later carried out their own community study, also in south London. Their team interviewed 800 subjects in their homes and also a group of psychiatric hospital patients. They found that early parental loss because of death was not associated with depression. When they examined early parental loss because of separation, they found it to be associated with depression in the hospitalized psychiatric patient group but not in the depressives in the community.[3] Thus, invoking Mechanic's concept of illness behavior, they suggested that early loss from separation was not an etiologic factor in depression but did provide a reason for sufferers to seek treatment.

Early Loss Due to Separation

However, early parental loss because of separation can be due to diverse causes — marital breakdown, illness in a parent requiring lengthy hospitalization, illness in the child (such as tuberculosis) leading to a year or more in a hospital, the child's having been evacuated during wartime, the father's having been away at war for two or three years, or the father's emigration to a new country ahead of his family. When Tennant and Bebbington examined their community data in terms of these different separation experiences, they found that depression appeared significantly associated with early separation but only with early separation that was due to marital discord or parental illness.[4]

In clinical studies over the past several years, it has been found that parental loss before 17 years of age is significantly associated with nonpsychotic, nonbipolar depression in both English and Canadian female psychiatric patients and in Canadian male patients.[5] This study has now grown to comprise 300 psychiatric patients suffering from nonpsychotic, nonbipolar depression, matched with 300 nondepressed and never-depressed gynecologic and orthopedic outpatients.[6] Significantly, more of the 300 depressives than of the 300 controls had experienced permanent separation from mother either before 11 years of age or before 17 years of age.[6,7] Also a significantly greater number of the depressives had experienced permanent separation from father before 17 years of age (even when the few who had experienced permanent separation from both mother and father were excluded). However, it is noteworthy that although there are significant differences between them and the controls, the percentage of nonpsychotic, nonbipolar depressives with such loss is small. Only 6.7% of the 300 depressives had experienced permanent separation from mother before 11 years and only 10% before 17 years of age, and only 12% had experienced permanent separation from father before 17 years of age. Tennant et al.[8] also found in their community psychiatric survey that "loss and deprivation" in combination accounted for only about 5% of the variance in the adult psychiatry morbidity and statistically had its strongest effect after 11 years of age.

Early Loss Due to Due to Death

In 1980 Lloyd's comprehensive review of all the then available studies was published.[9] She concluded that the majority of studies found an increased incidence of childhood loss events among depressives and also that "the childhood loss of a parent by death generally increases depressive risk by a factor of about 2 or 3." However, her conclusion in relation to loss by death is controversial.

Tennant et al.[10], also in 1980, reviewed the evidence that parental death in childhood predisposes to depressive disorders in later life. They found inconsistent results in the literature and attributed them to the methodological limitations in most of the studies. These were due largely to inadequate control for potentially confounding social variables. They concluded, differently from Lloyd, that "parental death in childhood appears to have little effect on adult depressive morbidity." Also, in their own community study, Tennant et al.[3] found that early parental loss because of death was not associated with depression.

In my own study, 300 nonpsychotic, nonbipolar depressives were matched for age, sex, marital status, and social class with 300 nondepressed controls. As well as being carefully matched, potential controls were screened to eliminate those with a past or current depressive episode. Thus, many of the potentially confounding social variables identified by Tennant et al. were eliminated. Parental loss because of death before 17 years of age was examined. However, there were no significant differences for early loss because of parental death at any time period for either sex or for either parent.[5,11]

In recent years a number of studies, drawing upon a sample of 6,795 referrals over the five-year period 1963–67, derived from the North East of Scotland Psychiatric Case Register, have been published by Birtchnell.[12] Within this sample were 160 women whose mothers had died before the patients reached the age of 11. The clinical case records of these women were exhaustively reviewed by Birtchnell, with special reference to the nature and quality of parental care received following the bereavement and the subsequent psychiatric history. A control series of 80 women, who were brought up by both natural parents, neither of whom had died before the patient was 26 and who were matched by decade of birth with the early-bereaved women, were randomly selected from the remainder of the original Case Register sample. The case records of these women were similarly reviewed, and special attention was paid to the quality of the relationship with each parent. The object of comparing early bereaved and nonbereaved patients was to ascertain whether there were clinical features that have a specific association with early bereavement.

From this study, Birtchnell[12] reached a number of negative conclusions. First, early death of mother does not affect personality. Second, early death of mother does not increase the predisposition to mental illness. Third, early death of mother in itself neither sensitizes the individual to stress nor affects the age at first breakdown. Fourth, early death of mother in itself does not affect the extent of involvement with psychiatric services. Fifth, early death of mother in itself does not affect the nature of psychiatric breakdown or the severity of depressive disorders.

Thus, in three large studies reported since 1980 — namely, those of Tennant et al.[3], Roy[5,11] and Birtchnell[12] — parental loss by death has not been found to be associated with depression. These results support the earlier conclusion of Tennant et al.[10] that "parental death in childhood appears to have little effect on adult depressive morbidity."

Specificity of Early Loss for Depression

Thus the evidence suggests that early parental loss because of separation is a risk factor for depression but that early parental loss because of death is not. The question then arises as to how specific early loss by separation is for depression. In a study to examine this, 102 neurotic depressive patients were matched with 102 patients suffering with other neuroses — obsessive-compulsive neurosis, hysterical conversion and dissociation, and phobic neuroses.[13]

Early parental loss by separation, but not by death, was significantly associated with the neurotic-depressive group. In another study, 94 nonpsychotic, nonbipolar depressives were matched with 94 nondepressed personality-disorder patient controls.[14] Again, early parental loss by separation, but not by death, was significantly associated with the depressed group.

Thus, there is some evidence that early parental loss because of separation may have some degree of specificity for depression rather than for other psychiatric disorders. However, the two studies cited above involved comparison only with other neuroses and personality disorders. Early parental loss is known to be associated with other psychiatric disorders, such as delinquency in adolescents and attempted suicide. But it is now increasingly being recognized that many adolescent delinquents at some time also suffer from depression and that many of those who attempt suicide have associated affective symptoms. Further research is needed to investigate the degree of specificity that early loss by separation may or may not have for nonpsychotic, nonbipolar depression.

Pre- and Postseparation Family Relationship

Early parental loss because of separation is not a unitary experience, and other factors are increasingly being recognized as important in determining the outcome. These include the quality of family relationship both before and after the separation, the reason for the separation, the age at which the separation occurred, and the quality of care during the separation. An attempt to evaluate these other factors was made in a recent study by Kennard and Birtchnell.[15] They used a postal questionnaire to identify 73 women in the community with early separation from mother and found no association with psychiatric disorder. However, the reason for this negative finding may well be that almost half of the women in the study had experienced only temporary separation as wartime evacuees and only 16 (21.9%) had experienced permanent separation from mother. But, interestingly, the group with early separation from mother due to unsatisfactory family circumstances had significantly higher scores on the Zung Depression Scale than those with separation due to external factors, such as wartime evacuation, mother's hospitalization, or mother's working away from home. Examining the relationship factors, Kennard and Birtchnell found that almost 40% of all the separated women had poor maternal relationships, compared with only 15% of controls without early separation from mother.

Kennard and Birtchnell make the point that it is highly likely that the poor preseparation relationships with the mother were linked with the parental disharmony that eventually led to the separation experience. Also, 44% of the separated women with poor preseparation maternal relationships had psychiatric symptoms at the time of interview. The investigators also found that 75% of the early-separated women with poor preseparation maternal relationships and poor substitute care had psychiatric symptoms at the time of interview, compared with 27% of early-separated women with poor preseparation relationships but adequate substitute care. Further, a significantly greater number of the women with two or more changes of care plus poor replacement care plus poor preseparation relationships had psychiatric symptoms at interview, compared to those with two or more changes of care plus poor replacement care but with adequate preseparation maternal relationships.

In a similar study, Adam et al.[16] compared 98 persons who had attempted suicide with 102 matched controls for the incidence of parental loss and family stability before the age of 25 years. Forty-eight percent of the attempted suicides had experienced loss of one or both parents early in life, compared with only 23.5% of control subjects. This is consistent with the findings of previous studies. However, in addition, Adam et al. collected detailed information on the family background relating to the presence or absence of adequate parental care. Family backgrounds were rated as stable, unstable or chaotic. A "stable" family was defined as one in which adequate parental care was consistently available without material hardship. An "unstable" family was one in which adequate parental care was inconsistently available for physical or emotional reasons, with or without material hardship. A "chaotic" family was one in which gross deprivation of adequate parental care was associated with prolonged separation from parental figures and often with material and emotional deprivation for prolonged periods. Where parental loss was noted, the research team applied their family stability ratings to the periods preceding and surrounding the time of the loss. Previous studies have been limited by a restricted focus on simple incidence rates for parental loss, without consideration of the quality of parental care before and after loss and in intact homes.

In the study by Adam et al.[16] the majority of those who had attempted suicide were rated as having had an unstable or chaotic long-term family environment, regardless of whether they had experienced actual parental loss. Furthermore, a high percentage of those who had experienced loss had unstable families before the experience of loss. This and the fact that most of those with intact homes who attempted suicide also had unstable families raised questions about the role of loss. Adam et al. concluded that family instability may be the principal etiologic variable and that the high incidence of loss may be an incidental finding. They further noted that loss has long been recognized to be at best a crude indicator of inadequacies in parental care, although its apparent simplicity and convenience of definition have perpetuated its use in research.

Early Loss and Psychotic Depression

Early parental loss has been considered mainly in relation to one type of depressive disorder—the commonly seen nonpsychotic, nonbipolar depression. However, the possible effect of early loss in psychotic depression has also been studied. In an early report, Perris[17] found that among his manic-depressive patients the mean age of onset was about ten years lower in the group who had experienced parental loss before 15 years of age. However, in a later study of 231 manic-depressives, this finding could not be replicated.[18]

In both of these studies, the percentage of early parental loss due to death was high and probably reflects the fact that the patients' parents lived mainly in the first half of the century, when treatment for medical conditions and affective disorders was not readily available or effective, lithium treatment was undiscovered, and two world wars occurred.

In their study, Brown et al.[2] found that in their depressed patients early parental loss because of death was associated with psychotic-like depressive symptoms and that early parental loss because of separation was associated with neurotic-like depressive symptoms. Brown et al. therefore argue for a role for early loss as a factor determining depressive symptom formation and severity. They speculate that early loss by death, being irreversible, leads to a sense of abandonment, while early loss due to separation, which is less irredeemable, leads to a sense of rejection. However, Birtchnell's recent study[12] compared the numbers of "neurotic" depressives and "psychotic" depressives with early parental loss due to death of the mother and found no significant difference. Birtchnell concluded, differently from Brown, that early death of the mother does not influence the severity of depressive disorders. Psychotic depression usually has a marked biological etiology, but there may be other determinants as well. Further research is needed to confirm or refute these findings.

Provoking and Protecting Factors

In their community study, Brown and Harris also measured life events and chronic difficulties, and the results led them to propose a vulnerability model for depression. They saw early parental loss as one of four vulnerability factors that made a woman vulnerable to develop depression in the face of adverse life events or chronic difficulties. The other three factors were unemployment, not having a good confiding marital relationship, and having three children under 14 years of age at home. These factors, being more frequent in the lower social classes, were thought to partly account for the fact that depression seems more common in lower-class than in upper-class women. Brown speculated that early parental loss had its predisposing effect for later depression by lowering self-esteem.

Although early parental loss because of permanent separation is a risk factor for depression, it is important to recognize that most depressives have not experienced an early parental loss and also to recognize that persons who have experienced early loss are not inevitably going to suffer from depression. As Kennard and Birtchnell demonstrated,[15] the great majority of the general population who have experienced nonpermanent early separation do not become depressed. This is almost certainly also the case for those who have experienced permanent separation. This may be because after the separation they received adequate parental care, as discussed earlier.

Also, risk factors for depression probably mainly increase the risk for a depressive episode at the time the subject experiences adversity. Paykel et al.[19] have demonstrated that depressives experienced three times as many life events in the six months before the onset of depression as did nondepressed controls. Life events can be divided into two main types, desirable and undesirable. Desirable life events are such events as winning a lottery, promotion, and marriage, while undesirable life events are such events as getting fired, marital separation, and death of a child. Paykel et al. showed that particularly undesirable life events and exits from the social field were associated with depression, whereas Brown et al.[1,2] demonstrated that particularly threatening life events or chronic difficulties were associated with depression. Even if adversity (in the form of undesirable life events) is experienced, there are probably a number of factors that, if present, may prevent or alleviate depression. These "protective factors" may include such things as good social supports, a good marriage, employment, good self-esteem, and personality strengths. Thus early parental loss because of permanent separation, although significantly associated with depression, is only one factor in the complex interaction between the individual and the environment.

References

1. Brown G, Harris T: *Social Origins of Depression*, Tavistock, London, 1978.

2. Brown G, Harris T, Copeland J: Depression and loss. *Br. J. Psychiatry*, 130:1–18, 1977.

3. Tennant C, Bebbington P, Hurry J: Parental loss in childhood: Relationship to adult psychiatric impairment and contact with psychiatric services. *Arch. Gen. Psychiatry* 38:309–314, 1981.

4. Tennant C, Hurry J, Bebbington P: The relation of childhood separation experiences to adult depressive and anxiety states. *Br. J. Psychiatry* 140:375–482, 1982.

5. Roy A: Role of past loss in depression. *Arch. Gen. Psychiatry* 38:301–302, 1981.

6. Roy A: Five risk factors for depression. *Br. J. Psychiatry* 150:536–541, 1987.

7. Roy A: Early parental separation and depression. *Arch. Gen. Psychiatry* 42:987–991, 1985.

8. Tennant C, Bebbington P, Hurry J: Social experiences in childhood and adult psychiatric morbidity: A multiple regression analysis. *Psychol. Med.* 12:321–327, 1982.

9. Lloyd C: Life events and depressive disorder reviewed. I: Events as predisposing factors. *Arch. Gen. Psychiatry* 37:529–535, 1980.

10. Tennant C, Bebbington P, Hurry J: Parental death in childhood and risk of adult depressive disorders: A review. *Psychol. Med.* 10:289–299, 1980.

11. Roy A: Early parental death and adult depression. *Psychol. Med.* 13:861–865, 1983.

12. Birtchnell J: Women whose mothers died in childhood: An outcome study. *Psychol. Med.* 10:699–713, 1980.

13. Roy A: Early parental loss in depressive neurosis compared with other neurosis. *Can. J. Psychiatry* 25:503–505, 1980.

14. Roy A: Specificity of risk factors for depression. *Am. J. Psychiatry* 138:959–961, 1981.

15. Kennard J, Birtchnell J: The mental health of early mother separated women. *Acta Psychiatr. Scand.* 65:388–402, 1982.

16. Adam K, Bouckoms A, Streiner O: Parental loss and family stability in attempted suicide. *Arch. Gen. Psychiatry* 39:1081–1085, 1982.

17. Perris C: A study of bipolar (manic-depressive) and unipolar recurrent depressive psychoses: II. Childhood environment and precipitating factors. *Acta Psychiatr. Scand.* 42:45–57, 1966.

18. Roy A: Parental loss in childhood and onset of manic-depressive illness. *Br. J. Psychiatry* 136:86–88, 1980.

19. Paykel E, Myers J, Dienelt M, et al.: Life events and depression. *Arch. Gen. Psychiatry* 21:753–760, 1970.

4

Depression: Bipolar or Unipolar?

Ralph A. O'Connell

EDITOR'S NOTE

One of the common diagnostic problems encountered in psychiatric practice is to be able to distinguish between bipolar and unipolar depression in those patients who have a history of previous episodes of depression but no clear-cut history of manic episodes. To meet the criteria for bipolar disorder, a depressed patient must manifest a dysphoric mood or loss of interest or the ability to experience pleasure, plus four of the required vegetative symptoms such as sleep disturbance, appetite disturbance, loss of sexual drive, or psychomotor changes; but he must also give a history of one or more manic episodes. A diagnosis of major recurrent depression also requires these elements of depression, but without a history of mania.

But what if there is no clear-cut history of mania? Does that preclude the possibility of bipolar disorder? Not necessarily. Such patients may have periods of considerable productivity, outgoingness, or expansiveness channeled in constructive directions. Episodes of elevated mood may be slight and readily missed, except by family members who know the patient well.

For practical purposes, the presence of a well-documented mania in the first-degree relative of a patient with major depressive episodes should raise the question of a bipolar disorder. The age of onset of bipolar disorders is significantly less than for unipolars: 20–25 years of age versus 40–45 years of age for unipolars. Women are more prone to unipolar disorders than are men. Bipolar patients may have a tendency to be endomorphic, heavy-set, with a history of hypertension, gout, or diabetes mellitus. They are somewhat more likely to experience retarded depression accompanied by increased sleep, lethargy, and weight gain, as opposed to the patient with unipolar depression, who is reportedly more anxious and agitated, with sleep loss, appetite and weight loss, and obsessive-compulsive features.

In treating the depressed phase of bipolar disorder one must, of course, be cautious lest the use of heterocyclic antidepressants stimulate a manic episode as the depression lifts; in such cases, the concomitant use of lithium may be critical. Lithium may also be effective as an adjunct to antidepressant medications in treating drug-resistant bipolar depression. It is also effective in preventing depression in both

29

bipolar and recurrent unipolar illness. Heterocyclic antidepressants are more effective in preventing recurrences in unipolar than in bipolar illness, and in fact, if not used in conjunction with lithium, may potentiate manic and hypomanic episodes in the latter.

The Value of Diagnosis

In medicine, diagnostic criteria are of value in relation to their ability to predict treatment outcome and prognosis. Without this, they are more or less academic. Psychiatry is in an evolutionary phase of increasingly more specific and reliable diagnostic criteria and, to a lesser degree, more specific treatments for these diagnoses. At the present time, the criteria for diagnosing the vast majority of psychiatric disorders are operational and not based on etiology. Thus, treatment based on etiology is not yet possible. Yet there is a substantial body of knowledge relating treatment outcome to specifically defined disorders, and this information has practical clinical implications. The major affective disorders represent one area in which there have been major advances in diagnostic classification in the past decade, with the separation of bipolar disorder and major depression. This chapter will review this area, especially the question of bipolar and unipolar depressions, their clinical differentiation, and the implications for treatment and prevention.

Historical Background

Affective disorders were recognized in the early medical literature. Kraepelin grouped all depressions under the umbrella of manic-depressive psychosis, whether or not mania was present in the clinical history. This was adopted in DSM-II, and most psychiatrists practicing today were trained in this classification. Kraepelin grouped all types of affective disorder under manic-depressive psychosis including affective personality disorders and involutional melancholia. In the early part of this century, several prominent psychiatrists were concerned about the overinclusiveness of the concept of manic-depressive psychosis; they included Adolf Meyer, Aubrey Lewis, and Karl Jaspers. Leonhard, in Germany, is given credit for separating bipolar and unipolar disorders in affective illness. Studies by Angst in Switzerland and Perris in Sweden confirmed his findings. It is now generally accepted that there are at least two types of major affective disorders—the bipolar disorders, requiring at least one episode of mania, and the recurrent unipolar depressions, without mania. These distinctions seem to have validity, but there may be subclassifications within the bipolar and unipolar groups as further evidence emerges.

Diagnostic Criteria

DSM-III incorporates the bipolar/unipolar distinction in the classification of major affective disorders. A bipolar disorder may be mixed, manic, or depressed, depending on the symptoms of the current episode. To be classified as bipolar depressed, the patient must meet the criteria for a current major depressive episode with a dysphoric mood or loss of interest or the ability to experience pleasure, plus four of the required vegetative symptoms (sleep disturbance, appetite disturbance, psychomotor changes, etc.), but there must also be a history of one or more manic episodes. The presence of mania, either in the current episode or by history, is the *sine qua non* of a bipolar disorder.

A major depression may be single or recurrent. The episodes must also meet the criteria for a major depressive episode. There must be no history of a manic episode for the disorder to remain in the unipolar depressive category. At any time in the clinical course, the presence of mania changes the diagnosis to bipolar. (Unipolar mania is thought by most clinicians to be extremely rare; family and epidemiological studies indicate that it is the same as bipolar disorder, so the term "unipolar mania" is not used.)

Clinical Distinctions

As noted above, if there is a history of mania, there is no difficulty in differentiating a bipolar disorder from a unipolar one. The clinical problem arises with a major depressive episode—either a first episode or one of several—in a patient with no history of mania. There are several differences between the two disorders that may be of help in predicting whether a specific patient's depression will eventually prove to be bipolar. Several studies indicate that the genetic predisposition to the bipolar and unipolar disorders is distinct. The genetic loading is stronger for the bipolar disorder. Some published pedigrees show the bipolar disorder running in families as an X-dominant trait. In these families, the evidence is quite convincing. However, there are well-documented cases of the transmission of bipolar disease from father to son—an impossibility with an X-linked trait. This poses the possibility of two subtypes of bipolar disorder. For practical purposes, the presence of well-documented mania in the first-degree relatives of a patient with major depressive episodes should raise the question of a bipolar disorder.

The age at onset of bipolar disorders is significantly less than for unipolars: 20 to 25 years for bipolars, 40 to 45 years for unipolars. Women are more prone to unipolar disorders than are men. For bipolar disorders, the distribution between the sexes is equal. Many clinicians feel there is, in general, a difference in personality type, and even in body type, between bipolars and unipolars. These have been described in the older literature. Bipolar patients, in their euthymic phase, are more outgoing, expansive, energetic, and prone to mood swings, which are cyclothymic and do not reach clinical proportions. Families often recognize these phases and describe them as regular for the patient. "Oh yes. Every spring he has a spell, goes to Florida, bets on the horses, and has to call home for money." Or they will recount a story indicative of what may be a mood swing, either high or low, that did not require treatment but in retrospect is significant. Bipolar patients may be extremely productive and successful if their energies and talents have been channeled successfully. There will be a history of business ventures, successes and failures, and other evidence of a cyclic personality. The bipolar patient may often be endomorphic in somatotype and heavy-set (especially around the middle), with a tendency to hypertension, gout, or diabetes mellitus. These characteristics are by no means diagnostic, but they are common enough to raise the suspicion of a bipolar disorder in a patient with no documented history of clinical mania.

Many patients seek treatment only for a depressive episode. Using the strict criteria for manic episode probably misses many bipolar patients who do not seek treatment for hypomanic episodes, especially if these episodes are not dysphoric and do not produce adverse social or financial consequences. The Research Diagnostic Criteria (RDC) of Spitzer et al. made a distinction between bipolar I and bipolar II. Bipolar II patients suffer from hypomania or mild mania but have not required hospitalization for this. These patients are similar to bipolar I patients in terms of family history and response to treatment. Akiskal has studied cyclothymic patients along the same lines and found that in many cases the history, clinical course, and response to treatment are similar to those of bipolar patients. It is highly probable that bipolar disorder exists along a spectrum, with only a certain group of patients meeting the more rigid criteria of a manic episode. Consequently, many unipolar patients may, in fact, be bipolar.

There are at present no biological tests that will reliably distinguish bipolar from unipolar patients. Studies on biogenic amine metabolism, neuroendocrine function, and lithium distribution show promise in separating the two disorders in certain experimental settings, but such tests are not yet clinically practical.

Does the clinical picture of the depressive episode help distinguish the bipolar from unipolar depression? Yes and no. No, not always, but yes, many clinicians report that the depressive episode of the bipolar depression is more likely to be a retarded depression with slowed psychomotor activity and often accompanied by increased sleep, lethargy, and weight gain—a picture of anergia. On the other hand, the patient with unipolar depression is reportedly more agitated and anxious, with sleep loss, appetite and weight loss, and obsessive-compulsive features.

Subtypes of Unipolar Depression

Winokur and his group have studied unipolar depressed patients and developed further subtypes based on family history. They have divided unipolar depressive disease into pure depressive disease (PDD), which refers to patients with a first-degree relative who has depressive disorder; depressive spectrum disease (DSD), in patients with a family history of alcoholism or antisocial personality; and sporadic depressive disease (SDD), in patients with no family history of depression, alcoholism, or antisocial personality. Studies using the dexamethasone suppression test show many more positive results in patients with PDD, indicating that this group may have a disease with different biological aspects. This type of categorization of depressive subtypes may prove fruitful in the future.

Course of Illness

Bipolar patients have an earlier onset of illness and suffer from more episodes over their lifetime than do unipolar patients. (This increased number of episodes is not dependent on the earlier onset.) The episodes, both manic and depressive, of bipolar patients are more frequent and the intervals between episodes shorter.

A question that often arises is: How many depressive episodes does a patient have to have before it is safe to say that he or she is definitely unipolar and not bipolar? Statistically, it seems to be quite safe to assume that a patient is unipolar after three successive depressive episodes without an episode of mania or hypomania. I have observed several patients who presented with clear-cut hypomania after many years and many episodes of depression.

The natural history of affective disorder is difficult to observe today. Most patients with severe episodes have been treated in one manner or another. Kraepelin observed 459 manic patients for more than 20 years and reported that 45% had only one episode; 30% had three or more episodes. Follow-up studies report varied figures as to type of first episode, number and duration of episodes, and duration of intervals. Much of this has to do with the intensity of observation and the definition of episodes. The vast majoiity of episodes remit, and the patient returns to his premorbid level of functioning (Kraepelin's "*restitutio ad integram*"). While this may be true in the strict sense of psychopathology, patients with untreated or severe, recurring illness suffer greatly from social and personal morbidity. Suicide is commonly reported in long-term follow-up studies; the rate is about 10% for bipolar patients and higher for those with unipolar recurrent depressions. Bipolar patients have an increased mortality from causes other than suicide when compared to a control population.

Implications for Treatment

What are the practical clinical implications of differentiating between bipolar and unipolar depression? This is a difficult question, and there are no definitive answers. The ideal situation would be specific and predictable treatment for the different subtypes of depression. It is to be hoped that this may occur in the future. At present, however, two clinical considerations — the treatment of the depressive episode and long-term preventive treatment — are worth discussing.

There are no essential differences in treatment for the depressive episodes of either bipolar or unipolar illness. The accepted guidelines for antidepressant use and psychotherapy are the same for both, although one must be especially cautious about the possibility of a manic swing occurring as depression lifts in bipolar cases. As mentioned above, the depressed phase of bipolar illness tends to be characterized by more psychomotor retardation and anergia. For such patients, the more stimulating, drive-enhancing tricyclics, such as desipramine or nortriptyline, may be helpful. Unipolar depressives, more likely to be agitated, may respond better to more sedating tricyclics, such as amitriptyline or doxepin. For patients with a more middle-ground picture of depression, imipramine or maprotiline may be indicated. The choice of antidepressant, in any event, is a function more of the clinical symptoms than of the diagnostic subtype.

Bipolar depressions may become hypomanic during a course of antidepressant therapy. This, in fact, is considered diagnostic by some. If a patient is known to be bipolar by virtue of a previous manic or hypomanic episode, it may be advisable to use lithium prophylactically during the antidepressant treatment phase.

Although by no means as effective as the tricyclic antidepressants (or the tetracyclics), lithium has been reported to have some antidepressant effect — especially in bipolar depressions. There are also several recent reports of patients unresponsive to tricyclics who show a rapid antidepressant response when lithium is added. Lithium should be considered as an adjunct to antidepressants, especially in treatment of resistant bipolar depressions.

The place of the monoamine oxidase inhibitors is still unclear in psychiatry. They are seldom used as a first choice in the major depressive disorders with endogenous or vegetative features. However, interest is growing in the use of MAOIs for the atypical depressions with prominent neurotic, hysterical, and hypochondriacal features. These may turn out to be a subtype of unipolar depressions with a different biological etiology.

ECT should still be considered for patients with major depressive disorders, especially those with acutely suicidal or delusional depressions. It is effective in both bipolar and unipolar depressions. Some studies have indicated that more ECT treatments are required for unipolar than for bipolar patients.

Psychotherapy is indicated concomitantly with antidepressants both for bipolar and for unipolar depressions. Patients in a major depression need support through the period of acute depression, a chance to ventilate feelings, and the opportunity to explore psychosocial factors that may be related to the episode. Several studies have now shown that, although antidepressants are effective in relieving the more vegetative symptoms of depression, psychotherapy is essential in restoring the patient to the premorbid or, at times, an improved level of function. Antidepressants should never be given in a vacuum. The extent of psychodynamic cause for any depressive episode can vary greatly. In some patients, stress factors may be obviously related to the episode; in others, less so. Often the stress factors are in fact secondary to the affective pathology and not causative. This is particularly true in bipolar patients. The patient seeks treatment during the depressive episode and relates the depression to a major social or financial loss recently experienced. Careful history usually reveals that the patient experienced a hypomanic episode before the depression and that the psychosocial stressors perceived as causing the depression were, in fact, the product of the hypomanic episode. In such situations, the correct diagnosis of a bipolar disorder greatly helps in planning adequate long-term treatment.

Long-Term Treatment

Affective disorders, bipolar or unipolar, tend to be recurrent in nature. Although this is true for the group as a whole, the decision to place a particular patient on long-term preventive treatment can be difficult. The therapeutic benefit has to be weighed against the cost, inconvenience, and risk of side effects. Several authors have recommended guidelines on when to start preventive treatment. They all involve an assessment of the number, severity, and intervals between previous episodes. If episodes are severe and debilitating, there is a greater need for preventive treatment. If, on the other hand, a patient and his family can recognize the prodrome of an affective episode, treatment can be initiated early and long-term treatment may not be necessary.

Lithium carbonate is effective in preventing both recurrent bipolar and unipolar illness. This finding has been replicated in several studies. Tricyclic antidepressants are effective in preventing recurrence of unipolar depression, but less so depressive episodes in bipolar illness. In fact, long-term use of antidepressants without concomitant lithium may potentiate manic or hypomanic episodes. It seems clear that lithium should be considered as a prophylactic treatment for both bipolar and unipolar illness. It is easy to administer and nontoxic if adequately monitored. The possibility of long-term renal changes has to be considered but, to date, these have not proved to be of major concern.

Another reason to consider lithium is the fairly high possibility that a patient with recurrent depressions may, in fact, be bipolar. Many patients with no history of hypomania do very well on long-term lithium, free of further recurrences and with no disturbing side effects. For such patients, long-term lithium maintenance can be rewarding.

The Future

The bipolar/unipolar dichotomy is now a generally accepted distinction in the affective disorders. Within these categories, further subtypes may emerge as data become available. The hope is that with the further delineation of affective subtypes, more specific knowledge of etiology will evolve and, following this, more specific and predictable treatment. Perhaps biological markers will be discovered for subtypes of illness, with high sensitivity and specificity. These markers may prove to be measures of biogenic amine metabolism, neuroendocrine challenge tests, sleep markers, or other correlates of neurobiological dysfunction. Family history, specific operational diagnostic criteria such as those introduced in DSM-III, and biological markers will, it is hoped, allow for much more specific and predictable treatment planning and prognosis.

Further Reading

Akiskal HS, Hirschfeld RMA, Yerevania BI: The relationship of personality to affective disorders: A critical review. *Arch. Gen. Psychiatry* 40:801–810, 1983.

Baastrup PC, Schou M: Lithium as a prophylactic agent. Its effect against recurrent depressions and manic-depressive psychosis. *Arch. Gen. Psychiatry* 16:162–172, 1967.

Diagnostic and Statistical Manual of Mental Disorders, Third Edition, American Psychiatric Association, Washington, DC, 1980.

Kraepelin E: *Manic-Depressive Insanity and Paranoia*, E. & S. Livingstone, Edinburgh, 1921.

Perris C: The distinction between bipolar and unipolar affective disorders. In Paykel ES (ed): *Handbook of Affective Disorders*, Guilford, New York, 1982.

Prien RJ: Lithium in the prophylactic treatment of affective disorders. *Arch. Gen. Psychiatry* 36:847–848, 1979.

Spitzer RL, Endicott J, Robins E: Research diagnostic criteria: Rationale and reliability. *Arch. Gen. Psychiatry* 35:773–782, 1978.

Winokur G: Persistent problems in the diagnosis of depression and their relationship to elitism in academic psychiatry. *Compr. Psychiatry* 23:495–504, 1982.

5

The Nature of Recovery and Relapse in Depressive Disorders

Martin B. Keller, Barbara Friedman, and Philip W. Lavori

EDITOR'S NOTE

Clinically most of us operate on the assumption that the majority of depressed patients we see will recover; however, we are all too familiar with the small but significant number of those who do not. Here the authors report the current level of knowledge about the prognosis for recovery from major depressive disorder (MDD). They also provide some information regarding the relapse rate.

About 50% of patients in the authors' study recovered within one year after the initial onset of symptoms; 28% recovered during the second year, 22% during the third, and 18% during the fourth. Nearly 63% of depressed patients recovered during the first four months following actual entry into the study/treatment program. About 20% of the nonbipolar patients appeared to have unremitting courses when followed up two years later, and ultimate prognosis for this group seemed poor.

An acute onset seems to predict early recovery. When a major depressive disorder is superimposed on an underlying low grade chronic depression, such patients usually recover more rapidly than patients with MDD alone; however, they are much less likely to recover as fully. It would appear that the longer the presence of depression prior to the initiation of treatment, the more likely the patient will be to remain depressed for a substantial period afterwards. Other predictors of chronicity include low family income, hospitalization, being married, and the medical center at which the patients were studied and treated.

The longer a patient remained well, the less his risk of relapse. Twelve percent of patients in this study relapsed within four weeks after recovery; 24% relapsed after

12 weeks. Clearly, recovered patients should be carefully monitored for some time after recovery.

Patients with three or more prior episodes of depression seemed to relapse more rapidly than those with fewer such episodes. An associated diagnosis of substance abuse or dependency increased the risk of relapse. Older patients were more prone to relapse than younger ones.

Double depression is a term used to describe a major depressive disorder superimposed on a preexisting chronic minor or intermittent depression of at least two years' duration. In the study, 88% of such patients recovered from the major depressive disorder episode; only 31% recovered from both the depressive episode and the chronic malady. This group of patients seems to enter treatment more quickly and recover more rapidly with treatment than patients with only MDD.

As with most such investigations, the specific factors that may account for rapid vs. slow recovery and the degree of risk of relapse are not explored. From clinical experience, we know that biological influences, flexibility versus rigidity of personality and the nature of the patient's environment all contribute to outcome.

Introduction

The purpose of this chapter is to discuss the phenomena of recovery and relapse from episodes of major depressive disorder (MDD). We will begin with a brief summary of the history of follow-up research on affective disorders, concentrating on the results and design characteristics of studies done to date. Then we will discuss the utility of life table and survival methods for analyzing the time to recovery and relapse in depressed patients participating in the naturalistic follow-up protocol of the NIMH-Clinical Research Branch of the Psychobiology of Depression (Collaborative Depression Study).[1]

History, Methodologic Review and Findings From Follow-up Studies On Affective Disorders

Kraepelin[2] used the clinical course as a validating principle to distinguish between the affective disorders (manic-depressive illness) and schizophrenia (dementia praecox). Kraepelin's nosologic distinction included the postulate that particular forms of affective disorders have a remitting course, with a return to premorbid levels of functioning during remission, which may be

followed by relapse or recurrence. In contrast, schizophrenia was characterized as invariably having a chronic and deteriorating course.

Most physicians are still taught that depression is a relatively short-lived,
acute disorder in which the natural course of the untreated episode ranges
between six and 12 months. Treated disorders are expected to be of much
shorter duration.

Published follow-up studies on affective disorders report wide disparities
in outcome. For example, the literature relating naturalistic short-term outcome studies on affective disorders describes an extremely wide range of
recovery from depression after one year of follow-up. Rates of recovery
range from 30% to 90%.[3-7] Review articles by Robins and Guze[8] and Klerman[9] on long-term prospective and retrospective follow-up studies show
rates of chronicity ranging from 1% to 28% for patients with severe depression who were followed for a minimum of two years. Table 1[2,3,10-24] summarizes these studies and their important sample and design characteristics.

Similar variation in outcome is found in the literature on relapse. In a
recent review of ten of the largest and most widely cited studies on relapse in
affective disorders, Zis and Goodwin[25] point out that the reported proportion of patients with a single episode ranges from 0% to 58%, whereas the
proportion of patients with multiple episodes ranges from 18% to 80%.
They demonstrate that these differences are in part attributable to the variations in diagnostic criteria at intake, the definition of recovery and relapse,
the methods of data collection, the sources of information, the length of
observation, and the patient population. Most of these considerations apply
as well to the studies of recovery that are listed in Table 1. We concur with
Zis and Goodwin's recommendation that the ability to generalize outcome
data on affective disorders can be greatly enhanced by standardizing these
methodologic parameters when designing follow-up research protocols.

The Use of Life Tables and Survival Analysis
in Follow-up Research

In order to illustrate how different data sets on follow-up may be utilized in
a more uniform manner, Lavori et al.[26] used life tables and survival analysis
to reanalyze the raw data presented in the literature on relapse in major
depressive disorder. They focused on 40 studies that provided information
on subsequent episodes, on intervals between episodes, and on relapse or
recurrence patterns. Some of the methodologic differences in the reports of
relapse were removed by the use of life tables and survival methods in the
reanalysis, thus furnishing a consistent format in which to better summarize
the available knowledge on patterns of relapse after recovery.

Even with the uniform reanalysis, there continued to be considerable differences in the overall results of individual studies. In spite of the wide disagreement over the cross-sectional rates of relapse, however, the reanalysis revealed that the risk of relapse declined steadily for the first one to three years after recovery in all studies. A declining hazard suggests that the subjects are not homogeneous with respect to initial risk. It appears that there are two or more risk groups, and that observed relapse during the first-year interval is due to the "high risk" group. This group is rapidly depleted by relapse, so the slower relapses come to fore in the second-year interval. This interpretation of the decline in interval-specific rates of relapse supports the hypothesis that distinguishing subgroups of patients with affective disorders by patterns of outcome may be valid. It is also possible that patients who remain well are "strengthened" by the remission through a kind of healing process, and thus the individual hazard of relapse falls over time.

Design of the Collaborative Depression Study

The Collaborative Depression Study is a naturalistic, prospective, longitudinal study of 1,000 patients in five collaborating centers. Patients were recruited when they were accepted for psychiatric treatment through the customary referral mechanisms at inpatient and outpatient psychiatric units in public and private settings associated with each of the five centers. All patients were at least 17 years of age at entry, were Caucasian, spoke English, had an IQ above 70, and did not have organic brain syndrome severe enough to preclude evaluation. Patients were admitted to the study if they had a Research Diagnostic Criteria (RDC)[27] diagnosis of major depressive disorder, mania, or schizoaffective disorder.

This is a naturalistic study in that patients are not randomly assigned to treatment groups and treatment is not administered by the investigators, but all treatment received by patients is systematically recorded. Decisions about treatment were made by individual clinicians and patients. We do know that there is wide variability in the intensity and type of somatotherapy and psychotherapy received by the subjects[28,29] and that a substantial proportion received levels of treatment far below current clinical and research standards. We are not yet able to comment specifically on how treatment affected the rates of recovery and relapse that have been reported to date. It is important to consider that the outcomes might have been better if all patients had received the best available treatment, yet it is necessary to recognize that in the real world of clinical practice many patients receive less than optimal treatment. The treatment received by our subjects, therefore, may fairly represent the treatment given to the larger population of depressed

TABLE 1
Studies Reporting Depressed Patients with a Chronic Course

Author (Year)	N	Years Observed	Prospect Obs. (Yrs)	F/U Interval	Percent Chronic	Diagnostic Criteria	Information Sources Intake	F/U	Preditors of Chronicity
Kraeplin (1921)[2]	899	10-44	0	—	4-5%	Author	—	—	
Lundquist (1945)[10]	319	10-30	0	?	9%	Sjobring	Records	Direct Records	Depressive Delusions Monotony
Huston 1 (1948)[11]	154	6.6	mean 5	6 months	9%	No	Direct	Direct(Q) FRC	No
Huston 2 (1948)[12]	93	6.5	mean 4.5	6 months	18%	No	Direct	Direct(Q) FRC	No
Stenstedt (1952)[13]	216	1-20	0	1-20	1-4%	Faergeman	Records	Direct(Q) RC	No
Watts (1956)[14]	570	8	8	8	14%	Author	Direct	Direct	No
Astrup (1959)[15]	115	5	0	5	8%	No	?	Direct(Q) C	Sex
Bratfos (1968)[16]	215	6	6	mean 6	20%	—	Records	Direct FCR	Age, Sex # Previous Episodes

Morrison (1973)[3]	325	3.3	3.3	6-12 mo.	20%	DSM II, Feighner	Records	Direct(Q) RC	No
Murphy (1974)[17]	37	8	5	mean 5	16%	Feighner	Direct	Direct FRdc	No
Akiskal (1978)[18]	136	max 10	3-4	7	10%	RDC, DSMII, Feighner	Direct FR	Direct FR	No
Venkoba (1977)[19]	102	3-13	3-13	3-13	9%	Author	Direct Records	Direct(Q) F	No
Shobe (1971)[20]	115	mean 18	mean 8	–	22%	Author	Direct	Direct CF	Sex
Winokur (1973)[21]	225	mean 4	mean 4	6-12 mo.	19%	DSM II, Feighner	Records	Direct(Q) FC	Sex, Age
Keller (1981)[22]	97	2	2	q 6mo.	21%	RDC	Direct Records	Direct Records	see text
Klerman (1980)[23]	91	4	4	6 mo-3 yrs	10%	DSM II	Direct Records	Direct Records	No
Bronisch (1985)[24]	50	6-8	0	mean 7	22%	ICD, RDC	Direct	Direct	No

Legend for Sources of Information:

Direct = From patient; Direct(Q) refers to the use of a questionnaire;

F = Family; R (or Records) + Clinical charts, and the like; C = Treating Clinician; dc = Death Certificate.

43

patients. The present analysis focuses on patients with an index diagnosis of major depressive disorder who were followed for two years.

The follow-up component of the Collaborative Depression Study has focused on the psychopathologic and psychosocial course and outcome. An important contribution of this study had been the development of standardized methods by which a longitudinal course can be described and understood. The Longitudinal Interval Follow-Up Evaluation (LIFE)[30] was designed as the follow-up instrument to assess the longitudinal course of intake diagnoses made with the SADS[31] and RDC. In this way, outcome measures for the follow-up have been defined by linking them to the diagnostic system employed at intake. The LIFE is a precoded, semistructured psychiatric interview that elicits information on psychopathology, nonpsychiatric medical illness, treatment, and psychosocial functioning over the previous 26 weeks. The ratings on psychopathology are made on a week-by-week basis by assessing change points in the patient's status. The weekly levels of psychiatric symptomatology are based on the number and severity of RDC symptoms for each diagnosis being assessed; therefore the same criteria are used to diagnose patients at the time of selection and at follow-up. Methodologic contributions of the Collaborative Depression Study also include the measurement of time to recovery and relapse and the construction of probability estimates for recovery and subsequent relapse, while controlling for period at risk and differentiating predictors of recovery and relapse.

Definition of Major Depressive Disorder (MDD), Major Depression, Recovery, and Relapse

Major depressive disorder and major depression: The RDC and *DSM-III*[31] delineated specific diagnostic criteria for functional psychiatric disorders that made it possible to operationalize definitions of outcomes such as recovery, relapse, and chronicity.

Williams and Spitzer,[33] in their annotated comparison of the *DSM-III* and the RDC, noted that the RDC for major depressive disorder, chronic minor depression, and intermittent depression are very similar to the *DSM-III* categories of major depressive episode and dysthymic disorder. (The reader is referred to that article for a detailed description of these diagnostic entities.) According to the RDC, a minimum of five specific symptoms must cluster for at least two weeks in order to diagnose a definite episode of MDD. In addition, the person must seek help or manifest significant functional impairment. The diagnosis of major depression in *DSM-III* is very similar, except that impairment is not required and one fewer symptom is required for a definite diagnosis. The subjects described in the rest of this article were all diagnosed as having a major depressive disorder according to the RDC. Therefore, it is important to bear in mind that some patients who met criteria for major depression according to *DSM-III* did not have a depression sufficiently severe to enter the Collaborative Study.

Recovery: The definition of recovery is made in terms of the psychiatric status ratings. To be considered recovered from an episode of MDD a patient must have no more than two of the symptoms of MDD at a mild degree but may have symptoms of another disorder. These criteria were selected somewhat arbitrarily in the absence of previous literature on this matter. Although they seem reasonable on clinical grounds, one could argue that the criteria should be more or less stringent. One of the unique strengths of this design is that the weekly psychiatric status ratings provide an opportunity to redefine recovery by raising or lowering the number of symptoms required or by shortening or lengthening the time required at these levels. Such flexibility of analysis will be of great value when comparing these data with future work by other investigators who may use different thresholds for defining recovery.

The quantitative scale of measuring a longitudinal course also provides more detailed information than does the recovered/nonrecovered dichotomy. For example, patients can be divided into those with complete recovery and those with residual recovery, as well as into different categories of partial remission.

Relapse: In the Collaborative Depression Study relapse was defined as meeting full (definite) RDC criteria for an affective episode of MDD, minor depression, hypomania, mania, or mania mixed with or cycling to depression.

Results on Recovery and Relapse From the Collaborative Depression Study

Time to recovery: "Recovery in Major Depressive Disorder"[34] uses regression models and life tables to describe recovery from MDD for 101 patients. Two different outcome variables are described: (1) duration from onset to end (either recovery or the end of the 12-month follow-up period), and (2) duration from study entry to end. The time to recovery from the onset of the episode of depression was protracted, since only about 50% of the patients recovered within the first follow-up year. The annual rates of recovery then declined steadily to 28% in the second year, 22% in the third year, and 18%

in the fourth year. In contrast, the speed of recovery from the entry into the study was more rapid, as 63% of patients recovered by four months. The recovery rates were about 20% each month for the first four months and then declined sharply for the remaining months of the one-year follow-up. These analyses identify the period of four months immediately after entry into the study as an extremely important time during the course of an episode of MDD. After a typically protracted illness, patients have a sharply accelerated rate of recovery for these four months.

Thus, life table analyses demonstrate that when duration is measured from the onset of the depressive disorder, the rate of recovery is extremely slow and maintains a fairly constant decline. In contrast, when the duration is measured from time of entry into the study, recovery is rapid for a period of four months and then slows considerably during the next eight months.

Patients who remain chronically depressed: Twenty percent of nonbipolar patients with an MDD have been found to have an unremitting course after two years of prospective follow-up.[35] This is inconsistent with Kraepelin's classic theory of manic-depressive insanity, which predicted recovery to the premorbid state. However, the finding is consistent with the results of several other studies listed in Table 1. The weekly longitudinal profile of symptom severity indicates that most of the unrecovered patients remain very depressed throughout the two-year period. The prospects for subsequent recovery appear to be poor since the interval-specific rates of recovery decline markedly after one year of prospective follow-up.

Predictors of recovery and chronicity: Several clinical variables were statistically significant predictors of recovery after one year of follow-up when measured from entry into the study. An acute onset predicts early recovery. The superimposition of an episode of MDD on an underlying, low grade chronic depression affects recovery rates, depending on the definition of recovery. If one defines recovery as the return to usual self, these patients recover from the major depressive disorder more quickly than those patients with MDD alone. However, if recovery is defined as complete remission from all depressive symptoms, both chronic and acute, these patients have a lower rate of recovery than the other patients since the underlying chronic depression has a pernicious course.

The strongest predictor of continued depression for two years of prospective follow-up is a long duration of the episode prior to entry into the research study. On the basis of these data we hypothesize that the experience of remaining depressed for an extended time reduces the patient's chances of recovery. This indicates that efforts at earlier treatment for depressed patients might decrease chronicity and suggests that clinicians should begin treatment of depression very soon after the onset of symptoms. Patients with an RDC secondary subtype of MDD had a substantially greater likelihood of chronic outcome than patients with primary depression. This association provides an example of the usefulness of follow-up studies in establishing the predictive validity of nosologic subtypes. Other predictors of continued chronic depression after two years of follow-up include a low family income, hospitalization, being married, and the university medical center at which patients were studied. The differences among the admitting research centers in recovery rates were not expected and we are unable to explain this finding to our satisfaction.[35]

Time to relapse: In "Relapse in RDC Major Depressive Disorder,"[36] Keller et al. used life tables to describe well periods and subsequent rates of relapse for 75 patients, who were followed for a minimum of one year after recovery from an episode of MDD. A high interval-specific rate of relapse shortly after recovery was detected. Twenty-four percent of patients relapsed within 12 weeks at risk and 12% of patients relapsed within four weeks at risk. The rate of relapse for patients still at risk declined steadily during the follow-up period. Thus, the longer the patient remained well, the lower the current risk for relapse. In "Predictors of Relapse in MDD,"[37] Keller et al. used a substantially larger sample that was followed for as long as two years to document that the rate of relapse following recovery from a major depressive episode is highest in the months immediately after recovery and declines steadily over the ensuing years. This finding indicates the clinical importance of closely monitoring patients in the immediate postrecovery period.

Predictors of relapse: Patients with three or more prior episodes of depression were found to have significantly shorter times from recovery to relapse than patients with fewer than three episodes prior to entry. The strength of association between the number of previous episodes of depression before study entry and the time to relapse indicates the prognostic importance of reliable history-taking. Furthermore, having three or more episodes obscures the predictive power of other clinical variables. Clinical predictors of relapse emerge only in patients who have just recovered from their first episode.

First episode patients with the primary RDC subtype of MDD had longer well intervals and thus lower relapse rates than secondary patients. Having a diagnosis of secondary MDD accelerates the speed of relapse by a factor of about five. Ninety-three percent of these secondary subjects had a previous history of substance abuse or dependence. Therefore, the primary/secondary distinction is a good prognostic indicator for clinicians to use in assessing risk of relapse in patients who have recovered from their first episode of depression. It also provides an example of the usefulness of follow-up studies in establishing the predictive validity of nosologic subtypes of MDD.

Younger subjects had longer well intervals, and hence lower relapse rates, than older patients. Each decade of age decreased the time from recovery to relapse by about 40%.

Recovery and relapse in double depression: Approximately 25% of subjects who enter the Collaborative Depression Study with a nonbipolar major depression meet criteria for "double depression," a syndrome in which a major depressive disorder is superimposed on a preexisting chronic minor or intermittent depression, known as a dysthymic disorder, of at least two years' duration. Data will be presented on the impact of the dysthymic disorder on recovery and relapse from the major depression, and on the course of the dysthymic disorder for those patients who recover from the major depression.

The phenomenon of double depression has recently begun to receive more attention in the literature. Keller and Shapiro[38] reported that cross-sectional recovery rates for patients with double depression differed markedly, depending on whether recovery was defined as recovery from the major depressive disorder alone (88%) or recovery from both the major depressive disorder and chronic minor depression (31%). There was an increased rate of recovery from the index episode of major depressive disorder in patients with a preexisting chronic depression (88%) compared to subjects with MDD alone (69%).

In a later report on 316 patients in the Collaborative Depression Study who were followed for a time period ranging between six months and two years, Keller et al.[39] described additional differences in the clinical course and outcome between patients with MDD alone and those with double depression. Patients with double depression had a significantly shorter duration of the MDD before entry into the study, and a shorter time to recover from the acute depression than the patients with MDD alone. Patients with double depression who recovered from the major depression had a significantly higher rate of relapse into subsequent RDC affective disorder following recovery than those with MDD alone. The chronic minor depression reduced the apparent effect of the known predictors of recovery and relapse from the MDD and predicted a pernicious course for the chronic depression. The patient with double depression who recovers from the acute disorder is poised between two outcomes — a complete recovery or a relapse into another affective episode. In the one-year period following recovery from the MDD, patients with double depression had a falling chance of recovery from the chronic minor depression and a rising chance of relapse into a major affective episode. In other words, the longer the time that the patient remains chronically depressed after recovery from the acute episode, the greater the likelihood that relapse will preempt full recovery.

Summary

An important conclusion from this work is that the factors predicting recovery from an episode of MDD are different than those factors predicting relapse following recovery. Furthermore, variables that predict time to recovery from the onset of an episode of depression differ from those that predict time of entry into a clinical research protocol. Finally, the presence of a preexisting or underlying chronic disorder has a profound effect on the course of the MDD and on the clinician's ability to predict the acute course. The few months immediately following a change in the patient's state (either recovery or relapse), are critical in the management of the patient's course of illness. Researchers should focus future intensive efforts on these critical periods.

References

1. Katz MM, Secunda SK, Hirschfeld RMA, Koslow SH: NIMH-Clinical Research Branch collaborative program on the psychobiology of depression. *Arch. Gen. Psychiatry* 36:765-771, 1979.

2. Kraepelin E: *Manic-Depressive Insanity and Paranoia*, Barkley RM (transl.), Robertson GM (ed.), E. & S. Livingstone, Edinburgh, 1921.

3. Morrison J, Winokur G, Crowe R, Clancy J: The Iowa 500: The first follow-up. *Arch. Gen. Psychiatry* 29:678-682, 1973.

4. Schapira K, Roth M, Kerr TA, Gurney C: The prognosis of affective disorders: The differentiation of anxiety states from depressive illness. *Br. J. Psychiatry* 121:195-198, 1972.

5. Paykel E, Dienelt M: Suicide attempts following acute depression. *J. Nerv. Ment. Dis.* 153:234-243, 1971.

6. Winokur G, Morrison J: The Iowa 500: Heterogeneity and course in manic-depressive illness (Bipolar). *Compr. Psychiatry* 16(2):125-131, 1975.

7. Cadoret R, Widner RB, North C: Depression in family practice: Long-term prognosis and somatic complaints. *J. Family Practice* 10:625-629, 1980.

8. Robins E, Guze SB: Classification of affective disorders: The primary-secondary, the endogenous-reactive and the neurotic-psychotic concepts. In Williams TA, Katz MM, Shield JA Jr. (eds): *Recent Advances in the Psychobiology of the Depressive Illness*, Washington, DC, DHEW Pub. No. (HSM) 70-9053, 1972.

9. Klerman GL: Other specific affective disorders. In Friedman AM, Kaplan HI, Saddock BJ (eds): *Comprehensive Textbook of Psychiatry*, Third Edition, Williams & Wilkins, Baltimore, 1980.

10. Lundquist G: Prognosis and course of manic-depressive psychosis: A follow-up study of 319 first admissions. *Acta Psychiatr. Scand.* (Suppl. 35):1-93, 1945.

11. Huston PE, Locher LM: Involutional psychosis: Course when treated and

when untreated with electric shock. *Arch. Neurol. and Psychiatr.* 59:385–394, 1948.

12. Huston PE, Locher LM: Manic-depressive psychosis: Course when treated and untreated with electric shock. *Arch. Neurol. and Psychiatr.* 60:37–48, 1948.

13. Stenstedt A: A study in manic-depressive psychosis: Clinical, social and genetic investigations. *Acta Psychiatr. Scand.* (Suppl. 79):1–111, 1952.

14. Watts CAH: The incidence and prognosis of endogenous depression. *Br. Med. J.* 1:1329–1397, 1956.

15. Astrup C, Fossum A, Holmbe R: A follow-up study of 270 patients with acute affective psychosis. *Acta Psychiatr. Scand.* (Suppl. 135), 4:1–65. 1959.

16. Bratfos O, Haug JO: The course of manic depressive psychosis: A follow-up investigation of 215 patients. *Acta Psychiatr. Scand.* 44:89–112, 1968.

17. Murphy GE, Woodruff RA, Heynic M, et al: Validity of the diagnosis of primary affective disorder: A projective study with a five year follow-up. *Arch. Gen. Psychiatry* 30:751–756, 1974.

18. Akiskal HS, Bitar AH, Puzantian VR, et al: The nosological status of neurotic depression: A prospective 3–4 year follow-up examination in the light of the primary-secondary and unipolar-bipolar dichotomies. *Arch. Gen. Psychiatry* 35:756–766, 1978.

19. Venkoba RA, Nammalvar N: The course and outcome in depressive illness: A follow-up study of 122 cases in Madurai, India. *Br. J. Psychiatry* 130:392–396, 1977.

20. Shobe FO, Brion P: Long-term prognosis in manic-depressive illness: A follow-up investigation of ill patients. *Arch. Gen. Psychiatry* 24:334–337, 1971.

21. Winokur G, Morrison J: The Iowa 500: Follow-up of 225 depressives. *Br. J. Psychiatry* 123:543–548, 1973.

22. Keller MB, Shapiro RW: Initial results from a one year prospective naturalistic follow-up. *J. Nerv. Ment. Dis.* 169(12):761–768, 1981.

23. Klerman GL: Long-term outcomes of neurotic depressions. In Sells SB, Crandell R, Roff M, Strauss JS, Pollin W. (eds): *Human Functioning in Longitudinal Perspective*, Williams & Wilkins, Baltimore/London, 1980.

24. Bronisch T: Depressive neurosis: Long-term prospective and retrospective follow-up study of former inpatients. *Acta Psychiatr. Scand.* 71:237–248, 1985.

25. Zis AP, Goodwin FK: Major affective disorder as a recurrent illness: A critical review. *Arch. Gen. Psychiatry* 36:835–839, 1979.

26. Lavori PW, Keller MB, Klerman GL: Relapse in affective disorder: A reanalysis of the literature using life table methods. *J. Psych. Res.* 18:13–25, 1984.

27. Spitzer RL, Endicott J, Robins E: Research diagnostic criteria: Rationale and reliability. *Arch. Gen. Psychiatry* 35:773–782, 1978.

28. Keller MB, Klerman GL, Lavori PW et al.: Treatment received by depressed patients. *JAMA* 248:1848–1855, 1982.

29. Keller MB, Lavori PW, Klerman GL et al.: Low levels and lack of predictors of somatotherapy and psychotherapy received by depressed patients. *Arch. Gen. Psychiatry 43*(5), 458–466, 1986.

30. Shapiro R, Keller MB: *The Longitudinal Interval Follow-up Evaluation (Life)*, Massachusetts General Hospital, Boston, 1979.

31. Endicott J, Spitzer RL: A diagnostic interview: The schedule for affective disorders and schizophrenia. *Arch. Gen. Psychiatry* 35:837–844, 1978.

32. *Diagnostic and Statistical Manual of Mental Disorders*, Third Edition, American Psychiatric Association, Washington, DC, 1980.

33. Williams JBW, Spitzer RL: Research diagnostic criteria and DSM-III: An annotated comparison. *Arch. Gen. Psychiatry* 39:1283–1289, 1982.

34. Keller MB, Shapiro RW, Lavori PW, Wolfe N: Recovery in major depressive disorder: Analysis with life table and regression models. *Arch. Gen. Psychiatry* 39:905–910, 1982.

35. Keller MB, Klerman GL, Lavori PW et al.: Long-term outcome of episodes of major depression: Clinical and public health significance. *JAMA* 252(6):788–792, 1984.

36. Keller MB, Shapiro RW, Lavori PW, et al.: Relapse in RDC major depressive disorder: Analysis with life table. *Arch. Gen. Psychiatry* 39:911–915, 1982.

37. Keller MB, Lavori PW, Lewis CE et al.: Predictors of relapse in MDD. *JAMA* 250:3299–3304, 1983.

38. Keller MB, Shapiro RW: Double depression: Superimposition of acute depressive episodes on chronic depressive disorders. *Am. J. Psychiatry* 139:438–442, 1982.

39. Keller MB, Lavori PW, Endicott J, et al.: Double depression: A two year follow-up. *Am. J. Psychiatry* 140:689–694, 1983.

6

The TRH Test in Psychiatric Disorders

Peter T. Loosen

EDITOR'S NOTE

There is still no standard test or set of tests that can be considered essential in psychiatric diagnosis and treatment. Many, such as the TRH test, are currently being evaluated. The TRH (thyrotropin-releasing hormone) test involves an assessment of the amount of TSH (thyroid-stimulating hormone) produced in response to the administration of a given dose of TRH. Studies suggest that in about 25% of depressed patients the TSH response is markedly attenuated or blunted. However, this response is not specific to major depressive disorders. Alcoholic patients, both during acute alcohol withdrawal and during prolonged abstinence, as well as certain borderline patients, also show such blunting; of course, many such patients also have an important affective component. This abnormal response is rarely seen among schizophrenics.

What does it mean? The abnormal TRH test is found more often among patients with a long duration of illness and a history of suicidal behavior. Perhaps it reflects a feedback mechanism defect, a hypothesis similar to that proposed to explain the abnormal dexamethasone suppression test observed in depression.

Does it possess clinical value? Some. When it is used in combination with the dexamethasone suppression test, a fairly high number of patients with affective disorder can be confirmed, although often the clinical findings alone are enough to provide a strategy for treatment. It may be of some limited value in overall treatment planning, since patients whose TRH tests fail to change in spite of clinical improvement seem to have higher relapse rates unless maintained on antidepressants for a long time.

Introduction

In recent years, the possible clinical utility of biological findings as laboratory markers has been increasingly investigated in biological psychiatry. To date, the dexamethasone suppression test (DST) serves as the best known example of such a marker.[1] It is not surprising that within this search for laboratory markers peptides have also been studied. There has been the direct measurement of peptides in body fluids,[2] and the use of peptides, such as LHRH or CRF, as challenge tests to elicit the response of their respective target hormones.[3,4] In psychiatric disorders, however, these tests have not met marker criteria such as acceptable specificity, sensitivity, and predictive value. Only one test, using a peptide, comes close to meeting such criteria: the TRH test. Our experience with this test will be the content of this brief review. (The reader is referred to our previous reviews for a more detailed description of this subject.[5,6])

Thyrotropin-Releasing Hormone (TRH) Test

Technique: The TRH test, that is, the measurement of serum thyroid-stimulating hormone (TSH) after administration of TRH, has been thoroughly investigated in both endocrine and psychiatric disorders. It is a safe, inexpensive, and rapidly accomplished standard procedure. The technique used by psychiatric investigators follows guidelines developed in endocrinology.[5,6] Variables to be considered and/or controlled are nutritional state of the subject, menstrual history, dose of TRH, rate and route of administration, and time of blood sampling. One may inject TRH at about 9 a.m. in a standardized dose (0.5 mg) after an overnight fast. The subject is placed in a recumbent position throughout the ensuing experiment. Intravenous administration of TRH is preferred to oral administration to avoid the potentially confounding variable of differential absorption. In regard to time of sampling, we suggest the collection of four blood samples for TSH assay: TSH 0, TSH 15, TSH 30, and TSH 45 minutes. It has been shown that this design will not produce false positive TSH results.[7]

Side effects, confounding variables, and patients at risk: The test provokes only mild and short-lasting subjective reactions. TRH side effects such as nausea, urinary urgency, flushing, and a general sensation of warmth occur immediately after TRH injection and coincide nicely with the sharply rising curve of TRH plasma levels.[8] They last for about two minutes. The half-life of exogenous TRH in human plasma is approximately 5 to 6 minutes.[9]

Several factors are known to affect the TSH response to TRH. The following may produce false positive results, i.e., TSH blunting: increasing age, being male, acute starvation, chronic renal failure, Klinefelter's syndrome, repetitive administration of TRH, and administration of glucocorticoids, thyroid hormones, opiates, salicylates, phentolamine, dopamine, and prodopaminergic agents, somatostatin and neurotensin.[5,6,10] In contrast, false negative results can occasionally be observed after administration of lithium, dopamine receptor blockers, iodine and iodine-containing contrast dyes, spironolactone and theophylline.[5,10] These factors need to be considered whether one performs the TRH test for psychiatric disorders or for strictly endocrinologic purposes. Moreover, there are three medical conditions which do not invalidate results, but pose a danger to the patient during administration of TRH. The first two concern high blood pressure and heart disease. TRH may induce a short-lasting increase in blood pressure during the first two minutes following injection.[11,12] This may be dangerous to patients with heart disease, and may explain the severe headaches and transient amaurosis reported to have ensued shortly after TRH injection in hypertensive patients.[13] The third condition concerns individuals with a history of seizure disorders. It is possible that such patients may experience a seizure following TRH administration.[14,15] We recommend taking special precautions (e.g., very slow injections and/or lowering of the TRH dose) when TRH is administered in these three conditions.

The TRH Test in Depression

Frequency, definition, and test-retest reliability: It is now clear from more than 55 studies involving more than 1200 patients that the TRH-induced TSH response is markedly attenuated ("blunted") in about 25% of depressed patients.[5,6,16] To explain this fault most usefully, we think that it is more helpful to classify patients as "blunted" or "non-blunted" than to compare group means. We have studied 73 normal men and women from 20 to 70 years of age; their mean age was 39.6 ± 1.4 ($\bar{x} \pm$S.E.M.) years. Subjects with a personal or family history of mental illness were excluded. Since the lowest Δmax TSH (i.e., the maximum increase in serum TSH above baseline) in the normal population was 5.6 μ/ml, we arbitrarily defined a blunted response as a Δmax TSH less than 5.0 μ/ml. Using this definition, we found TSH blunting in 13 of 50 (26%) patients, both men and women, with primary depression.[5] Obviously, the definition of blunting will largely influence its frequency; higher frequencies were observed when TSH blunting was defined as a Δmax TSH smaller than 6 or 7 μ/ml.[7]

Only a few patients have been retested during a second episode of depression or even a second time in a continuing episode. So far as can be determined, however, test-retest reliability of a blunted TSH response is acceptable.[17,18]

Specificity and state-trait considerations: TSH blunting is not specific for depression. Table 1 summarizes specificity data from our laboratory. As shown, we also observed the fault in some patients with alcoholism, both during acute alcohol withdrawal[19] and during prolonged abstinence,[18] as well as in some patients with borderline personality disorders.[20] Common to these three disorders are, of course, severe affective disturbances. The absence of TSH blunting in patients with schizophrenia, however, suggests that the fault is not merely a correlate of mental stress. Here it is worth noting that recent data from other investigators demonstrate the occurrence of TSH blunting in some schizophrenic patients, but at a frequency much lower than in depression or alcoholism.[6]

Is TSH blunting in depression limited to the acute state of the disorder (state marker) or can it also be observed during remission (trait marker)? Several independent groups of investigators[5,6] have addressed this question. One of the resulting reports has been particularly revealing. Targum demonstrated that only eight of 19 patients with primary depression normalized their TSH response at the time of symptomatic recovery.[21] Moreover, Brambilla et al.[22] found that two of six phenotypically normal first-degree relatives of an affective proband showed blunting. Thus, in some TSH-respon-

TABLE 1
Frequency of TSH Blunting in Various Diagnostic Groups

	Number		
	Total	TSH Blunting	%
Depression	50	13	26
Schizophrenia	13	0	0
Alcoholism			
— Acute Withdrawal	12	6	50
— Post Withdrawal	14	5	36
— Prolonged Sobriety (>2 years)	29	9	31
Borderline Personality Disorder	15	7	47

Definition of TSH blunting ($\triangle$ max TSH < 5.0 μU/ml) was based on the study of 73 normal volunteers of whom none had shown a blunted TSH response.[5]

ders the fault is related to the trait of high vulnerability to depression, whereas in others it is a function of the acute state of this disorder. In a similar way, TSH blunting has been observed in alcoholic patients both during acute withdrawal[19] and after prolonged sobriety.[18] (See also Table 1.)

Sources of variance: Presumably all the factors listed above which influence the TSH response in normal subjects or in nonpsychiatric patients can influence the response in psychiatric patients as well. Thus, the need for age- and sex-matched control groups is obvious. Other factors tend to be uncommon, e.g., renal failure or Klinefelter's syndrome. An exception is nutritional state, and one must control for this in light of the profound appetite disturbances which often accompany depression. We and other investigators have appraised several additional factors as to their relevance for TSH blunting in depression (Table 2). In short, there seems to be no association between the TSH response to TRH and age, severity of depression, previous intake of antidepressant drugs,[5,6] and the patient's height, weight, and body surface.[17] (The latter study was necessary because TRH is usually injected in a standard dose, as opposed to a dose related to body weight.) Nor does the

TABLE 2
Factors Associated With a Reduced TSH Response in Depression

Clinical Factors:

1) Age	no
2) Body surface	no
3) Antidepressant drugs	no
4) Severity of illness	no
5) Subtypes of depression:	
a) primary vs. secondary	unknown
b) unipolar vs. bipolar	no
6) Duration of illness	yes
7) State-Trait occurrence	yes
8) History of violent suicide attempts	yes

Endocrine Factors:

1) Serum thyroid hormone elevation	no
2) Serum cortisol elevation and DST abnormalities	no
3) Dopamine	no
4) Somatostatin	unknown
5) TRH pharmacokinetics	unknown
6) Basal TSH and 24-hr. TSH rhythm	unknown
7) Neurotensin	unknown

TRH test presently seem to aid in the distinction between primary and secondary depression (though the majority of TSH blunting seems to occur in patients with primary depression) or between unipolar or bipolar subgroups.[5,6] There is, however, evidence suggesting that TSH blunting is associated with prolonged duration of illness[23] and a history of suicidal behavior.[24-26] Linkowski et al.[26] extended these findings by showing that the TSH response was virtually absent in patients with a history of violent suicidal behavior, whereas it was normally distributed in those with nonviolent suicidal behavior. In endocrinological terms, it seems unlikely that TSH blunting in depression is the result of increased levels of serum thyroid hormones or cortisol, or of enhanced dopaminergic activity. First, depressed patients with TSH blunting are almost always euthyroid.[5,6,16] Some patients may, paradoxically, show a blunted TSH response and low thyroid hormone levels suggesting a disturbance in feedback inhibition. The concept of a disturbed feedback relationship is further supported by our preliminary finding[27] that pretreatment with a single oral dose of thyroid hormones attenuates the TSH response in normal subjects, but not in depressed patients. Second, depressed patients are often cortisol hypersecretors.[1] However, there has been no clear association shown between cortisol hypersecretion and TSH blunting in several studies that investigated this matter.[5,6] Third, dopamine, whose inhibitory functions on TSH secretion have been well described,[28] does not seem to play a major role in patients with TSH blunting because the prolactin response is usually normal in these patients.[5,6,17]

Prediction of outcome: The TRH test has been used to assess the (clinical) response to standard antidepressant treatment (e.g., tricyclics, ECT), and to predict early relapse after remission induced by such treatment. In several studies[16,21,29,30] TRH was administered during depression and during recovery, the change in maximum ΔTSH between first and second testing serving as the endocrine variable. It was found that an increased maximum ΔTSH on second testing correlated well with a favorable clinical response.[16,29] Furthermore, a persistently low maximum ΔTSH predicted early relapse, usually within six months.[16,29,30] Kirkegaard has recently reviewed these studies in detail.[16] He demonstrated that, by optimizing both test conditions and TSH assay, only 15% of patients are misclassified due to individual and methodological variations. (The reader is referred to that article for a detailed description of the clinical usefulness of the TRH test as a predictor of treatment outcome.) The findings of Krog-Meyer et al.[30] are of interest in an additional way. These investigators reported that the danger of early relapse, as predicted by a persistently low maximum ΔTSH during symptomatic recovery, could be prevented by long-term administration of amitriptyline.

The TRH Test and Other Putative Biological Markers

Information gained from comparing the TRH test with other putative biological markers may be helpful in two ways: It may aid in a better understanding of the pathophysiology of TSH blunting and, perhaps, allow a more refined use of the TRH test as a clinical marker.

TRH test and DST: To date, nine independent groups of investigators have administered both the DST and the TRH test to patients with major depression. Their results indicate that cortisol nonsuppression after dexamethasone and TSH blunting do not show any clear association, suggesting that neither abnormality is an (endocrine) epiphenomenon of the other.[5,6] Three of these studies[31-33] are also of interest. They showed that a higher sensitivity can be achieved in identifying depressed patients if the DST and TRH test are used together. For example, in the study by Extein et al.,[31] 30% of patients were abnormal on both tests, 34% showed TSH blunting, and 20% failed to suppress on the DST. Only 16% were normal on both tests. Targum et al.[33] found 33% of depressed patients (and 89% of nondepressed patients) to be normal on both tests. However, it still remains to be determined whether the predictive value of a combined TRH test and DST is greater than the predictive value of either test alone.

TRH test and monoamine measures: Monoamines are thought to play a role in the pathophysiology of depression.[34,35] They are also, being neurotransmitters, intimately involved in neuroendocrine regulation.[5] It is thus not surprising that several investigators have assessed one or another measure of monoamine function together with the TRH test. As reviewed in detail elsewhere,[6] data regarding urinary excretion of 3-methoxy-4-hydroxyphenylglycol [MHPG] (a norepinephrine metabolite) and the TSH response are equivocal. However, Gold et al.[36] reported a significant negative correlation between TSH response and 5-hydroxyindoleacetic acid [5-HiAA] (a serotonin metabolite) levels in cerebrospinal fluid of depressed patients. Robertson et al.[37] found a significantly reduced uptake of labeled serotonin in blood platelets of euthyroid depressed patients with TSH blunting as compared to normal controls.

Significance of TSH Blunting

The blunting TSH response in some depressed, alcoholic, and borderline patients may have both pathophysiologic significance and practical clinical value, though at present both offer potential possibilities rather than actual results. Moreover, it is important to recall that the observation of TSH blunting in depression may be valuable in one way while a blunted response in the other conditions may be valuable in quite another way.

Pathophysiologic significance: A prominent difficulty in studying brain function in man, apart from its complexity, is the fact that, for obvious reasons, the human brain cannot be studied directly. Thus, "windows"[38] have been utilized. Here, the neuroendocrine system—more precisely TSH secreted by the anterior pituitary gland—provides an important mode of access. In brief, the thyrotroph cells in the anterior pituitary are regulated not only by feedback messages from the periphery (e.g., thyroid hormones, cortisol) but also, via the portal venous system, by hormones secreted by neurons in the hypothalamus. These hormones are TRH, somatostatin, and possibly neurotensin. They are regulated at least in part by neurons from other brain regions which depend for transmission upon the secretion of substances of traditional interest to the psychiatrist—acetylcholine, norepinephrine, dopamine, serotonin, etc. Thus, if the relevant physiologic connections were known, one could make inferences from measurement of TSH about activity of transmitters in the brain. However, as we have pointed out in another place, "it is difficult to draw conclusions about amine transmitters from pituitary hormone measurements. At every level of the system there are complex interactions of multiple factors of opposing signs."[5]

In addition to the neuroendocrine window strategy,[38] one can assemble sufficient evidence to posit two preliminary endocrine hypotheses for TSH blunting. The first hypothesis suggests that TSH blunting in depressed patients may be due to chronic hypersecretion of (endogenous) TRH. In this condition, the thyrotroph cells in the anterior pituitary are thought to become hyporesponsive to TRH, possibly because of down-regulation of thyrotroph-cell TRH receptors. After TRH challenge, these patients then show TSH blunting. This hypothesis rests partly on studies in which TRH was given chronically to normal subjects.[5,6] The second hypothesis regards the status of the thyrotroph cells, which may be disordered or may receive increased inhibitory input in patients with TSH blunting. The notion that thyrotroph cells are primarily disordered is presently not testable. However, we have discussed elsewhere in detail the evidence that they may receive increased inhibitory input in patients with TSH blunting.[5,6]

Clinical utility: During the last decade, the employment of neuroendocrine strategies and the search for biological markers have emerged as two salients of psychiatric research. This effort, however, has produced some confusion. Neuroendocrine measures, as shown above, rest upon complex physiological processes; the notion of biological markers is based on concepts that are only vaguely defined as to their application to psychiatric research. As we[5,39] and others[38] have pointed out, biological findings should be called markers only after they have fulfilled certain stringent criteria, such as acceptable validity, sensitivity, specificity, and predictive value. Biological markers are also defined as state or trait markers. A state marker (e.g., the DST) is an aspect of an illness. By definition it is not present before or after the illness. Its utility lies in aiding in diagnosis. In contrast, a trait marker will be present before, during and after an illness. It helps, therefore, in assessing the likelihood of (or the vulnerability for) an illness. With this consideration in mind, what can be said about the TSH blunting in both depression and alcoholism? It is sometimes a state marker and sometimes a trait marker. The fact that, as a state marker, it can occur in depression and (acute states of) alcoholism without persisting into remission suggests that it may play a role in the pathophysiology of these conditions, though the interpretation of mechanism is uncertain and, possibly, heterogeneous in nature. The fact that, as a trait marker, TSH blunting can occur in depressed patients in remission and in abstinent alcoholics suggests that it may be helpful in identifying subjects with high vulnerability for these conditions. In addition to its possible use as a state or trait marker, TSH blunting has shown promising clinical utility in several ways. The phenomenon may aid in: (a) assessing the response to standard antidepressant treatment; (b) predicting outcome to such treatment; (c) assessing the risk for violent suicide attempts; and (d) describing the relationship between different psychiatric disorders.

Summary

An important conclusion from this work is that the TRH test has excellent research and empirical clinical value. For years investigators and clinicians have suspected relationships between the thyroid axis and behavior, especially in the affective state, but investigations of these relationships have suffered from the criticism that no disorder in thyroid axis function could be identified. This criticism can now be removed. However, if one assumes that depression must be understood as a process (and the clinical course of the disease strongly supports this view), then the study of process requires longitudinal observation. Here, it is worth recalling that the majority of studies cited in this review are based on the administration of TRH during the acute illness, and that only in a few studies were patients retested during symptomatic recovery. Clearly, what is needed are longitudinal studies using multiple testings with a variety of biological markers and repeated, careful assessment of the state of the disorder over an extended period of time. Such studies are likely to clarify further our present knowledge in regard to test-retest reliability of TSH blunting, its state or trait nature, its usefulness for monitoring treatment response and predicting outcome, and its possible association with duration of the disease and suicidal behavior. They are also likely to show whether the TSH response has a seasonal variation and whether it is affected by long-term antidepressant treatment.

References

1. Carroll BJ: The dexamethasone suppression test for melancholia. *Br. J. Psychiatry* 140:292–304, 1982.

2. Rubinow DR et al.: CSF somastatin in affective illness. *Arch. Gen. Psychiatry* 40:409–412, 1983.

3. Winokur A et al.: Variability of hormonal responses to a series of neuroendocrine challenges in depressed patients. *Am. J. Psychiatry* 139:39–44, 1982.

4. Gold PW et al.: Psychiatric implications of basic and clinical studies with corticotropin-releasing factor. *Am. J. Psychiatry* 141:619–627, 1984.

5. Loosen PT, Prange AJ Jr.: Serum thyrotropin response to thyrotropin-releasing hormone in psychiatric patients: A review. *Am. J. Psychiatry* 139:405–416, 1982.

6. Loosen PT: The TRH-induced TSH response in psychiatric patients: A possible neuroendocrine marker. *Psychoneuroendocrinology* 10:237–260, 1985.

7. Schlesser MA et al.: The thyrotropin-releasing hormone stimulation test: A methodological study. *Psychiatry Res.* 9:59–67, 1983.

8. Loosen PT, Youngblood WW, Dew B: Plasma levels of exogenous TRH in normal subjects and two patients with TSH blunting. *Psychopharmacol. Bull.* 19:325–327, 1983.

9. Bassiri RM, Utiger RD: Metabolism and excretion of exogenous TRH in humans. *J. Clin. Treat.* 52:1616–1621, 1973.

10. Wenzel KW: Pharmacological interference with in vitro tests in thyroid function. *Metabolism* 30:717–732, 1981.

11. Zaloga GP et al.: Diagnostic dosages of TRH elevate BP by non-catecholamine mechanisms. *Arch. Intern. Med.* 144:1149–1152, 1984.

12. Borowski GD et al.: Blood pressure response to TRH in euthyroid subjects. *J. Clin. Endocrinol. Metab.* 58:197–200, 1984.

13. Drury PL et al.: Transient amaurosis and headaches after TRH. *Lancet* I:218–219, 1982.

14. Maeda K, Tanimoto K: Epileptic seizures induced by TRH. *Lancet* I:1058–1059, 1981.

15. Dolva LO, Riddervold F, Thorsen RK: Side effect of TRH. *Br. Med. J.* 281:532, 1983.

16. Kirkegaard C: The thyrotropin response to thyrotropin-releasing hormone in endogenous depression. *Psychoneuroendocrinology* 6:189–212, 1981.

17. Loosen PT, Kistler K, Prange AJ Jr.: Use of the TSH response to TRH as an independent variable. *Am. J. Psychiatry* 140:1145–1149, 1983.

19. Loosen PT, Prange AJ Jr, Wilson IC: TRH (Protirelin) in depressed alcoholic

men: Behavioral changes and endocrine responses. *Arch. Gen. Psychiatry* 36:540–547, 1979.

20. Garbutt JC et al.: The TRH test in borderline personality disorder. *Psychiatry Res.* 9:107–113, 1983.

21. Targum SD: The application of serial neuroendocrine challenge studies in the management of depressive disorder. *Biol. Psychiatry* 18:3–19, 1983.

22. Brambilla F et al.: Neuroendocrine correlates and monoaminergic hypothesis in primary affective disorders (PAD). In Brambilla F, Racagni G, de Wied D (eds): *Progress in Psychoneuroendocrinology*, Elsevier/North-Holland, New York, 1980, pp. 235–245.

23. Takahashi S et al.: Thyrotropin-responses to TRH in depressive illness: Relation to clinical subtypes and prolonged duration of depressive episode. *Folia Psychiatr. Neurol. Jpn.* 28:355–365, 1974.

24. Agren H: Biological markers in major depressive disorders: Clinical and multivariate study. *Acta Univ. Uppsaliensis.* Abstracts of Uppsala Dissertations from the Faculty of Medicine, 405, 1981.

25. Kjellman BF: The function of the hypothalamic-pituitary-thyroid axis in affective disorders. Dissertation available from the Karolinska Institute, Department of Psychiatry and Medicine, St. Goran's Hospital, Stockholm, and University of Linkoping, Department of Psychiatry, Stockholm, 1983.

26. Linkowski P et al.: Thyrotropin response to thyreostimulin in affectively ill women: Relationship to suicidal behavior. *Br. J. Psychiatry* 143:401–405, 1983.

27. Loosen PT, Wilson IC, Prange AJ Jr.: Endocrine and behavioral change in depression after TRH: Alteration by pretreatment with thyroid hormones. *J. Affective Disord.* 2:267–278, 1980.

28. Burrow GM et al.: TRH and dopamine interaction affecting pituitary hormone secretions. *J. Clin. Endocrinol. Metab.* 45:65–72, 1977.

29. Langer G et al.: Evidence of neuroendocrine involvement in the therapeutic effects of antidepressant drugs. In Brambilla G, Racagni G, de Wied D (eds.): *Progress in Psychoneuroendocrinology*, Elsevier/North-Holland, New York, 1980, pp. 197–208.

30. Krog-Meyer J et al.: Prediction of relapse with the TRH test and prophylactic amitriptyline in 39 patients with endogenous depression. *Am. J. Psychiatry* 141:945–948, 1984.

31. Extein I, Pottash ALC, Gold MS: Relationship of thyrotropin-releasing hormone test and dexamethasone suppression test abnormalities in unipolar depression. *Psychiatry Res.* 4:49–53, 1981.

32. Rush AJ et al.: Relationships among the TRH test, REM latency and dexamethasone suppression tests: Preliminary findings. *J. Clin. Psychiatry* 44:23–29, 1983.

33. Targum SD, Sullivan AC, Byrnes SM: Neuroendocrine interrelationships in major depressive disorder. *Am. J. Psychiatry* 139:282–286, 1982.

34. Coppen A et al.: Abnormalities of indoleamines in affective disorders. *Arch. Gen. Psychiatry* 26:474–478, 1972.

35. Schildkraut JJ: The catecholamine hypothesis of affective disorders: A review of supporting evidence. *Am. J. Psychiatry* 122:509–522, 1965.

36. Gold PW et al.: Pituitary thyrotropin response to thyrotropin-releasing hor-

mone in affective illness: Relationship to spinal fluid amine metabolites. *Am. J. Psychiatry* 134:1028–1031, 1977.

37. Robertson AG et al.: Biological markers for depressive illness. *Psychopharmacol. Bull.* 18:120–122, 1982.

38. Carroll BJ: Neuroendocrine functions in psychiatric disorders. In Lipton MA, DiMascio A, Killman FK (eds): *Psychopharmacology: A Generation of Progress*, Raven Press, New York, 1978, pp. 487–497.

39. Prange AJ Jr., Loosen PT: Somatic findings in affective disorders: Their status as risk factors. In Regier DA, Allen G (eds): *Risk Factor Research in the Major Mental Disorders*, U.S. Government Printing Office, Washington, DC, 1981.

7

The Risk of Misdiagnosing Physical Illness as Depression

Mark S. Gold and Peter Herridge

EDITOR'S NOTE

Physical illnesses commonly present as psychiatric disturbances. Some statistics are particularly pertinent: For example, in one study nearly 10% of patients seeking help in psychiatric outpatient facilities subsequently revealed physical illnesses accounting for their psychopathological symptoms. In another study, among patients admitted to a state hospital, as many as 46% had physical illnesses which had been previously unrecognized and which were related to their psychiatric disorder.

Missing a physical diagnosis in a psychiatric patient is not the exclusive failing of psychiatrists; it is estimated that 48% of physical disorders are overlooked by psychiatrists but that 32% are missed by nonpsychiatric physicians, and nearly 84% by nonmedical social agencies.

Many psychiatrists are not equipped to deal with physical illnesses. For many, general medical training may be a distant memory; for others, it may never have been adequate and, even when it has been, keeping up to date is extremely difficult. On the other hand, placing one's faith blindly in the diagnostic acumen of other medical specialists can often provide a false sense of security for the treating psychiatrist.

In this chapter, the authors highlight certain clues to help the clinician be more alert to the possibility of hidden physical disease. For example, no matter how closely the patient's condition corresponds to *DSM-III* categorization, this does not automatically rule out physical disorder. Depressive symptoms are particularly common as nonspecific manifestations of organic disease. Cancer, diabetes, hypoadrenalism, hyper- and hypoparathyroidism, hyper- and hypothyroidism, infectious mononucleosis, infectious hepatitis, and a variety of other disorders are important culprits, contributing to or aggravating existing psychopathology.

It is unlikely in the near future that psychiatrists will assume overall diagnostic responsibility for their patients. However, we must be assured that adequate physical investigations have been carried out by competent others and continue to remain on guard for the emergence of signs and symptoms of physical disorder.

Introduction

One of the more recent discoveries of modern psychiatry is that the majority of psychiatric disorders show a remarkably low response to initial treatment.[1] The rates of relapse of patients who are systematically followed for a period of a year or more is disconcerting.[1,2] Such relapses are troublesome for both the patient, who must ask·for further treatment or switch physicians, and the physician who must encounter a less cooperative patient while trying to determine why the initial treatment failed.

One of the major reasons for treatment failures is that many patients are being treated for psychiatric disorders when, in fact, they are suffering from physical illness or drug or alcohol abuse.[3-6] Psychiatric symptomatology can be, and frequently is, the first manifestation of a reversible physical illness. Contrary to the beliefs of most psychiatric and nonpsychiatric physicians, patients whose psychiatric symptoms mask physical illness are not rare.[3-6] While many psychiatrists contend that they have "never seen one," it has, in fact, been repeatedly documented by many different authors that physical illness needs to be vigorously excluded before a psychiatric diagnosis can be made.[3-6]

It is assumed by the *DSM-III* committee, and it is clear from looking at the *DSM-III* differential diagnosis trees, that physical illnesses must be ruled out before proceeding through the decision tree. If a physical illness is found to be the etiology of the psychiatric symptoms then the diagnosis must move into the section on organic mental disorders. Unfortunately, the most common misdiagnoses and the state-of-the-art workup for each are never addressed.

Misdiagnosis: Is It Really a Problem?

Hall et al.[3] studied 658 consecutive psychiatric outpatients and found that 9.1% of these patients had medical disorders that produced the psychiatric symptoms. Additional patients in whom medical disorders were mostly or partially causative were discussed but not quantified. Forty-six percent of these patients could have been identified by their initial treating physicians. In another study of outpatients, Koranyi[5] excluded all patients who were immediately hospitalized as well as those patients who failed to complete a comprehensive assessment. He started with an initial sample of 2,670 patients; a final sample of 2,090 patients who had been completely evaluated was examined. Forty-three percent of these patients were suffering from one or several major physical illnesses, 46% of which were undiagnosed at the time of referral. Of the total population 7.74% had a physical illness which was causative of the psychiatric symptoms. Herridge[6] studied 209 consecutive admissions to an inpatient unit and found that at least 5% had major physical illnesses which were causative of and presented as a psychiatric disorder.

Hall et al.[4] conducted a prospective study of 100 admitted state hospital patients. Patients with known physical disorders along with sociopathic personality disorders and persons with significant histories of alcohol or drug abuse were omitted. An intensive search for causative physical illness revealed that 46% of the patients had a previously unrecognized and undiagnosed physical illness that was specifically related to their psychiatric symptoms and either caused these symptoms or substantially exacerbated them. Hall notes that, "28 of 46 patients evidenced dramatic and rapid clearing of their psychiatric symptoms when medical treatment for the underlying physical disorder was instituted. Eighteen patients were substantially improved immediately following medical treatments."[4] Similar findings were found by Hoffman,[7] who reported that, of 215 patients referred to a specialized medical psychiatric inpatient unit for further evaluation, the referring diagnosis was inaccurate in 41% of the cases, and 24% of cases were changed from physical to psychiatric or from psychiatric to physical illness.

Both psychiatrists and nonpsychiatrists fail to diagnose physical illness. Koranyi[5] reported that of all the sources referring patients to his outpatient clinic, nonpsychiatrists failed to find 32% of physical illness in referred patients, while psychiatrists missed 48% of physical illness in referred patients. Most striking was that 83$\frac{1}{2}$% of all patients referred by social agencies or who were self-referred had undetected physical illness at the time they were seen in the outpatient department. Physicians are better than the patients themselves and other mental health workers in diagnosing physical illness, but their overall performance is poor by any standards.

These studies clearly show that physical illness is either a precipitant or associated condition which needs to be considered in any diagnostic formulation. More sophisticated and provocative testing techniques have been used successfully to help diagnose thyroid disease[8] and identify low dose drug and alcohol abuse in our psychiatric patients. These new tests will increase the percentage of detected medical illnesses.[9]

Why Misdiagnosis Exists

The factors which lead to diagnostic errors are important and need to be scrutinized in detail. Despite the fact that they are physicians, many psychiatrists are particularly unequipped to deal with physical illness in their patients. Klein et al.[10] feel that errors in diagnosis "cannot be attributed to random sloppiness, bad faith, or lack of desire to help a patient to the utmost." They propose a variety of reasons, including simple lack of knowledge, educational lag in residency training programs, lack of continuing medical education, and resistance to new information. This can lead to a selective rejection of certain facts of the case so that the patient will more easily fit into the physician's specialty or orientation, and permits the psychiatrist to maintain his allegiance to certain schools of psychiatric and/or medical thought. This often results in a distortion and misperception of the patient and his sometimes obvious physical illness.

McIntyre and Romano[11] found that less than 35% of practicing psychiatrists give their patients a physical examination. Thirty-two percent of psychiatrists admitted that they felt incompetent to perform even a rudimentary physical. The numbers actually may be much greater. As a result, when psychiatric patients are examined by psychiatrists, the examination is, at best, perfunctory and not directed towards searching out medical disorders which could present with psychiatric symptoms.

Most psychiatrists use the same means of sidestepping these issues as nurses, social workers, psychologists, and other nonmedical psychotherapists. They all consult either the patient's family doctor, internist, pediatrician, or gynecologist for a medical clearance to rule out physical disorders. This practice unfortunately is, in our opinion, a grave mistake. Reliance on the other medical specialists has been suggested by Hall et al.[3,4] and Koranyi[5] to provide "a false sense of security for the treating psychiatrist."[4] Koranyi[5] used this procedure in the past and rejected it because, "My early practice consisting of a referral for routine medical consultation proved to be insufficient and unsatisfactory." He prefers to have the psychiatrist perform the examination personally because "a thorough and unprejudiced physical examination with the appropriate biochemical screening is a singularly important act to be performed with the greatest thoroughness on all patients." He goes on to state that "the examiner must continually entertain the question what 'other than obvious' might be the cause or contributing factor to the presenting symptom?" Sadly, few psychiatrists act or think in this manner.

The previously cited studies refer only to physical illnesses which present as psychiatric disorders and were, in whole or in part, causative of the psychiatric symptoms. Physical illness can cause or worsen psychiatric symptoms to a variable extent. Some disorders which present exclusively with psychiatric symptoms are wholly causative of the psychiatric symptomatology. Proper treatment of these disorders, if they have not progressed to an irreversible stage, should result in a total clearing (a cure) of all the psychiatric symptomatology without institution of psychiatric treatment. Consequently, psychiatric symptoms which develop in reaction to previously existing illness will be considered only in passing. Other disorders exacerbate or in part cause the observed psychiatric symptomatology; when they are treated, there is a significant but only partial clearing of the psychiatric symptoms. Still other illnesses are concomitant with and unrelated to the psychiatric disorders; when they are treated, there is no effect on the psychiatric symptoms. Finally, there are psychiatric illnesses that are often treated incorrectly as medical disorders by nonpsychiatric practitioners.

Many disorders are truly on the borderline between psychiatry and internal medicine and neurology. Most of them are not detectable by physical examination or by "routine" laboratory screening alone. The correct diagnosis may not be made unless the attending physician is aware of the existence of these diseases and actively pursues the diagnosis through aggressive specialized chemical testing. As many as 50 or 100 patients with apparently similar symptomatology may have to be tested to find one patient with a physical disorder. We feel that this search is always worth it. Many times such an intensive search is dismissed by our informed colleagues as a search for "zebras" and not justified on a cost-effective basis. However, it is interesting to note the behavior of these same colleagues when they or members of their family develop psychiatric symptoms. They insist that no stone be left unturned in the search for a physical and "more easily treatable" cause of these symptoms.

Specificity of Presenting Psychiatric Symptoms

From the previously cited studies and many others, it becomes clear that no matter how closely the first presentation of a psychiatric patient may conform to classical *DSM-III* descriptive criteria, one cannot assume that the patient is suffering from a psychiatric disorder.

This nonspecificity of medical disease causing specific syndromes is particularly true for depressive disorders. The differential diagnosis of depression is long and involved. Giannini et al.[12] list 91 possible disorders which can present as depression. Hall[13] lists 24 medical illnesses that frequently induce depression and 77 medical conditions which can present as depression. Below various medical disorders which can present psychiatrically and mimic depressive illness are reviewed.

AIDS: The neurologic disease produced by the AIDS virus may initially be manifested by symptoms that mimic functional psychiatric syndromes. Psychiatric symptoms are most often seen in AIDS patients with opportunistic infections and in some patients precede other manifestations of AIDS.

These symptoms may be related to systemic infection, primary cerebral infection or metabolic abnormalities. Persons who have not developed the standard criteria for the diagnosis of AIDS may present with symptoms such as insomnia, anxiety, irritability, emotional lability or even paranoid delusions or severe depressive symptoms.

The mental symptoms in AIDS may remain static or become exacerbated by metabolic problems or progress to severe dementia or to a severely apathetic, negative, and withdrawn state which may erroneously be thought to be dementia.

The carcinoid syndrome: Carcinoid tumor may be confused with major depression, hypomania, major depression with psychosis, or anxiety. It may not always be accompanied by spontaneous flushing of the upper body precipitated by consuming certain foods or alcohol, epinephrine administration, excitement, or exertion. An attack may be accompanied by abdominal pain and diarrhea. The syndrome accompanies a variety of tumors which occur in the gastrointestinal tract and lungs. These tumors secrete various biologically active substances including dopamine, histamine, ACTH, and serotonin. Serotonin-secreting tumors are most common.

If this disorder is included in the differential diagnosis, the diagnosis may be confirmed by an increased urinary excretion of 5-hydroxyindoleacetic acid (5-HIAA), which normally does not exceed 9 milligrams daily.

Cancer: Many malignant tumors may present to the psychiatrist with depressive symptomatology, many meeting *DSM-III* criteria months or even years earlier than physical symptoms or signs.

Central nervous system tumors present with psychiatric symptomatology especially if they occur in the temporal and frontal regions. The most common symptom is a change in personality. Left-sided tumors present more frequently as irritability or depression, while tumors of the parietal and occipital lobes tend to be relatively silent. Limbic system tumors can present as depression, delusions, assaultive behavior, and confusional states. A high index of suspicion is indicated when the patient presents in an atypical fashion with a personality change, shows signs of depression with a weight loss greater than 20 pounds, or is unresponsive to a first trial of standard psychiatric treatment.

Diabetes mellitus: In Hall et al.'s study[4] certain patients with diabetes mellitus presented psychiatrically and met the diagnostic criteria for major depression, as well as for other disorders. Koranyi[5] noted that diabetes may present as depression, sexual dysfunction, and/or marital problems. The diagnosis is made by demonstrating an elevated fasting blood sugar or an abnormal response to a glucose load at one and two hours.

Illicit drugs: Conservative sources estimate that 18- to 25-year-olds have the highest percent of illicit use in all drug categories. However, drug use is also epidemic in 25- to 40-year-olds and correlates much closer with income (the higher or lower the income the more drug abuse) than with the chief complaint.

A recent study found that 17% of all high school seniors had tried cocaine within 30 days of the survey. Recent estimates are that one out of ten people in the U.S.A. have an addiction to alcohol and that 15% of all people have either a drug or alcohol problem.

Drug and alcohol abuse and withdrawal may imitate depressive illnesses. Furthermore, hospitalized psychiatric patients sometimes abuse drugs in the hospital, resulting in confusing changes in function and severe exacerbations of their illnesses. The only way to make the drug abuse diagnosis is to be constantly aware of the frequency of drug and alcohol problems. Simply questioning the patient without testing is both naive and dangerous. Drug intoxication, drug withdrawal, and sequelae of drug abuse should be actively eliminated from consideration.[9] They commonly present as depression and may meet *DSM-III-R* criteria for major depression. They can, however, resemble any known psychiatric symptom, from psychosis to mild anxiety states, and must be considered in all psychiatric disorders no matter how classical the presentation. Asking the patient about existence and extent of drug use is necessary but anecdote should never be confused with fact. Drug use, drug intoxication, and drug withdrawal diagnosis can only be made by blood or urine testing.

Prescription drugs: Psychiatric symptoms occur in at least 2.7% of patients taking prescription medication on a regular basis, according to the Boston Collaborative Drug Surveillance Study of 9000 patients.

Hyperadrenalism (Cushing's syndrome): Cushing's syndrome may present as an affective illness with or without psychosis, euphoria, or anxiety. In one study using structured interviews and RDC criteria, depression was present in 83% of patients with endogenous Cushing's syndrome who met RDC criteria for either mania and hypomania prior to the depression.

Hypoadrenalism (Addison's disease): Hypoadrenalism commonly presents psychiatrically as depression or organic brain syndrome. The diagnosis is usually made on the basis of low diurnal serum cortisol or low 24-hour urine cortisol excretion; it is easily treated with steroid replacement therapy.

Hypoglycemia: Many patients diagnose themselves as hypoglycemic in order to explain their depressive symptomatology. There is little proof that all such patients have symptomatic hypoglycemia. However, there are several conditions which can cause symptomatic hypoglycemia, the most prominent of which are insulinoma and the exogenous administration of insulin. Insulinoma is probably the most frequent cause of symptomatic hypoglycemia and may produce bizarre behavior, which may be indistinguishable from schizophrenia, depression, dementia, or anxiety attacks. The diagnosis depends on simultaneous documentation of increased plasma insulin and hypoglycemia using a five-hour glucose tolerance test.

Hyperparathyroidism/hypoparathyroidism: The psychiatric disturbances seen in hyperparathyroidism are directly related to the serum calcium levels. Serum calcium levels of 12 to 16 mgs per 100 ml are associated with psychiatric changes. Hypoparathyroidism with resultant low serum calcium levels most commonly presents as an organic brain syndrome, but may appear to be delirium tremens or depression with psychosis. Diagnosis of both hyperparathyroidism and hypoparathyroidism is first suspected upon seeing an abnormal serum calcium level on routine blood screening or from a history of thyroid or parathyroid disorders in the family and/or previous thyroid or parathyroid surgery.

Hyperthyroidism: Hyperthyroidism may present resembling panic disorders, anxiety, neurosis, and mania. It is not realized that hyperthyroidism frequently presents as depression. The diagnosis of hyperthyroidism is made by the classical signs and symptoms of hyperthyroidism along with elevated T_3 and T_4, a depressed level of TSH, and a low TSH response to TRH administration.

Hypothyroidism: Hypothyroidism has been classically associated with psychosis in the form of "myxedema madness." It is also associated with depression and organic brain syndromes. Gold and Pearsall[8] have demonstrated that there is a subtle form of hypothyroidism, "subclinical hypothyroidism," in which all the thyroid function tests including T_3, T_4, T_3 uptake, and TSH are normal in the presence of exaggerated TSH response to administration of intravenous TRH. Patients with an augmented ΔTSH and titers of thyroid autoantibodies have successfully been treated with thyroid hormone alone. Furthermore, a discrete syndrome, "symptomless autoimmune thyroiditis" (SAT) exists in 7–15% of inpatients and outpatients who meet *DSM-III* criteria for major depression.

Metal poisonings: Heavy metal poisonings can occur with environmental exposure, pica, or poisoning with a wide variety of metals, including magnesium, copper, zinc, manganese, lead, mercury, thallium, bismuth, aluminum, arsenic, and bromides. Most consistently they produce an organic brain syndrome but can mimic major depression.

Unless actively looked for with heavy metal screens by atomic absorption or plasma emission spectroscopy of urine and blood, metal poisoning will not be found or properly treated. If it is detected and treated early enough, the psychiatric symptoms are, for the most part, reversible.

Huntington's chorea: There is a high incidence of symptoms resembling both mania and depression in patients with Huntington's chorea. This was noted even in Huntington's original article of 1872, in which he noted, "The tendency to insanity and sometimes that form of insanity which leads to suicide is marked." As in other diseases, from hypothyroidism to folate or B$_{12}$ deficiency, psychiatric manifestations of this disease can occur well before any of the choreiform movements or any of the signs of dementia.

Infectious mononucleosis: Infectious mononucleosis may be followed by a syndrome which is identical to a major depressive episode. The diagnosis of infectious mononucleosis is made by a positive heterophile or mono spot test. A single negative test *never* excludes the diagnosis.

Infectious hepatitis: Psychiatric symptomatology before, during, or after infectious hepatitis of any type, either A, B, or non-A non-B, can range from mild lethargy to major depression. There are even some reports of suicide and acute delusional mania following hepatitis.

Multiple sclerosis: Multiple sclerosis is a demyelineating neurologic disease characterized by lesions which are separated in space and time within the central nervous system. It has been associated with a wide variety of psychiatric symptomatology, including mania and depression.

Pancreatic carcinoma: Of all the malignant tumors that present psychiatrically, pancreatic carcinoma is the most notorious.[14] The first signs of the tumor are often severe depression with crying spells, insomnia unresponsive to sleeping medication, and anxiety associated with the fear that the patient has a very serious illness.[14]

Panhypopituitarism: Psychiatric presentations are common in pituitary failure and usually present with depression and lack of libido.

Post concussion syndrome: The post concussion syndrome occurs as the aftereffect of brain damage from severe head injury. It may present psychiatrically as anxiety, depression, excess anger, loss of emotional control, mood swings from euphoria to depression, and social disinhibition. Lesions of the left hemisphere, especially the left temporal lobe, tend to produce more psychiatric symptoms, as well as intellectual deficits. Affective and behavioral symptoms are more frequently observed in right hemisphere damage.

Syphilis (general paresis): At one time syphilis accounted for 10–20% of all admissions to state hospitals for the insane. This makes penicillin one of the most important psychiatric treatments and the VDRL and STS the most important psychiatric laboratory tests of all time.

Systemic lupus erythematosus: Systemic lupus erythematosus is a relatively uncommon disease which occurs in 2–3 per 100,000 population with a 9 : 1 ratio favoring females. It presents between ages 10 and 70 and may be accompanied by a wide variety of psychiatric symptoms, including mania, depression, schizophreniform or schizophrenic psychosis, and organic brain syndrome. It may often be labeled as a conversion disorder. It is ignored or overlooked in young females presenting with psychiatric symptoms and complaining of arthralgias, despite the fact that arthralgias are the most common first presentation of this disorder.

Vitamin deficiencies: Among the better known vitamin deficiencies associated with psychiatric symptoms are folate[4,14] and vitamin B_{12} deficiency,[14] as well as niacin (nicotinic acid) deficiency. Folic acid deficiency presents with depression, fatigue, and lassitude. Marked deficiency can present with burning feet, restless leg syndrome, and/or a depression which is unresponsive to antidepressant therapy. Coppen and Abou-Saleh[15] found a higher rate of affective morbidity in those patients with low folate levels as compared to those patients with normal folate levels in patients treated in a lithium clinic. Hall,[4] in his prospective study of hospitalized state psychiatric patients, found three cases of folate deficiency, two of which presented as RDC schizophrenia and one as RDC schizoaffective disorder. Normal CBC folate deficiency occurs frequently and is often misdiagnosed and mistreated.

Vitamin B_{12} deficiency may also present psychiatrically in the absence of any signs of anemia or bone marrow changes, and may present neurological-ly as a peripheral neuropathy or myelopathy (subacute combined degenera-tion). It has been known to present with a wide spectrum of psychiatric disorders, including apathy, irritability, depression, dementia, confusional states, paranoid states, and schizophreniform psychosis.[14]

Patients who develop a zinc deficiency may become "frankly depressed," complain of lost interest in food, and show weight loss.

Frequency of Occurrence of Nonpsychiatric Illness Presenting as Psychiatric Symptoms

Depression symptoms caused by drug, alcohol, and other substance abuse appear to be the most common cause of psychiatric misdiagnosis and mis-treatment (see figure 1). As a general category, endocrine disorders are most frequently associated with depressive symptoms. Provocative testing will make this point even more clear in the future. The next most commonly involved organ system is the central nervous system. Toxic and withdrawal disorders are found third most commonly. Nutritional disorders and infec-tious diseases are the next most common. Cancer and metabolic disorders like Wilson's disease, acute intermittent porphyria, G6 PDase deficiency, and polycystic ovaries are found but are rare unless the patient has an unusual presentation, recent treatment failure, atypical features, or a weight loss of 20 pounds or more.

To reduce misdiagnosis and mistreatment of depression, a complete phys-ical, neurological, and endocrinological examination should be performed by a physician who is fluent in both psychiatry and internal medicine. This should not be the kind of perfunctory examination mentioned earlier in this chapter, but one directed toward finding physical illnesses that can cause or exacerbate psychiatric symptoms. One should especially examine for thyroid abnormalities, carotid bruits, arteriosclerotic changes in the retinal vessels, cardiac murmurs, abdominal bruits, and skin and nail fold changes.

While the laboratory is becoming an important component of any evalua-tion,[9] it does not replace the physician. Lab tests are ordered to correspond to and confirm the major issues in the differential. The bias is to actually rule out a possible diagnosis by testing rather than relying solely on clinical impression, which we find inaccurate in about 25% of cases. No tests are routine, with the exception of admission blood levels of all medications the patient is taking.

The practice of psychiatry is likely to change radically in the future. We hope that the information contained here and reported elsewhere in greater detail[16] will help present and future psychiatrists to more easily make this change.

WHEN "DEPRESSION" ISN'T

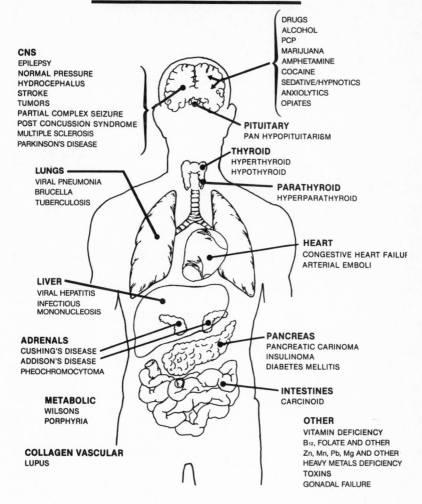

CNS
EPILEPSY
NORMAL PRESSURE
HYDROCEPHALUS
STROKE
TUMORS
PARTIAL COMPLEX SEIZURE
POST CONCUSSION SYNDROME
MULTIPLE SCLEROSIS
PARKINSON'S DISEASE

DRUGS
ALCOHOL
PCP
MARIJUANA
AMPHETAMINE
COCAINE
SEDATIVE/HYPNOTICS
ANXIOLYTICS
OPIATES

PITUITARY
PAN HYPOPITUITARISM

THYROID
HYPERTHYROID
HYPOTHYROID

LUNGS
VIRAL PNEUMONIA
BRUCELLA
TUBERCULOSIS

PARATHYROID
HYPERPARATHYROID

HEART
CONGESTIVE HEART FAILUR
ARTERIAL EMBOLI

LIVER
VIRAL HEPATITIS
INFECTIOUS
MONONUCLEOSIS

ADRENALS
CUSHING'S DISEASE
ADDISON'S DISEASE
PHEOCHROMOCYTOMA

PANCREAS
PANCREATIC CARINOMA
INSULINOMA
DIABETES MELLITIS

METABOLIC
WILSONS
PORPHYRIA

INTESTINES
CARCINOID

OTHER
VITAMIN DEFICIENCY
B12, FOLATE AND OTHER
Zn, Mn, Pb, Mg AND OTHER
HEAVY METALS DEFICIENCY
TOXINS
GONADAL FAILURE

COLLAGEN VASCULAR
LUPUS

References

1. Shapiro RW, Keller MB: Initial 6 month follow-up of patients with major depressive disorder. *J. Affective Disord.* 3:205–220, 1981.

2. Hamilton M: The effect of treatment on the melancholias (depressions). *Br. J. Psychiatry* 140:223–230, 1982.

3. Hall RCW et al.: Physical illness presenting as psychiatric disease. *Arch. Gen. Psychiatry* 35:1315–1320, 1978.

4. Hall RCW et al.: Unrecognized physical illness prompting psychiatric admission: A prospective study. *Am. J. Psychiatry* 138:629–635, 1981.

5. Koranyi EK: Morbidity and rate of undiagnosed physical illness in a psychiatric clinic population. *Arch. Gen. Psychiatry* 36:414–419, 1979.

6. Herridge CF: Physical disorders in psychiatric illness: A study of 209 consecutive admissions. *Lancet* II:949–951, 1960.

7. Hoffman RS: Diagnostic errors in the evaluation of behavioral disorders. *JAMA* 248:964–967, 1982.

8. Gold MS, Pearsall HR: Hypothyroidism — or is it depression? *Psychosomatics* 24:646–654, 1983.

9. Gold MS, Pottash AC, Extein I: The Psychiatric Laboratory. In Bernstein JG (ed): *Clinical Psychopharmacology*, John Wright PSG, Boston, 1982, pp. 29–58.

10. Klein DF, Gittelman R, Quitkin F, Rifkin A: *Diagnosis and Drug Treatment of Psychiatric Disorders: Adults and Children*, Williams and Wilkins, Baltimore, 1980, p. 849.

11. McIntyre JW, Romano J: Is there a stethoscope in the house (and is it used)? *Arch. Gen. Psychiatry* 34:1147–1151, 1977.

12. Giannini AJ, Black HR, Goettsche RL: *Psychiatric, Psychogenic, and Somatopsychic Disorders Handbook*, Medical Examination Publishing Company, New York, 1978, p. 316.

13. Hall RCW: *Psychiatric Presentations of Medical Illness*. Spectrum, New York, 1980, p. 421.

14. Jefferson JW, Marshall JR: *Neuropsychiatric Features of Medical Disorders*, Plenum, New York, 1981, p. 383.

15. Coppen A, Abou-Saleh MT: Plasma folate and affective morbidity during long term lithium therapy. *Br. J. Psychiatry* 141:87–89, 1982.

16. Gold MS, Lydiard RB, Carman JS (eds): *Advances in Psychopharmacology: Predicting and Improving Treatment Response*, CRC Press, Boca Raton, FL, 1984.

8

The Diagnosis of Depression in the Elderly

Thomas A. Ban and Michael H. Ebert

EDITOR'S NOTE

Psychiatric morbidity is disproportionately high among the elderly. Depression is the most frequently encountered nonorganic disorder in this age group; it is often associated with physical illness. Suicide is especially common among elderly white males. Physical disease, specific life events, and disease affecting the central nervous system contribute significantly to the occurrence of depression. It is particularly interesting that right-handed patients with single ischemic lesions affecting the left frontal cortex reveal a high incidence of depression (without a previous history of depression), in contrast to patients with lesions affecting other parts of the brain.

The criteria for the diagnosis of depression here are essentially the same as those for its diagnosis in any age group. Insomnia, restlessness, and psychotic manifestations, such as delusions, are more common in elderly depressions than in mood disorders among younger patients; retardation is less common. Bodily concerns, constipation, indecisiveness, and overall inefficiency are frequently seen.

Differential diagnosis is critical. Physical illnesses can present themselves in the form of depression. Depression can appear in the form of somatic symptoms. One should be on the alert for multiple sclerosis, normal pressure hydrocephalus, temporal lobe tumor, endocrine disorders such as hypothyroidism, adrenal insufficiency, and hyperparathyroidism, and metabolic disorders involving a decrease in serum sodium and/or potassium or an increase in serum calcium. Pseudodementia refers to a condition that mimics organic dementia. However, it is sudden or subacute, not chronic; it signals an underlying depression and can sometimes be diagnostically confirmed by the dexamethasone suppression test; it is reversible, being amenable to antidepressant treatment regimens.

Introduction

While individual life span has remained unchanged, average life expectancy at birth has increased four times during recorded history.[1] As a result of the rapid increase in average life expectancy at birth during the last 100 years, more than 200 million of the 3 billion people living today are aged, i.e., 65 years old or older.[2]

In the United States, average life expectancy at birth increased from 50 years in 1900 to 73 years in 1967; and, while 200 years ago about 80% of Americans had died before reaching age 60, today 80% of deaths occur after this age.[3] Consequently, there are approximately 25 million people 65 years of age and over, and it is estimated that by the year 2025, their total number will rise to at least 42 million.[4,5] This means that one in nine Americans is already over 65, and that in 50 years this figure is expected to increase to one in five.[6]

The drastic shift in the age distribution of the general population has focused attention on gerontology (a term introduced by the Russian medical scientist Elie Metchnikoff), the scientific study of the aging process, and on geriatrics (a term introduced by the American pediatrician Ignaz Nascher), the medical specialty concerned with the study, prevention, and treatment of pathological conditions of the aged.[3] Gerontology deals with primary aging or senescence, which is a biologic process rooted in heredity. Geriatrics deals with secondary aging or senility, i.e., defects and disabilities resulting from disease.[7]

Morbidity in the Aged

Medical illness occurs in a disproportionately high percentage in the aged. While individuals over age 65 make up 13% of the general population, they account for more than 30% of the visits to internists in the United States.[5] The same 13%, elderly Americans, are responsible for nearly one-third of overall health expenditures[8] and account for over 40% of acute hospital bed days.[9]

Psychiatric morbidity, like morbidity for other medical illness, is also disproportionately high in the aged.[10] During the first half of the century, a threefold increase in the number of people over 65 years of age in the U.S. was associated with a ninefold increase in the number of first admissions from this age group to mental hospitals. In spite of the sharp reduction in admission rates to mental hospitals for all age ranges from 1958 to 1968, first admission rates in 1965 were about 70 per 100,000 for the age group under 65, 100 per 100,000 for the age group 65 to 74, and as high as 200 per 100,000 for the age group 75 to 84.[11,12]

It is estimated that of every 1,000 persons 65 years of age or older in the United States, at least nine are living in mental hospitals and 27 in nursing or rest homes. Approximately 60% of these institutionalized patients suffer from organic mental disorders, and possibly as many as 90% of allegedly nonpsychiatric nursing home patients show psychopathologic symptoms.[10] In addition, a study in Baltimore from the early 1960s showed that 12% of the noninstitutionalized population over age 65 suffered from mental illness.[14] In San Francisco, the figure was 15%.[15] An even higher 20 to 45% prevalence rate was suggested by Busse and Pfeiffer.[7]

Medical illness frequently coexists with and complicates psychiatric illness in the aged. One survey showed that 80% of the elderly patients admitted to a psychiatric unit had at least one significant physical illness, including congestive heart failure, stroke, respiratory infection, peripheral neuritis, neoplasm, cirrhosis and/or malnutrition.[16]

Mental Illness in the Aged

Psychiatric illness in the elderly is not restricted to the effects of structural changes of the brain and diseases of the cerebrovascular system. Functional disorders are also commonly encountered in aged patients.[17] It is estimated that approximately 4% of the aged between 65 to 74 years old, and 20% of 75 years of age and older have organic mental impairment, and an additional 15% of the older people have functional psychiatric disturbances.[18]

Prevalence of depression: Depression, one of the most common psychiatric disorders, with a worldwide prevalence of 3%, is the most frequent among the functional disorders in the aged. There is no consensus, however, regarding the prevalence of depression in elderly people.[19] Thus, while Gianturco and Busse[20] estimate that nearly one-third of people over 60 experience depressed mood to some degree, Gurland and Cross[21] suggest that only 2 to 13% suffer from a "true major clinical depression."[22]

Prevalence figures for depression differ in community-based and institutionalized psychogeriatric patients. According to Crook,[23] the prevalence of depression may be on the order of 13% in the community among elderly persons,[24] while it may exceed 30% in medical settings.[25] Furthermore, it is estimated that about 50% of the patients over age 65 admitted to mental hospitals or psychiatric units of general hospitals are hospitalized primarily because of depression.[26] In keeping with this are the findings that affective disorders are present in somewhat more than 50% of hospitalized psychogeriatric patients in the age group between 60 and 70. There is a sharp decrease, however, in the occurrence of depressive illness in patients over the age of 80,[27] but in the population over the age of 80 with physical illness, the prevalence of depression remains 50%.[28]

Prevalence of suicide: It is reasonable to assume that the high increase of depression is responsible, at least in part, for the high suicide rate in old age. This is best exemplified by the finding that those over age 65 account for 25% of all suicides, even though they constitute only 13% of the total population.[29] Although the peak age for suicide in women is between 45 and 54, suicides increase continuously with age among white men in the United States.[30] Since suicide occurs at a higher rate among elderly men than among older women,[22] one can understand that in the study of Sendbuehler and Goldstein[29] the highest suicide rates were found in age groups above 55 years old, rising progressively from 32 per 1,000 in the 50 to 54 age group to 48 per 1,000 in the age group above 74. As with suicide, depression may be responsible, at least in part, for the high prevalence of alcoholism in psychogeriatric patients.[31,32]

Genetic factors: Sufficient evidence suggests that more than half of all depressed geropsychiatric patients experience the first depressive episode after the age of 60.[33] Since the morbidity risk for patients of depressive probands was 9.3% with a late onset and 15.7% with an early onset of the disease, and since the morbidity risk for first degree relatives of depressive patients was 8.3% with a late onset and 20.1% with an early onset,[34] Mendelwicz[35] proposed that depressive disorders appearing in the old age group may be genetically different from depressive disorders in the young age group. He suggested that polygenic inheritance, i.e., a combination of multiple interacting genes and environmental factors, may play a role in late onset depression. This would explain the relatively low morbidity risk for affective disorders in the parents and first degree relatives of depressed psychogeriatric patients.[36]

Psychogenic factors: It is a common contention, but not conclusively proven, that psychogenic factors play an important role in a considerable proportion of elderly depressions. Until such evidence is confirmed by properly designed clinical experiments, life events can only be considered of etiologic significance if Jaspers' three criteria of "pathological reaction" are fulfilled.[37] Accordingly, an adequate precipitating factor must stand in a close time relationship with the reactive state. There must also be a meaningful connection between the content of the experience and those of the abnormal reaction. Finally, the (depressive) reaction must be reversible, i.e., disappear when the primary cause for the reaction is removed. The majority of patients who fulfill Jaspers' criteria are diagnosed as "adjustment disorder with depressed mood" (300.00) in the *DSM-III*.[38] In the 9th edition of the International Classification of Diseases (ICD-9), the same patients might be diagnosed as suffering from brief (309.0) or prolonged (309.1) depressive reaction or neurotic depression (300.4).[39]

Somatic illness: Irrespective of psychogenic factors, there are indications that somatic disease may play a role in the onset of depressive manifestations in a considerable proportion of the elderly.[40,41] Although the causal relationship between the two is far from being established, Salzman and van der Kolk[22] contend that myocardial infarction or the diagnosis of cancer produce depressive symptoms, and the more severe this disease, the more profound the depression. They also suggest that depressive symptoms of varying intensity may also accompany chronic disease such as stroke, arthritis, diabetes, or glaucoma. As the chronic illness becomes increasingly incapacitating, a state of emotional hopelessness and helplessness sets in, signaling a true depressive illness. In medically ill elderly patients, concurrent depression appears to reduce life expectancy.[42]

Central nervous system disorders: Included among somatic disease are disorders of the central nervous system. Recognition of their possible role in triggering depression yielded *DSM-III* diagnoses of primary degenerative dementia (simple onset) with depression (290.21), and multi-infarct dementia with depression (290.43). Nevertheless, the fact remains that such a relationship has been revealed to date only for arteriosclerotic brain disease (multi-infarct dementia) and not for senile dementia (primary degenerative dementia).[17,43] Paradoxically, in ICD-9, a depressed type is recognized only for senile dementia (290.2) and not for arteriosclerotic dementia.

Corresponding with the association between depression and arteriosclerotic brain disease are the findings that depressive disorders which meet *DSM-III* criteria for either major depression or dysthymic disorder occur in approximately 20–25% of post-stroke patients. In this context, it is of both heuristic and practical importance that Robinson, Lipsey, and Price[44] revealed a significant relationship in these patients between depression and the site of the lesion. In a study of right-handed patients with single ischemic lesions and no history of depressive disorder, 6 of 10 patients with left frontal lesions had symptoms of major depression, while only 2 of 20 patients with other lesion locations manifested depressive symptoms. Furthermore, among the patients with left frontal lesions there was a strong positive correlation between the proximity of the lesion on CT scan to the frontal pole and severity of depression.

Diagnosis of Depression

The diagnosis of major depressive episode in the *DSM-III* is based on the presence of dysphoria or loss of interest in all or almost all social activities and pastimes.[38] In addition to the obligatory mood disturbance, which does not necessarily need to be the dominant symptom, the patient also needs to experience at least four of the following symptoms nearly every day for a period of at least two weeks: (1) poor appetite or significant weight loss, or increased appetite or significant weight gain; (2) insomnia or hypersomnia; (3) psychomotor agitation and retardation; (4) loss of interest or pleasure in usual activities; (5) loss of energy; (6) feelings of worthlessness or inappropriate guilt; (7) complaints or evidence of diminished ability to think or concentrate; and (8) recurrent thoughts of death or suicide attempt. However, even if these criteria are fulfilled, the diagnosis of major depressive episode cannot be made if bizarre behavior or preoccupation with a mood-incongruent delusion or hallucination dominates the clinical picture; if the depressive manifestations are superimposed on either schizophrenia, schizophreniform disorder, or a paranoid disorder; and/or if the depressive syndrome is due to any organic mental disorder or uncomplicated bereavement. These diagnostic criteria of the *DSM-III* apply to all adults (and, with some minor modification, also to children), regardless of whether they are young or aged.

According to Salzman and van der Kolk,[22] the 14 most frequently encountered depressive manifestations in psychogeriatric patients are: (1) anergy, (2) anhedonia, (3) anorexia and weight loss, (4) early morning awakening or insomnia or hypersomnia, (5) feelings of helplessness, hopelessness, worthlessness, (6) guilt, shame, self-reproach, (7) loss of libido and potency, (8) depressed mood, (9) nihilistic or somatic delusions or paranoid persecutory delusions, (10) psychomotor retardation or agitation, (11) recrimination, (12) decreased self-esteem, (13) aches and pains without an organic basis, and (14) suicidal thoughts and preoccupations. No verified information is available, however, on the frequency of these manifestations.

Information is also limited on the frequency of different depressive syndromes in the aged. However, there are some indications that dysthymia associated with insomnia, restlessness, and psychotic manifestations is relatively more prevalent in the aged than in younger patients. While dysthymia associated with anhedonia and motor retardation is probably less frequent, dysthymia with increased bodily concerns, constipation, indecisiveness, and inefficiency is commonly seen in psychogeriatric patients.[10]

Depressive subtypes in the elderly were described by Skodol and Spitzer,[45] and recently Meyers and Greenberg[46] reported on the high prevalence of delusional depression in elderly patients. In 152 consecutively admitted *DSM-III*-diagnosed elderly major depressives, delusional depression (corresponding with major depressive episode with psychotic features) was seen in 67 (44%). Delusional patients were significantly older at age of onset, but not at the age of their index admission. Utilizing the median age of onset of 60 as a cutoff, only 17 (24%) of the 70 early onset patients were delusional compared to 50 (61%) of the 82 late onset patients. No evidence for an aging effect was found. Delusional early onset patients were not significantly older at the time of their index admission than nondelusional early onset patients. In both sexes there was a trend for an increase in the prevalence of delusions with a later age of onset.

There is virtually no information on the biological correlates of depressive subtypes and/or syndromes in psychogeriatric patients. However, there are indications that increased 3-methoxy-4-hydroxy-phenyl-glycol (MHPG) concentrations in the urine,[36,47] decreased testosterone and estrogen levels in the serum,[32,48] and increased monoamine oxidase (MAO) activity in both plasma and platelet[49] are more frequently seen in aged than in young depressed patients.

Differential Diagnosis

Since depressive illness is usually amenable to treatment in the elderly, recognition of depressive syndromes is of crucial importance. However, diagnosing depression can be a challenge, particularly in this population, because of difficulty in distinguishing depressive from somatic symptoms and signs. Some physical illness produces symptoms suggestive of depression. Depression, in turn, may be manifested in symptoms suggestive of physical illness.[50]

Medical illness mimics depression: Many neurological, endocrine, and metabolic disorders produce symptoms which can be mistaken for depression, and if treated as such remain refractory to antidepressant drugs.[51] Among the neurological disorders, some of the episodic symptoms of multiple sclerosis such as fatigue, weakness, and bizarre complaints may be confused with depression.[52] Normal pressure hydrocephalus may resemble a form of agitated depression.[53] The headaches, vague paresthesias, and lapses of memory following unrecognized seizures may suggest a diagnosis of depression in cases of tumors of the temporal lobe.[54]

Endocrine disorders mimic depression more frequently than neurological diseases. Patients with hypothyroidism may look depressed because of their slow movements and speech,[55] while patients with adrenal insufficiency are often misdiagnosed as depressed because of their persistent complaints of fatigue, weight loss, and diminished activity.[51] The same applies to patients with hyperparathyroidism who exhibit symptoms of lethargy, fatigue, and lack of spontaneity.[56]

While both neurological and endocrine disorders occur with a considerably greater frequency in the young than in the old, metabolic and nutritional disorders that mimic depression are considerably more frequent in the elderly than in other patients.[54]

Among the metabolic disorders, those with a decrease in serum Na and/ or K, as well as those with an increase in serum Ca are the ones which may stimulate depressions. Among the nutritional disorders, patients with amnesia due to iron, folate or B_{12} deficiency are frequently labeled as "depressive" in their early stages. Furthermore, depressive manifestations often precede other signs of malignancies in patients with cancer of the pancreas or the gut.[51]

In the context of medical illness, consideration must also be given to drugs used in the treatment of somatic disease that induce depression as a side effect. Elderly patients are especially sensitive to these depressive effects. Among the most frequent classes of drugs which may induce depression are the antihypertensives, nonsteroidal anti-inflammatory agents, and anticancer drugs.[57]

Depression mimics medical illness: While medical illness may mimic depression, it is considerably more frequent that depression mimics somatic illness. Most common symptoms for both masking and expressing depression are pain, particularly in the head, neck, or back; gastrointestinal symptoms such as constipation or flatulence; and genitourinary symptoms such as a burning sensation upon urination.[22] Whereas no accurate prevalence figures are available, it is estimated that in the United States one-half to two-thirds of patients over 40 years of age seen by general practitioners may suffer from masked depression.[58]

Masked depression is not a clinical diagnosis, but simply a term indicating that the clinical picture is strongly suggestive of depression. Originally, it was applied only to endogenous depression. Later, however, it was extended to include also psychogenic depression.[59] Pathognomonic characteristics of masked depression are the phasic appearance of autonomic and/or other somatic signs and symptoms, diurnal fluctuations, mild inhibition of thinking process and drive, dysthymic mood changes, fatigue, sleep disturbance, and an anxious sense of failure or nonspecific apprehensiveness.

Pseudodementia mimics organic dementia just as masked depression mimics medical illness. In view of this, one might consider pseudodementia as a special form of masked depression. In the differentiation of depressive pseudodementia and true dementia, probably the most important factor is that the onset of true dementia is usually insidious, while that of pseudodementia is sudden or subacute. Cross-sectionally, a lack of cooperation, emotional lability, reduced mental alertness, recent memory impairment, confabulations, confusion, and disassociation are characteristic of true dementia, while somatic symptoms such as anorexia, weight loss, insomnia, and headache with a sense of distress are characteristic of the pseudodementia of depression. In true dementia, the course of illness is continuous and prolonged, while in pseudodementia, it is restricted to a limited period. During this limited period, the severity of cognitive impairment fluctuates in depression while it remains constant in demented patients.[10,60] In case of difficulties of differentiation on exclusively clinical grounds, the dexamethasone suppression test (DST) has been employed in confirming the diagnosis of primary affective illness. However, because cortisol levels are sometimes elevated in patients with primary degenerative dementia, elevated cortisol levels 16 to 17 hours after the oral injection of 1 mg of dexamethasone may not always indicate the presence of depression. On the other hand, transient improvement after administration of oral methylphenidate (2 to 8 mg) or intravenous sodium amobarbital (75 mg per ml given at a rate of 1 ml per minute) usually excludes true dementia and favors pseudodementia of depression.[60]

References

1. Dublin LI, Lotka AJ, Spiegelman M: *Length of Life*, Ronald Press, New York, 1969.

2. Hun N: The importance of social care in the aged. In Tariska I (ed): *Neuropsychiatric Disorders in the Aged*, Medicina, Budapest, 1967.

3. Butler RN: *Why Survive? Being Old in America*, Harper and Row, New York, 1975.

4. Brotman HB: Population projections. Part I: Tomorrow's older population (to 2000). *J. Gerontol.* 17:203–209, 1977.

5. Jarvik LE: Introduction. In Crook T, Copen G (Eds.): *Physician's Guide to the Diagnosis and Treatment of Depression in the Elderly*, Powley, New Canaan, CT, 1983.

6. Sloane RB: Psychiatric problems of the aged. *Cont. Educat.* 11:42–47, 1978.

7. Busse EW, Pfeiffer E: Functional psychiatric disorders in old age. In Busse EW, Pfeiffer E (eds): *Behavior and Adaptation in Late Life*, Little, Brown, Boston, 1969.

8. Lamy PP: *Prescribing for the Elderly*. Littleton, Boston, 1969.

9. Besdine RW: The data base of geriatric medicine. In Rowe JW, Besdine RW (eds): *Health and Disease in Old Age*, Little, Brown, Boston, 1982.

10. Ban TA: *Psychopharmacology for the Aged*, Karger, Basel, 1980.

11. Kramer M, Taube C, Starr S: Pattern of use of psychiatric facilities by the aged. Current status, trends and implications. In Simon A, Epstein LJ (eds): *Aging in Modern Society* (Psychiatr. Res. Report No. 23), American Psychiatric Association, Washington, 1968.

12. Kuhlen RG: Aging and life adjustment. In Birren JE (ed): *Handbook of Aging and the Individual*, University of Chicago Press, Chicago, 1957.

13. Mayer-Gross W, Slater E, Roth M: *Clinical Psychiatry*, Cassell, London, 1960.

14. Pasamanick B: A survey of mental disease in an urban population. An approach to total prevalence by age. *Ment. Hosp.* 46:567–572, 1962.

15. Simon A: Mental health of community-resident hospitalized aged. In Simon A, Epstein LJ (eds): *Aging in Modern Society* (Psychiatr. Res. Report No. 23), American Psychiatric Association, Washington, 1968.

16. Simon A, Epstein LJ (eds): *Aging in Modern Society* (Psychiatr. Res. Report No. 23), American Psychiatric Association, Washington, 1968.

17. Roth M: The natural history of mental disorders in old age. *J. Ment. Sci.* 101:281–301, 1955.

18. Jarvik LF: Aging and psychiatry. *Psychiatr. Clin. North. Am.* 5:5–9, 1982.

19. Blazer D: The epidemiology of depression in late life. In Breslau LD, Haug MR (eds): *Depression and Aging: Causes, Care and Consequences*, Springer, New York, 1983.

20. Gianturco D, Busse E: Psychiatric problems encountered during a long-term study of normal aging volunteers. In Isaac A, Post F (eds): *Studies in Geriatric Psychiatry*, Wiley, New York, 1978.

22. Gurland B, Cross P: Epidemiology of psychopathology in old age: Some implications for clinical services. *Psychiatr. Clin. North Am.* 5:11–26, 1982.

22. Salzman C, van der Kolk B: Treatment of depression. In Salzman C (ed): *Clinical Geriatric Psychopharmacology*, McGraw-Hill, New York, 1984.

23. Crook T: Geriatric psychopharmacology. An overview of ailments and current therapies. *Drug Development Research* 5:5–24, 1985.

24. Gurland BJ, Golden G, Dean L: Depression and dementia in the elderly of New York City. In: *Planning for the Elderly in New York City*, Community Council of Greater New York, New York, 1980.

25. Cheah KC, Beard QV: Psychiatric findings in the population of a geriatric evaluation unit: Implications. *J. Am. Geriatr. Soc.* 28:153–156, 1980.

26. Myers JN, Sheldon D, Robinson JS: A study of 138 elderly first admissions. *Am. J. Psychiatry* 120:244-249, 1963.

27. Roth M: Classification and etiology of mental disorders of old age. In Kay DW, Ash B (eds): *Some Recent Developments in Psychogeriatrics*, Headley Bros., Ashford, 1971.

28. Davenmuehle RH, Vervoerdt A: Physical illness and depressive symptomatology. *J. Am. Geriatr. Soc.* 10:932-947, 1962.

29. Sendbuehler J, Goldstein S: Attempted suicide among the aged. *J. Am. Geriatr. Soc.* 25:245-248, 1977.

30. Schmidt CW: Psychiatric problems of the aged. *J. Am. Geriatr. Soc.* 22:355-356, 1974.

31. Joffe JR: Functional disorders in the elderly. *Hosp. Pract.* 1:93-102, 1976.

32. Lipton MA: Age differentiation in depression: Biochemical aspects. *J. Gerontol.* 31:293-299, 1976.

33. Dunn G, Gross D: Treatment of depression in the medically ill patient. A case report. *Am. J. Psychiatry* 134:448-449, 1977.

34. Hopkinson G: A genetic study of affective illness in patient over 50. *Br. J. Psychiatry* 110:244-254, 1964.

35. Mendlewicz J: The age factor in depressive illness: Some genetic considerations. *J. Gerontol.* 31:300-303, 1976.

36. Ban TA: The treatment of depressed geriatric patients. *Am. J. Psychother.* 32:93-104, 1978.

37. Jaspers K: Causal and meaningful connections between life history and psychoses (Transl. by J. Hoenig). In Hirsch SR, Shepherd M (eds): *Themes and Variations in European Psychiatry*, University Press of Virginia, Charlottesville, 1974.

38. *Diagnostic and Statistical Manual of Mental Disorders*, Third Edition, American Psychiatric Association, Washington, DC, 1980.

39. *International Classification of Diseases*, Ninth Edition, World Health Organization, Geneva, 1977.

40. LaBruzza AL: Physical illness presenting as psychiatric disorder: Guidelines for differential diagnosis. *J. Operational Psychiatr.* 12:24-31, 1981.

41. Tsuang MT, Perkins K, Simpson JC: Physical diseases in schizophrenia and affective disorder. *J. Clin. Psychiatry* 44:42-46, 1983.

42. Kay DWK: Outcome and cause of death in mental disorders of old age. A long-term follow-up of functional and organic psychoses. *Acta Psychiatr. Scand.* 38:249-276, 1962.

43. Kay DWK, Bergman K: Physical disability and mental health in old age. *J. Psychosoc. Res.* 10:3-12, 1966.

44. Robinson RG, Lipsey JR, Price JR: Mood disorders in post stroke patients. Presented at the 138th Annual Meeting of the American Psychiatric Association, May 18-24, 1985, Dallas, Texas.

45. Skodol AE, Spitzer RL: Depression in the elderly: Clinical criteria. In Breslau LD, Haug MR (eds): *Depression and Aging: Causes, Care and Consequences*, Springer, New York, 1983.

46. Meyers BS, Greenberg RM: Delusional depression in the elderly. Presented at

the 138th Annual Meeting of the American Psychiatric Association, May 18-24, 1985, Dallas, Texas.

47. Schildkraut JJ, Keeler BA: MHPG excretion in depressive disorders. Relation to clinical subtypes and desynchronized sleep. *Science* 181:762-763, 1973.

48. Vogel W, Klaiber EL, Broverman DM: Roles of the gonadal steroid hormones in psychiatric depression in men and women. *Prog. Neuropsychopharmacol.* 2:487-503, 1978.

49. Robinson D: Monoamine oxidase inhibition and the elderly. In Raskin A, Robinson D, Levine J (eds): *Age and the Psychopharmacology of Psychoactive Drugs*, Elsevier, New York, 1981.

50. Ban TA: Chronic disease and depression in the geriatric population. *J. Clin. Psychiatry* 45 (Suppl. 2):18-23, 1984.

51. Hollister LE: Depressed medical patients: Diagnostic and treatment challenges. In Ayd FJ (ed): *Clinical Depressions: Diagnostic and Therapeutic Challenges*, Ayd Medical Communications, Baltimore, 1980.

52. Goodstein RK, Ferrell RB: Multiple sclerosis — presenting a depressive illness. *Dis. Nerv. Syst.* 38:127-131, 1977.

53. Rosen H, Swiger ME: Depression and normal pressure hydrocephalus: A dilemma in neuropsychiatric diagnosis. *J. Nerv. Ment. Dis.* 163:35-40, 1976.

54. Ban TA, Guy W, Wilson WH: The psychopharmacological treatment of depression in the medically ill patient. *Can. J. Psychiatry* 29:461-466, 1984.

55. Taylor JW: Depression and thyrotoxicoses. *Am. J. Psychiatry* 132:552-553, 1975.

56. Nobel P: Depressive illness and hyperparathyroidism. *Proc. R. Acad. Med.* 67:1066-1067, 1974.

57. Salzman C: Depression and physical disease. In Crook T, Cohen GD (eds): *Physician's Guide to the Diagnosis and Treatment of Depression in the Elderly*, Powley, New Canaan, CT, 1983.

58. Lesse S: Unmasking the masks of depression. In Ayd F (ed): *Clinical Depression: Diagnostic and Treatment Challenges*, Ayd Medical Communications, Baltimore, 1980.

59. Kielholz P, Poldinger W, Adams C: *Masked Depression*, Deutscher Arzter-Verlag, Koln, 1982.

60. Goodnick P, Gershon S, Salzman C: Dementia and memory loss in the elderly. In Salzman C (Ed.): *Clinical Geriatric Psychopharmacology*, McGraw-Hill, New York, 1984.

9

The Treatment of Depression in the Elderly

Thomas A. Ban and Michael H. Ebert

EDITOR'S NOTE

In elderly, depressed patients, psychopharmacologic agents—in conjunction with short-term psychotherapy—constitute the primary treatment modality. As effective as these may be, they may produce distressing side effects if not employed judiciously. Adverse drug reactions and drug-drug interactions are common. There is no evidence that any of the heterocyclic antidepressants is superior in its clinical effectiveness than any other; however, some of the more recently developed ones may induce fewer undesirable side effects, a particularly important consideration in this age group.

By and large, elderly patients require lower dosages of a given antidepressant to achieve a therapeutically potent blood level; in part, this is due to the diminished metabolism of the drugs in the liver. One must be cautious, however, not to err by giving too little of an antidepressant. Secondary amine drugs are probably preferable to tertiary amine ones, since they seem to show less age-related pharmacokinetic variability and possess lower protein-binding capacity.

Carefully used, MAO inhibitors can have a place in the treatment of certain elderly depressed patients, especially those with hypochondriasis, somatic anxiety, irritability and anergia. Mesterolone, a synthetic hormone, may be useful to enhance activity and performance and reduce somatic complaints among elderly males with low testosterone levels.

An interesting observation is the fact that poststroke patients with specific damage in the left frontal lobes manifest depression, whereas less depression is seen among similar patients without left frontal lobe involvement. Treatment planning must take into consideration accompanying or underlying physical and neurological disease, such as multiple sclerosis, diabetes mellitus, chronic liver disease, and the like. The antipain potential of some of the antidepressants may prove valuable in the management of patients who suffer with depression and chronic pain, such as those with chronic rheumatoid arthritis.

Introduction

The primary treatment modality of depression in elderly patients is pharmacological. Some short-term psychotherapeutic techniques are reported to be helpful, but procedures that aim to affect fundamental personality changes should not be used. The same applies to other psychodynamically based approaches to treatment. Thus, according to Hollender,[1-3] if a senescent person turns to the past and develops protective mechanisms against injuries of self-esteem, one "should not tamper with these defenses unless adequate substitutes can be provided" for replacing them. On the other hand, when the older person suffers from deprivation of realistic needs, "everything possible should be done to fill these needs."

While psychotherapeutic approaches have only limited, if any, application, psychopharmacological treatments may lead to iatrogenic diseases. This is especially true if they are administered without careful consideration of the actual manifestations of the depressive syndrome and/or without an adequate knowledge of other concomitant medications that the patient is taking because of coexisting physical disease.[4] But even if all possible precautions are met, adverse drug reactions and drug-drug interactions are frequent because of the alterations in pharmacokinetics and changes in receptor tissue sensitivity. An optimal therapeutic ratio can only be achieved by using the fewest drugs the patient needs.[5]

Empirical Approaches to Treatment

The prevailing approach to the pharmacotherapy of depression is empirical. Reviewers of treatments agree that cyclic or monoamine uptake inhibitor antidepressants are the ones most extensively employed, followed by monoamine oxidase inhibitors (MAOI).[5-9]

Cyclic antidepressants: There are 10 cyclic antidepressants available in the United States for clinical use in elderly depressed patients. They include eight first generation tricyclic compounds (four secondary amines — amoxapine, desipramine, nortriptyline, and protriptyline — and four tertiary amines — amitriptyline, doxepin, imipramine, and trimipramine), and two second generation heterocyclic compounds (maprotiline, and trazodone). In addition, there are several other second generation cyclic antidepressants, including citalopram, fluoxetine, fluvoxamine, and mianserin, in clinical investigation. While there is no conclusive evidence that any of the cyclic antidepressants is superior to another in overall therapeutic effects, there are indications that some of the second generation antidepressants may offer advantages insofar as side effects are concerned. Nevertheless, the fact remains that "none of these compounds appear to offer substantial hope of dramatic advance."[10]

Pharmacokinetic factors: A number of pharmacokinetic factors have practical implications for treatment with cyclic antidepressants in the aged. One of the most important is the 40–50% reduction in intestinal blood flow with an effect on the absorption of cyclic antidepressant drugs.[11] Although much less drug is absorbed, there is still considerably more drug available in the unbound form to interact with target organs because of the general fall in plasma proteins and the consequent decrease in protein binding capacity in the aged.[12] This is far from being compensated for by the increase in fat tissue (25% in males and 50% in females), which provides for an increase in storage for fat-soluble cyclic antidepressants.[13] Another important change of pharmacokinetic significance is the considerable loss of liver mass, with a decrease in the activity of the cytochrome oxidase system, responsible for the metabolism of drugs.[14,15] Cyclic antidepressants also reduce glomerular filtration (responsible for elimination) to approximately one-third of that seen in young middle-aged individuals.[16]

Because of the effects of aging on drug distribution, protein binding, and metabolic clearance, it is helpful in some clinical situations to obtain plasma levels of psychotropic drugs. One should keep in mind, however, that most assays of plasma level of a drug reflect total concentration (bound and unbound), rather than free concentration, which is the more relevant parameter with regard to CNS effects.

Corresponding with the pharmacokinetic changes are the results of Nies et al.[17] They found that patients over 65 have higher plasma levels of amitriptyline, imipramine, and desipramine than younger patients, even after considerable reduction in the dosages of these drugs. They also revealed that three weeks pass before the elderly reach steady state blood levels, whereas in younger patients steady state levels are attained within five to ten days with the same drugs.

Pharmacokinetic changes are coupled with increased receptor sensitivity. Because of this, pharmacologic treatment should commence with one-third to one-half the recommended adult dosage of the drug and increase slowly and gradually to obtain an optimal therapeutic response. Even with all possible precautions, however, the risk of toxic effects is greater and the incidence of adverse reactions is higher in the old than in the young,[18] to the extent that patients over 70 are likely to experience twice as many adverse drug reactions as patients under 50.[19]

The problem is further compounded by the age-related changes in reflex functions. Impairment of baroreceptor reflexes is considered to be responsible for the increased incidence and severity of postural hypotension following the administration of cyclic antidepressants.[20]

It is unfortunate that the extreme caution exercised may create problems. Prescription of dosages below the therapeutic range are frequently encountered in elderly patients treated with cyclic antidepressants.[21] This was shown by Friedel and Raskind,[22] who found low plasma levels associated with a lack of clinical response in doxepin-treated depressed elderly patients.

There are no generally accepted guidelines for the selection of cyclic antidepressants for depressed elderly patients. It is not uncommon, however, to give preference to secondary amine drugs,[9] because of the common contention that they show less age-related pharmacokinetic variability[21] than tertiary amine compounds. While this is the case for nortriptyline,[23] it does not necessarily apply to other secondary amine antidepressants.[11]

Another pharmacokinetic factor in favor of treatment with secondary amines in elderly patients is their lower protein binding capacity. By employing an ultrafiltration technique with labeled compounds, protein-binding capacity was estimated at 96% for imipramine and amitriptyline (both tertiary amines), 95% for nortriptyline, 92% for protriptyline, and 90% for desipramine (secondary amines). Protein-binding, however, varies among individuals; this variation explains in part some of the difficulties encountered in correlating plasma concentrations with clinical response.[24]

Pharmacodynamic factors: Sedation, histamine (H_1) receptor blockage, and anticholinergic potency need to be carefully considered prior to prescribing a cyclic antidepressant to elderly patients.

Most sedating among the available tricyclic antidepressants is doxepin, followed by amitriptyline and trimipramine. The least sedating is protriptyline, followed by desipramine. In fact, there are indications that protriptyline may even exert some mild stimulating action. H_1-receptor blockage may account for the sedating effect of tricyclic antidepressants and contribute to their hypotensive and appetite-stimulating action. Among the various tricyclic antidepressants, doxepin is by far the most strongly antihistaminic, followed by amitriptyline. Other tricyclic antidepressants are considerably less potent H_1-receptor blockers. While the desirability of sedation in the treatment of depression depends on the prevailing clinical manifestations, anticholinergic properties as a rule can result in serious and undesirable side effects in psychogeriatric patients. A rough ranking of tricyclic antidepressants, in descending order of anticholinergic potency based on central and peripheral muscarinic cholinergic receptor binding, is as follows: amitriptyline, doxepin, trimipramine, imipramine, nortriptyline, and desipramine. Amitriptyline is 20 times more potent in blocking muscarinic acetylcholine receptors than protriptyline or desipramine.[25] Anticholinergic potency of second generation antidepressants is even lower than of the first generation secondary amine drugs.

Monoamine oxidase inhibitors: In spite of the recognized increase in monoamine oxidase (MAO) activity with aging, monoamine oxidase inhibitor (MAOI) antidepressants are used considerably less frequently than cyclic antidepressants in the treatment of depressed elderly patients. Nevertheless, the fact remains that MAOI antidepressants such as isocarboxazid, phenelzine, and tranylcypromine are well tolerated in psychogeriatric patients.[26] The finding that frequently seen symptoms in depressed elderly patients, such as hypochondriasis, somatic anxiety, irritability, and anergia, respond favorably to MAOI drugs[27] favors the contention that increased MAO activity may play a role in the pathophysiology of these symptoms.[28] It has been noted that the stimulant effects of tranylcypromine are useful in some psychogeriatric patients,[29] and that depressed outpatients over 60 respond more favorably to phenelzine than do depressed outpatients under 60.[30]

One possible reason for the limited use of MAOI drugs is the potential danger of hypertensive crisis, the result of an interaction between MAOIs and tyramine-containing foods and/or other drugs.[31] While the occurrence of such an interaction is extremely rare, frequently encountered adverse effects with MAOIs are dizziness[32] and postural hypotension, particularly noted in patients over 50.[30] In spite of these adverse effects, MAOIs have been safely and effectively employed in the treatment of depressed psychogeriatric patients.[5,29,33] Furthermore, because of their low atropine-like effects,[34] they offer distinct advantages when anticholinergic effects are intolerable.

Rational Approaches to Treatment

Two major lines of research have opened new paths for a rational approach to the pharmacotherapy of depression in the aged. One is based on a better understanding of the phenomenological aspects of depression in elderly patients, while the other is based on a better understanding of the age-related biological changes that are of possible relevance to depressive illness.

Phenomenological Aspects of Depression

Exploration of the phenomenological aspects of depression in elderly patients has revealed a high prevalence of delusional depression.[35] It has also been recognized that in the treatment of delusional depression traditional cyclic antidepressants do not suffice and need to be combined with a neuroleptic. This has brought to attention the need for "transition compounds" which combine antidepressant with neuroleptic effects. The only available antidepressant compound in the United States that fulfills criteria of a "transition compound" is amoxapine, a tricyclic dibenzoxazepine. In the course of its metabolic breakdown, this unique compound hydroxylates into a dopamine receptor blocker with possible antipsychotic effects. It remains to be seen, however, whether amoxapine can offer real advantages over ECT or drug combinations in the treatment of delusional depression of the aged.[36]

Biological Changes in Aged

Biological changes in depressed psychogeriatric patients with possible therapeutic implications include the lowering of plasma testosterone concentrations; increased MAO activity; and decreased norepinephrine (NE), dopamine (DA), and serotonin (5HT) levels at functionally active receptor sites.

Low testosterone concentrations: Some elderly depressed men exhibit normal production but abnormally elevated metabolic clearance of testosterone. To attain the normal testosterone-estradiol ratio in these patients it is necessary to increase the testosterone production by 70%. A possible alternative is the administration of a synthetic exogenous hormone to correct relative testosterone deficiency.[37] One such substance is mesterolone, a synthetic androgen that produces similar effects to CNS stimulants in low dosage, and to antidepressants in high dosages on the quantitative EEG.[38] Treatment with mesterolone produced a tendency for improvement in activity and performance, along with a decrease in somatic complaints, in a group of aging males. However, no relationship between testosterone concentrations and therapeutic effects could be revealed.[39]

Increased MAO activity: It has been noted that patients with major depression and a reversible dementia syndrome have high platelet MAO activity similar to that seen in depressives with primary degenerative dementia. Based on this observation, Alexopoulos et al.[40] hypothesized that in some elderly patients, a reversible dementia syndrome develops when the pathophysiological changes of depression are added to an early asymptomatic dementia process.

Considering that, in clinical practice, a reversible cognitive dysfunction is virtually indistinguishable from an irreversible cognitive dysfunction, a trial with an MAOI antidepressant is warranted in patients with primary degenerative dementia, especially if the dementia syndrome is associated with platelet MAO activity in the high range. Furthermore, since the increase in MAO activity is restricted to the Type B enzyme, it is likely that deprenyl, a selective Type B enzyme inhibitor, is more suitable in the treatment of these patients than nonspecific MAOIs.

Changes in neurotransmitter stores, metabolism, and receptor mechanisms in the central nervous system are all part of the normal aging process. For example, dopamine content of brain tissue declines with age in several species, including man. Dopamine receptors are lost from the corpus striatum during aging.[41] Indeed, Parkinson's disease may be an accelerated form of aging of the central nervous system. Although less well documented, similar changes occur in brain norepinephrine and serotonin systems. Even though the mechanisms are not well understood, some have suggested that these changes in neurotransmitter function may be related to the incidence and form of major depression in the elderly.

Norepinephrine deficiency: In poststroke patients a significant relationship was found between depression and left frontal lesions.[42] The depression seen in these patients was attributed to the depletion of norepinephrine (NE) because only left anterior lesions, induced experimentally in rats, were associated with a depletion of NE in the locus ceruleus.

Favoring the NE deficiency hypothesis of depression in poststroke patients are the results of Robinson, Lipsey, and Price.[42] They found that nortriptyline, a specific NE reuptake inhibitor, was superior in its therapeutic effects to an inactive placebo in the treatment of patients with poststroke depression. However, because no specific 5HT reuptake inhibitor was included in the comparison, findings of this clinical trial could not provide conclusive evidence for the NE deficiency hypothesis of poststroke depression. If the NE deficiency hypothesis of poststroke depression could be supported by further evidence, one should consider using selective NE reuptake inhibitors in treatment.

Decreased 5HT responsivity: Substantial evidence has been given for a decreased responsivity to 5HT in the elderly; therefore, a relative deficiency of 5HT is another possible factor linked with old age depression.[43]

Serotonin (5HT) is produced from the amino acid tryptophan content of digested protein. The transport system responsible for carrying tryptophan from the blood into the brain has a lower affinity for tryptophan than for eight other neural amino acids. Therefore, increased amounts of tryptophan enter the brain only if the relative concentration of tryptophan in relationship to other amino acids is increased. Some have recently raised the possibility that cerebral 5HT levels might be influenced by dietary constituents. The possibility that consistent dietary manipulation might keep brain serotonin levels high and prevent depression in geropsychiatric patients remains to be seen.

The contention that 5HT deficiency plays a role in some depression is substantiated by the findings that L-tryptophan reverses the reduction of time spent in rapid eye movement sleep associated with insomnia, a cardinal symptom of depression in the elderly.[44] Piracetam, a nootropic agent, was found to enhance brain tryptophan levels in mice,[45] but it remains to be seen whether it can enhance the antidepressant effects of tryptophan in the elderly.

Depression Coexisting with Medical Illness

A large number of elderly patients suffer concurrently from depression and one or more other diseases.[21]

Neurological and endocrine disorders: The CNS disorder most frequently associated with depression in the aged is Parkinson's disease, and it is uncertain whether levodopa, the agent most commonly used to treat these patients, reduces depression by stimulating catecholamine release or aggravates it by decreasing 5HT levels. Irrespective of therapeutic implications, concomitant administration of levodopa and an MAOI may cause a significant rise in blood pressure, whereas concomitant administration of an antiparkinson agent with a tricyclic antidepressant may produce excessive anticholinergic effects.[46]

Diabetes mellitus is frequently encountered in old age; if it is associated with depression, the primary treatment of choice is a cyclic antidepressant drug. MAOIs should not be used since they significantly modify the response of insulin; hydrazines potentiate and prolong insulin-induced hypoglycemia, while nonhydrazines only delay the time of recovery. To prevent severe hypoglycemic stupor and/or hypotensive collapse, the dosage of insulin needs to be reduced if, for some reason, a MAOI is absolutely indicated as part of the treatment regimen.[47]

Ocular and oral diseases: Precipitation of a glaucomic attack by the administration of an antidepressant is rare. Therefore, chronic glaucoma which can be managed with cholinergic eye drops is not a contraindication for the use of cyclic or MAOI antidepressant drugs.[48] The same applies to dental caries, despite the fact that cyclic antidepressants may induce or aggravate dry mouth.[49]

Gastrointestinal and hepatic diseases: Although pyrosis commonly occurs, treatment with cyclic antidepressants produces a reduction of gastric secretion and acid production, together with a slowing of gastric emptying and small bowel transmit time — all of which may have a favorable effect on gastric ulcer patients. While the drug-induced relaxation of the esophageal sphincter may aggravate hiatal hernia, the drug-induced decreased of intestinal motility may result in constipation that, if ignored, can lead to adynamic ileus with resultant serious consequences.[50,51]

Cyclic antidepressants are primarily metabolized in the liver, and their concentrations increase with chronic liver disease. Consequently, there is a marked CNS sensitivity in hepatic insufficiency and intolerance to cyclic antidepressant drugs.[5] Insofar as MAOIs are concerned, the *PDR* warns that phenelzine should not be given to patients with a history of liver disease or with abnormal liver function test. Although phenelzine as a rule does not impair hepatic function, on rare occasions it has been associated with allergic hepatitis.

Cardiovascular disorders: In spite of their effect on the cardiovascular system, cyclic and MAOI antidepressants should not be withheld from cardiac patients. However, when evident, cardiac decompensation should always be treated prior to the initiation of antidepressant therapy. In case of ischemic chest pain, concurrent administration of a β-adrenergic receptor blocker may be necessary.[52] Treatment should be started with both drugs at low dose levels; dosage is then titrated upward until therapeutic levels are attained.

Because of their quinidinelike action, cyclic antidepressants should be used with caution in patients with changes in cardiac condition. Regardless of the drug chosen it should also be borne in mind that cyclic antidepressants interact significantly with antidysrhythmic drugs, such as procainamide.[53]

Hypertension is probably the most frequent concurrent illness with depression. Therefore it is of particular importance that cyclic antidepressants inhibit the uptake of guanethidine and its congeners into the neuronal terminal. By preventing accumulation of action sites, cyclic antidepressants antagonize the antihypertensive effect of these drugs. Since doxepin at low doses (100 mg per day) does not appear to block the antihypertensive effect of guanethidine, it is the drug of choice for concurrent therapy.[21] Among the other antihypertensives, clonidine may cause a paradoxical rise in blood pressure in patients undergoing concurrent treatment with cyclic antidepressants, and reserpine or methyldopa may induce depression to the extent that treatment with these substances may prevent and/or interfere with the therapeutic effect of cyclic antidepressants.[48]

Genitourinary and renal diseases: Cyclic antidepressants may induce urinary retention in patients with prostatic hypertrophy. Because the retention is usually promptly relieved by the administration of bethanechol (25 mg tid), prostatic hypertrophy is not a contraindication to treatment with cyclic antidepressants.[21]

In contradistinction to hepatic insufficiency, cyclic antidepressants are well tolerated in patients with renal damage. There is, however, an increased CNS sensitivity to these drugs.[21]

Pain and rheumatoid arthritis: It has long been recognized that an association exists between chronic pain and depression, and patients with chronic pain frequently respond favorably to the administration of a cyclic antidepressant. While neuroleptics may potentiate the therapeutic effect of narcotic analgesics in the management of persistent pain (e.g., inoperable cancer), combined administration of a neuroleptic and a cyclic antidepressant may be therapeutically effective without a narcotic analgesic in the treatment of denervation dysesthesias, such as postherpetic neuralgia, anesthesia dolorosa, and peripheral neuropathy. The analgesic action can also be potentiated by the addition of an antihistaminic drug.[54]

Facial pain and muscular contraction headache characterized by bilateral symmetrical tension in the frontal and occipital muscles seem to be particularly responsive to antidepressant drugs. Taking into consideration that these patients are prone to become addicted to analgesics, one should not withhold the prescription of an antidepressant too long, especially when sleep is disturbed.

Antidepressants may also have a therapeutic effect on the pain associated with rheumatoid arthritis. While cyclic antidepressants decrease the gastrointestinal absorption of phenylbutazone, a drug used in the treatment of rheumatoid arthritis, they increase blood levels by interfering with the metabolism of the drug.[55]

References

1. Hollender MH: Role of the psychiatrist in homes for the aged. *Geriatrics* 6:243–250, 1951.

2. Hollender MH: Individualizing the aged. *Soc. Casework* 33:337–342, 1952.

3. Hollender MH: Early psychologic reactions associated with organic brain disease in the aged. *N. Y. State J. Med.* 59:802–809, 1958.

4. Palmer JD, Bessler R: Drug-drug interaction: A general discussion about how and where drugs may interact in the body. *Ariz. Med.* 31:89–93, 1974.

5. Ban TA: *Psychopharmacology for the Aged*, Karger, Basel, 1980.

6. Gerner RH: Present status of drug therapy in depression in late life. *Clin. Neuropharmacol.* 7 (Suppl. 1):168–169, 1984.

7. Petrie WM, Ban TA: Pharmacology for the elderly. *Prog. Neuropsychopharmacol.* 5:335–342, 1981.

8. Petrie WM, Ban TA: Drugs and the aged. In Burrows GD, Werry JS (eds): *Advances in Human Psychopharmacology*, JAI Press, London, 1984.

9. Salzman C, van der Kolk B: Treatment of depression. In Salzman C (ed): *Clinical Geriatric Psychopharmacology*, McGraw-Hill, New York, 1984.

10. Crook T: Geriatric psychopharmacology: An overview of ailments and current therapies. *Drug Dev. Res.* 5:5–24, 1985.

11. Friedel RO: Pharmacokinetics in the geropsychiatric patient. In Lipton MA, DiMascio A, Killman KM (eds): *Psychopharmacology: A Generation of Progress*, Raven Press, New York, 1978.

12. Wallace S, Whiting B, Runcie J: Factors affecting drug binding in plasma of elderly patients. *Br. J. Clin. Psychopharmacol.* 3:327–330, 1976.

13. Gregerman RI, Bierman EL: Aging and hormones. In Williams RH (ed): *Textbook of Endocrinology*, Saunders, Philadelphia, 1974.

14. Kato R et al.: Variation in the activity of liver microsomal drug metabolizing enzymes in rats in relation to the age. *Biochem. Pharmacol.* 13:1037–1051, 1964.

15. Triggs EJ et al.: Pharmacokinetics in the elderly. *Eur. J. Clin. Pharmacol.* 8:55–62, 1975.

16. Briant RH: Drug treatment in the elderly: Problems in prescribing rules. *Drugs* 13:225–229, 1977.

17. Nies A et al.: Relationship between age and tricyclic antidepressant plasma levels. *Am. J. Psychiatry* 134:790–793, 1977.

18. Raskind MA, Eisdorfer C: Psychopharmacology of the aged. In Simpson LL (ed): *Drug Treatment of Mental Disorders*, Raven Press, New York, 1975.

19. Seidl LG et al.: Studies on the epidemiology of adverse drug reactions, III: Reactions in patients on a general medical service. *Johns Hopkins Med. J.* 119:299–315, 1966.

20. Johnson G et al.: Comparative effects of lithium and chlorpromazine in the treatment of acute manic states. *Br. J. Psychiatry* 119:267–276, 1971.

21. Ban TA: Chronic disease and depression in the geriatric population. *J. Clin. Psychiatry* 45:18–23, 1984.

22. Friedel RO, Raskind MA: Relationship of blood levels of Sinequan to clinical effects in the treatment of depression in aged patients. In Mendels J (ed): *Sinequan: A Monograph of Recent Clinical Studies*, Excerpta Medica, Amsterdam, 1975.

23. Friedel RO: The pharmacotherapy of depression in the elderly: Pharmacokinetic considerations. In Cole JO, Barrett JE (eds): *Psychopathology in the Aged*, Raven Press, New York, 1980.

24. Barga O et al.: Plasma protein binding of tricyclic antidepressants in man. *Biochem. Pharmacol.* 18:2135–2143, 1969.

25. Richelson E: Tricyclic antidepressants and neurotransmitter receptors. *Psychiatr. Ann.* 9:16–32, 1979.

26. Raskind MA, Robinson DS, Levine J (eds): *Age and the Pharmacology of Psychoactive Drugs*, Elsevier, Amsterdam, 1981.

27. Robinson DS: Age-related factors affecting antidepressant drug metabolism and clinical response. In Nandy K (ed): *Geriatric Psychopharmacology*, Elsevier, Amsterdam, 1979.

28. Tyrer P: Towards rational therapy and monoamine oxidase inhibitors. *Br. J. Psychiatry* 128:354–360, 1976.

29. Kral VA, Papetropoulos D: Treatment of geriatric patients. In Kline NS, Lehmann HE (eds): *Psychopharmacology*, Little, Brown, Boston, 1965.

30. Robinson DS et al.: Phenelzine plasma levels, pharmacokinetics and clinical outcome. *Psychopharmacol. Bull.* 17:154–157, 1981.

31. Van Praag HM: Psychotropic drugs in the aged. *Compr. Psychiatry* 18:429–442, 1977.

32. White KL: Tranylcypromine. *Psychopharmacol. Bull.* 17:157–159, 1981.

33. Ashford JW, Ford CV: Use of MAO inhibitors in elderly patients. *Am. J. Psychiatry* 136:1466–1467, 1979.

34. Snyder SH, Yamamura HI: Antidepressants and the muscarinic acetylcholine receptors. *Arch. Gen. Psychiatry* 34:236–246, 1977.

35. Meyers BS, Greenberg RM: Delusional depression in the elderly. Presented at 138th Annual Meeting of the American Psychiatric Association, May 18–24, 1985, Dallas, Texas.

36. Ban TA: Pharmacological perspectives in therapy of depression in the elderly. Presented at the XIIIth International Congress of Gerontology, July 12–17, 1985, New York.

37. Vogel W, Klaiber EC, Broverman DM: Roles of the gonadal steroid hormones in psychiatric depression in men and women. *Prog. Neuropsychopharmacol.* 2:487–503, 1978.

38. Itil TM et al.: Male hormones in the treatment of depression: Effects of mesterolone. *Prog. Neuropsychopharmacol.* 2:457–467, 1978.

39. Kaiser E et al.: The measurement of the psychotropic effects on an androgen in aging males with psychovegetative symptomatology: A controlled double-blind study with mesterolone versus placebo. *Prog. Neuropsychopharmacol.* 2:505–515, 1978.

40. Alexopoulos GS et al.: Depression with reversible dementia. Presented at the 138th Annual Meeting of the American Psychiatric Association, May 18–24, 1985, Dallas, Texas.

41. Joseph JA, Roth GS: Age-related alterations in dopaminergic mechanisms. In Samuel D et al. (eds): *Aging*, Raven Press, New York, 1983.

42. Robinson RG, Lipsey JR, Price JR: Mood disorders in poststroke patients. Presented at the 138th Annual Meeting of the American Psychiatric Association, May 18–24, 1985, Dallas, Texas.

43. Beregi E: The biology of aging. In Tariska I (ed): *Neuropsychiatric Disorders in the Aged*, Medicina, Budapest, 1967.

44. Hartman E, Cravens J: The effect of long-term administration of psychotropic drugs on human sleep. *Psychopharmacology (Berlin)* 33:153–245, 1973.

45. Giurgea CE: *Fundamentals to a Pharmacology of the Mind*, Charles C Thomas, Springfield, IL, 1981.

46. Ban TA, Hollender MH: *Psychopharmacology for Everyday Practice*, Karger, Basel, 1981.

47. Cooper AJ, Ashcroft G: Potentiation of insulin hypoglycemia by MAO antidepressant drugs. *Lancet* I:407–409, 1966.

48. Ban TA, Guy W, Wilson WH: The psychopharmacological treatment of depression in the medically ill patient. *Can. J. Psychiatry* 29:461–466, 1984.

49. Bassuk E, Schoonover S: Rampant dental carries in the treatment of depression. *J. Clin. Psychiatry* 29:163–165, 1978.

50. Clarke IMC: Adynamic ileus and amitriptyline. *Br. Med. J.* 2:531–532, 1971.

51. Tyber MA: The relationship between hiatal hernia and tricyclic antidepressant: A report of five cases. *Am. J. Psychiatry* 132:653–654, 1975.

52. Jefferson JW: Lithium carbonate-induced hypothyroidism: Its many faces. *JAMA* 242:271–272, 1979.

53. Bigger JR, Jr et al.: Cardiac antiarrhythmic effect of imipramine hydrochloride. *N. Engl. J. Med.* 296:206–208, 1977.

54. Merskey H, Hester RA: The treatment of chronic pain with psychotropic drugs. *Postgrad. Med. J.* 48:594–598, 1972.

55. Dyer HR: Psychotropic drugs in rheumatology. *JAMA* 226:1752–1754, 1973.

10

Principles of Psychotherapy With Depressed Patients

Anthony Storr

EDITOR'S NOTE

Loss is an important trigger for depression. So is personality vulnerability, with both developmental and genetic contributants. Certain personality traits, such as lack of self-confidence and self-assertion, can appear in childhood and persist to character- ize adults with depression-prone personalities. Such individuals are somewhat timid and excessively sensitive to disapproval; they often retreat from challenges and prob- lems; they usually repress aggression, tending to turn it inwardly against themselves; they appear to have low self-esteem — regardless of accomplishments — and persist- ently depend on others to provide love, recognition, and reassurance.

Contemporary environmental factors also contribute to clinical depression. Par- ticularly vulnerable are women without other adults in whom to confide, those at home with three or more children under the age of 14, those in poor living and housing conditions, and women who have lost mothers prior to the age 11.

Psychotherapy has certain goals: to help the patient make sense of his disorder; to clarify the meaning of life events from earliest memories onward; to demonstrate how present difficulties relate to lifelong adaptational problems. The therapist can help the patient change, through insight, those problems which can be changed within himself, and to live more effectively with those that cannot by understanding, dealing with — or avoiding — social factors that aggravate his vulnerability to depres- sion.

The depressed patient is often compliant in therapy. One must keep in mind the importance of exposing aggressive impulses, but do so in a way that will not threaten the therapeutic relationship. Do not take the readily formed positive transference at face value; this is often motivated by fear more than affection. Use rapport and transference to help the patient cultivate a better sense of his own worth.

Introduction

Depression is probably the commonest symptom for which patients seek help from a psychiatrist. As every psychiatrist knows, depression varies in severity from a transient, trivial diminution in vitality to a profound, psychotic state of melancholia in which the patient is deluded and inaccessible. Since the advent of electroplexy, of effective antidepressant drugs, and of lithium, there has been a tendency among psychiatrists to treat episodes of depression by using these relatively simple methods without seeking psychodynamic explanations for the condition or offering any form of psychotherapy. In this chapter, I shall try to show that psychotherapy has an important part to play in the treatment of even severe cases of recurrent depression.

The Depressive Personality

Every human being is susceptible to depression as a consequence of bereavement, disappointment, or failure. The loss of a loved person provokes — and is expected to provoke — depression in the most robust of us. Disappointments in love or disappointment at being passed over for a sought-after position are common precipitants of depression in many people. Failure to pass an examination is a frequent cause of depression in young people, as is failure in business in older individuals. What these different precipitants have in common is that they all involve the loss of something or someone in which the individual concerned had invested emotional energy and which were therefore bound up with his or her self-esteem. The rate at which a person recovers from the depression induced by these commonplace hazards of ordinary life varies with the severity of the loss itself. It is my impression that today, when most children in Western society can be expected to survive and flourish as adults, the loss of a dearly loved child is one of the worst bereavements that anyone can suffer. The depression induced by such a loss may, even in normal people, be prolonged for two or more years, and there is a sense in which some parents may never wholly recover from such a loss.

However, the severity of the loss experienced is not the only factor concerned in either the profundity or the duration of these so-called "reactive" depressions. Differences in personality are equally important. Some people become much more easily depressed than others in response to what may appear to be trivial precipitants. In such cases, the depth and duration of the depression are also often excessive. For example, a man or woman may become suicidally depressed after what appears to be no more than a passing dispute with a spouse. We designate such people depressive personalities.

Endogenous versus Reactive Depression

The notion of an exclusively endogenous depression—that is, depression coming on for no discernible reason whatsoever—should, I think, be dropped. The word "endogenous" is simply a cloak for ignorance. The more one investigates cases of depression, the more likely one is to discover the trigger that provoked a particular episode. Brown[1] and his coworkers recorded a number of patients with depression whose illness did not appear, at first sight, to have been provoked by major difficulties in life or severe life events. However, further investigation of these cases revealed that many of the female patients had in fact been exposed to traumas of a kind that did not come within the categories laid down by the researchers. For example, a woman had to leave her job on account of rheumatoid arthritis which, she had been told, was incurable—a life event that might be expected to provoke depression in most people. Another had become depressed upon hearing that a male coworker on whom she had a crush was already married.

Patients themselves are not always able easily to identify what factors initiated a particular attack, and this is one reason why a psychotherapeutic investigation is needed. As patients begin to understand themselves better during the course of psychotherapy, they begin to recognize their vulnerabilities and understand the emotional precipitants of depression. Very often, a tactless or unfeeling remark on the part of someone close to the patient which is perceived as damaging to self-esteem may cause him to feel disregarded, unloved, despised, or rejected. The patient himself may have repressed the incident only to have it recalled during the course of psychotherapy. In such instances, the patient may despise himself for his sensitivity and add to his depression by feeling that he ought not to have overreacted in this way, that any "normal" person would not be so foolish. I do not believe that even the severest attacks of depression come on spontaneously without any external precipitating cause. This is not to deny that genetic factors, biological periodicity, and other internal factors may be equally important, but simply to affirm that some kind of trigger is necessary for the depressive reaction to occur.

It is worth noting that, during the last 50 years, more and more illnesses and abnormalities that were alleged to be the consequence of built-in flaws in the individual have been shown to be caused by external agents. For example, the defects now known to be caused by maternal rubella were thought to be inborn defects. Many forms of cancer, most notably cancer of the lung, are the consequence of noxious agents only recently identified. The importance of dietary fiber in the prevention of diseases of the bowel has only been demonstrated within the past few years. The fact that severe stress of the kind experienced by prisoners of war and concentration camp victims can cause both physical and mental illness which may not appear for many years after the stress is relieved was only fully realized when research conducted after World War II revealed it to be so. The more we learn about both mental and physical disorders, the more we find that previously unrecognized external factors are important causal agents. Until I am proved wrong, I shall continue to believe that both severe and mild depressive reactions require some external stimulus of a noxious kind to provoke them.

Vulnerability of the Depressive Personality

Why are some people precipitated into profound depression by external stimuli which the normal person will soon recover from, shrug off, or disregard? The answer to this question cannot be given either completely or with certainty. That genetic factors play a part is almost certain. According to Kagan,[2] temperamental differences between infants can be demonstrated from the earliest days after birth. What Kagan calls "inhibition to the unfamiliar" can be demonstrated as early as eight months, and tends to persist throughout childhood. Inhibited children are restrained, watchful, and gentle. If a stranger appears, they stop playing and observe the stranger warily. They tend to have more nightmares and unusual fears than uninhibited children, and are usually passive if attacked by another child. Because they are highly sensitive to reprimands, they tend to be unusually obedient and compliant. Inhibited children show more marked physiological reactions to stress. Thus, they are more susceptible to allergic reactions and to constipation. Inhibited male children tend to avoid traditional masculine sexual activities in adolescence, to choose less masculine vocations in adulthood, and to remain introverted and anxious in new social situations.

A number of these temperamental traits are rather characteristic of adults with depressive personalities. Because they appear so early in the child's life, they are more likely to be part of his or her inheritance rather than the result of faulty rearing, although I am not disputing that the infant's earliest experiences may be of importance. People who are particularly prone to depression and who do not habitually employ "manic defenses" tend to be uncertain of themselves, overcompliant, and extremely sensitive to real or imagined disapproval or aggression from others. Like the inhibited children, they tend to retreat from new situations or problems, rather than attack them. Because they are so sensitive to disapproval, they dare not "stand up" to other people and tend to get pushed around by them. This masochistic stance toward others means that such people repress their own aggression. They dare not show aggression to those who are close to them for fear of incurring further disapproval and loss of love. This is probably the origin of the well-recognized fact that, during an attack of depression, the sufferer tends to turn his aggression inward against the self, to reproach himself for all his past sins, and to declare that his illness is entirely his own fault.

As Freud pointed out in his classic paper, "Mourning and Melancholia,"[3] the reproaches that the depressed person levels at himself are usually explicable as reproaches that he would like to have directed at someone close to him, but which he dares not express for fear of antagonizing someone upon whose love he is dependent.

To be so sensitive to disapproval argues that the person who is prone to depression has little or no built-in self-esteem. Those who are particularly liable to overreact to comparatively minor failures or losses by being plunged into profound and long-lasting depression seem to lack any inner resources to turn to in the face of misfortune. For them, failure in an examination or rejection by a possible sexual partner precipitates feelings of total hopelessness. Such people behave as though they believe that there are no second chances in life, as though they were completely dependent for maintaining their self-esteem upon the success of whatever enterprise they happen to be temporarily engaged in, without taking into account past successes or future possibilities. It is as if any love or recognition which they had had in the past counted for nothing, as if there was nothing inside themselves to which to turn, no sense of being intrinsically worthwhile. It is worth recalling that many psychotically depressed patients complain that there is a void inside them, an emptiness which can never be filled. This apparently delusional statement is in fact a symbolic one, a metaphor expressing a psychological truth.

Although in our present state of knowledge it is difficult to prove, I think it reasonable to assume that the normal child who is welcomed, loved, and recurrently made much of, gains a sense of his own worth from these repeated experiences. This sense of worth becomes so much a part of himself that even shattering failures and losses do not leave him with the feeling that he is worthless.

I am suggesting that Kagan's inhibited infants may be those who later become depressive personalities, and that, however much they may in fact be loved by their mothers during their first few years of life, they lack the ability to incorporate that love, to make it part of their inner worlds. They therefore fail to develop the kind of self-esteem that will see them through reverses in life without experiencing intolerable depression. We do not know enough about psychology, physiology, or genetics even to suggest what this defect is or how it is mediated.

What is clear is that those with depressive personalities remain dependent upon external sources for maintaining self-esteem. Like drug addicts, they require recurrent "fixes" to keep them on an even keel. The "fixes" which they demand are not drugs, but reassurances that they are loved and are successful in the external world.

Social Reasons for Vulnerability to Depression

In recent years, Brown and his colleagues have demonstrated that there are also social factors that determine a person's vulnerability to severe depression following loss. Thus, women who have no other adult in whom they can confide are more prone to clinically definable depression. So are women who have at home with them three or more children under the age of 14. Lack of any job outside the home (which clearly often goes hand in hand with having small children at home) is another factor, and so is poor housing. Knowing that these social factors affect whether a person's reaction to loss is "normal" or turns into a case of depression requiring psychiatric intervention is clearly important in deciding treatment.

Brown also discovered that those women who had lost their mothers before they had reached the age of 11 were more vulnerable to depression in the wake of traumatic life events. This is a particularly interesting finding that requires explanation. Psychoanalysts have so emphasized the importance of early childhood in determining character that psychiatrists have tended to underestimate the significance of later events. If it is confirmed that loss of the mother at as late as 10 years of age renders a person more liable to react to subsequent losses with severe depression, it follows that the child's character is not as clearly defined by the age of five as psychoanalytic theory suggests.

It also raises the question of whether subsequent losses somehow trigger a similar reaction to earlier losses. Loss of the mother is usually a significant loss in anyone's life, and may be presumed to be more significant the earlier it occurs. Do subsequent losses inevitably take on the quality of that most significant loss, even when they are not directly connected with it?

Clinical experience suggests this to be so. Repeated traumatic experiences of any kind in a person's life tend to recall earlier ones and to be treated as more similar than is often the case. Every psychiatrist must have seen women who complain that men always let them down, or men who make the same accusation about women. Although each instance of rejection or hurt may in fact occur for different reasons, they all tend to be gathered together under the same emotional umbrella. This means that even trivial instances of supposed rejection may be treated as if they were much more serious than they are.

One reason why a person may be plunged into severe depression by a loss which seems comparatively trivial is, therefore, that the trivial loss awakens echoes of a previous loss that was highly significant. Brown writes, "There may in depression be some kind of 'induced sensitivity' that makes subsequent episodes more likely. . . . "

Psychotherapy of the Depressive Personality

Persons in the midst of a severe episode of depression are often beyond the reach of formal psychotherapy while the episode lasts. There is little point in attempting formal psychotherapy with persons who are suffering from a depressive illness when they are retarded or are expressing either hypochondriacal delusions or delusions of total worthlessness. Some patients in this condition actually repudiate any attempt to contact them, appearing to prefer to be left alone in their misery. However, others are grateful for being listened to, even if they are convinced that they have committed the unforgivable sin and are condemned to eternal punishment. Because we now have effective physical methods of treatment for severe depression, we are apt to underestimate the importance of talking to, and listening to, psychotic patients. The fact that a doctor is prepared to take what they say seriously is important to many deluded patients, who will often express their gratitude for this when they have recovered from the psychotic episode. But the period between attacks of depression is, of course, the time when more formal psychotherapy can be most effective.

The Aims of Psychotherapy with Depressive Patients

One aim of psychotherapy with any type of patient is to make sense out of his disorder. In order to do this, the therapist must familiarize himself with the patient's history and development from his earliest memories onward. Every patient in psychotherapy needs to be furnished with a coherent narrative of his life in order to make his personality and his disorder comprehensible. Various psychotherapeutic "schools" may emphasize different factors as being of particular importance in causing the patient to have become the way he is. Some analysts might postulate that the way the patient was handled during the first few months of life was all-important; others may lay greater stress upon later periods.

In our present state of knowledge, we cannot accurately determine how much the liability to depression is to be attributed to nature and how much to nurture. What is important is that the characteristics of the depressive personality are usually manifested early, and that the patient's emotional development and interaction with other people are generally fairly consistent. For example, the patient's fear of showing aggression to those upon whom he is emotionally dependent usually manifests itself early in life. Following upon this, it is usually not difficult to demonstrate a more general inhibition of aggression of such a kind that the patient has lacked independent initiative, and has perhaps been inclined to give up too easily in the face of tasks or problems. As Seligman[4] has demonstrated, learned helplessness goes hand in hand with depression.

Demonstrating to the patient that his present difficulties are related to the way in which he has developed as a person since childhood is only a first step in psychotherapy, but it is an important one. By gaining insight into the structure of his personality the patient comes to feel that, however unhappy his life may be at times, it at least makes sense in terms of his history and personality.

Armed with the knowledge of the importance of social factors in increasing vulnerability to depression, the therapist may become aware of such factors operating in his patients. Although no therapist can provide new housing, enough money to pay for child care, or a new spouse, the therapist's awareness of how a lack of these amenities contributes to the depth and prolongation of depression will influence how he responds to the various subjects of his patient's discourse. It is only when one knows what to look for that one picks up what is important. Many depressed patients blame themselves so severely for what they consider "weakness" that they do not realize that normal people also react to adverse social circumstances with depression, and are often relieved when this is pointed out.

Insight into Vulnerability

As patients gradually become more and more aware of their own vulnerability, this becomes somewhat modified. Insight may not abolish emotional overreaction, but it does enable patients to take a more detached attitude. Instead of being overwhelmed by the emotion of the moment, the patient is, as it were, able to stand back and observe his own emotions — perhaps with regret, perhaps with a certain wry humor. "There I go again!" is a healthier attitude than, "This is the end of the world."

Moreover, insight into vulnerability may enable patients to avoid certain situations which provoke depression. For example, the punitive superego so characteristic of such a patient may compel her to visit her cantankerous, elderly mother in spite of the fact that every visit is followed by severe depression. When the connection has been established, it may be that she can decrease the frequency of her visits without too much guilt, or even come to regard them as disagreeable chores rather than daughterly duties that she feels she ought to enjoy, but actually hates.

It is difficult, but not impossible, for the depressive patient to learn that episodes of depression are always transient. Most people who are at all seriously depressed believe that they will never recover from a particular attack. Moreover, they often feel that being depressed is in some sense a more authentic condition than feeling cheerful or "normal." In this way they may be partially right, especially if they belong to that group of depressives who habitually try to ward off depression by overwork or other defensive maneuvers. There are some patients who have to come to terms with the fact that they are chronically depressed, and that a large part of their lives is a struggle against this condition. The more patients can admit this, the less are they overwhelmed with depression when it episodically becomes worse. Depression resembles other episodic complaints like asthma. When the patient is well he tends to deny the fact that he has a disability and is therefore less prepared for the recurrence of an attack and less inclined to take precautionary measures to deal with it. I am sure that it is wrong to tell patients to "forget all about it" once an attack of depression is over, or say, "You may never get another attack." It is preferable to treat the liability to depression as a disability with which the patient has to come to terms, just as he might have to come to terms with being an asthmatic or an alcoholic. In all these conditions, the patient has to learn to live with something which he would much rather be without but which cannot entirely be eliminated.

It is only when patients learn to accept their susceptibility to depression that they can also accept the fact that episodes of severe depression invariably come to an end. It is those who deny the possibility of further attack who are overwhelmed by the attack when it does come and who cannot believe that it will ever be over. Denial is a mechanism of defense that is both dangerous and ineffective.

Transference in the Psychotherapy of Depression

Depressive patients of the kind I have been writing about are often labeled "good" patients because of their tendency toward compliance. Their anxiety to please the therapist and their capacity for repressing aggression make them appear to be nicer than they are. One very important positive gain which can be achieved in psychotherapy is the realization that the expression of aggressive feelings need not necessarily bring about the end of a relationship. If the therapist manages to bring to the surface the aggressive impulses which are buried within every depressive, to aid their expression toward the therapist, and to prove by continuing understanding and compassion that he is still concerned and ready to help, he will be providing a learning experience for the patient that may well prove invaluable.

One useful opportunity for exposing aggressive impulses recurs in every period of psychotherapy of any length. I am referring to the times when therapy is interrupted by the therapist's vacation. On the therapist's return, the patient will usually say that he has been more depressed or has suffered in other ways. It is generally possible to demonstrate that the patient has felt aggressive toward the therapist for abandoning him, and also to show that the expression of such aggressive feelings is not a serious threat to the relationship.

Depressive patients appear to form positive transferences very easily. It is important not to take this entirely at face value. When patients are initially suspicious or hostile, analysis of their negative transference feelings is essential if therapy is to proceed. In the case of depressive patients, what appear to be positive emotions toward the therapist consist partly of compliance and ingratiation, and are thus the product of fear rather than of love. Analysis of these pseudo-positive emotions usually brings forth aggressive feelings of which the patient was previously unaware.

I referred earlier to the fact that patients with depressive personalities remained dependent upon outside sources of self-esteem. It appeared probable that these patients, for one reason or another, had failed to incorporate any sense of their own worth during babyhood and early childhood, even in instances where parental love had seemed adequate. How far are depressive patients, during long-term psychotherapy, able to experience the therapist as a loving parent and thus acquire the kind of built-in self-esteem which they should have acquired much earlier in life?

Our knowledge is not yet adequate to answer this question fully. What one can say is that there are certainly some patients who do incorporate the therapist in this way and who thus acquire a sense of their own worth which they did not previously possess. I have the impression that these are patients who, in actuality, did suffer from neglectful or unloving parents. The transference situation gives such patients a second chance, a corrective emotional experience in which they learn that at least one other person values and appreciates them. Moreover, this other person accepts the aggressive, assertive aspects of their personalities as well as the compliant, "good" aspects. However, even these patients, who may gain a great deal from psychotherapy, seldom entirely lose their tendency to become unduly depressed in adversity. Some degree of vulnerability to depression remains with them.

The Therapeutic Value of Achievement

One way in which depressive personalities ward off depression is by repeated achievement. This is especially true of gifted people, who may often be, in the world's eyes, extremely successful. However, examination of what they actually do often reveals that their attitude toward work is compulsive. They so easily get depressed if they are not working and achieving that they dare not take holidays, or cannot enjoy holidays if they are not perpetually active. They tend to work very long hours and to leave themselves no time for family life or relaxation, which they dismiss as a waste of time. Often, such people go to bed very late in the hope that they will instantly fall asleep, thus leaving no time for morbid thoughts to enter their minds. Whether or not personalities of this kind display obvious hypomanic symptoms, they are employing a manic defense against depression. Such a defense is often quite effective for long periods.

The fact that repeated achievement can be the consequence of hypomanic overactivity has tended to discredit work as therapy for depression. Yet depressive personalities often underachieve because they have no confidence in their abilities or denigrate their achievements instead of being proud of them. Many depressives possess unrealized potentials and benefit greatly from recognizing these and putting them to use. Sometimes one finds that such people have prematurely abandoned occupations and leisure activities that they might have enjoyed because they underestimated their capacities or set themselves impossible standards. It is very important for depressives to have some rewarding occupation to turn to that they can still pursue when depression threatens, or when they are already mildly depressed. Intellectuals can often be encouraged to write. Even keeping a diary is valuable, as it enables the writer to objectify his moods and thus to detach himself from them to some extent. Others may benefit from learning to play a musical instrument — again, something to which they can turn even when feeling low. Cultivating one's garden is a rewarding occupation that requires no interaction with others and that brings a sense of achievement to people of all ranges of intelligence. The point I want to emphasize is that, although work can be a compulsive activity that prevents the person from facing himself and his problem, it can also be a way for the depressive to realize more of his true potential and thus acquire a greater sense of his own worth. Freud, when asked to define normality, did so in terms of the ability to love and the ability to work. Psychotherapists have tended to overemphasize object relationships and to undervalue work as a legitimate source of self-esteem.

It is encouraging to learn that, in some clinics in the U.S. specializing in the treatment of affective disorders, every patient is offered some form of psychotherapy, even when receiving lithium or antidepressants. I hope this practice will become more general. Patients with recurrent depression can often gain considerable benefit from psychotherapy whether or not they are also receiving other forms of treatment.

References

1. Brown GW, Harris T: *Social Origins of Depression: A Study of Psychiatric Disorder in Women*, Tavistock, London, 1978.
2. Kagan J: *The Nature of the Child*, Basic Books, New York, 1984.
3. Freud S: Mourning and Melancholia, *Standard Edition*, Vol. XIV, Norton, New York, pp. 239–258.
4. Seligman MEP: *Helplessness*, W.H. Freeman, San Francisco, 1975.

Further Reading

Alvarez A: *The Savage God*, Weidenfeld & Nicolson, London, 1971.
Arieti S, Bemporad J: *Severe and Mild Depression: The Psychotherapeutic Approach*, Tavistock, London, 1980.
Bagley C: Occupational status and symptoms of depression. *Social Science and Medicine* 7:327–339, 1973.
Eitinger L, Strom A: *Mortality and Morbidity after Excessive Stress*, Universitesforlaget, Oslo, 1973.
Flach FF: *The Secret Strength of Depression*, J. B. Lippincott, Philadelphia and New York, 1974; Bantam Books, New York, 1975.
Fromm-Reichmann F: Intensive psychotherapy of manic-depressives. *Conf. in Neurol.* 9:158–165, 1949.
Reynolds DK, Farberow NL: *Suicide: Inside and Out*, University of California Press, Berkeley and Los Angeles, 1978.

11

Cognitive Therapy for Depression

Robin B. Jarrett and A. John Rush

EDITOR'S NOTE

Cognitive therapy has received a good deal of attention as one psychotherapeutic tactic for the treatment of depression. It is a highly structured approach which presumably permits rapid improvement from depression and offers a chance to prevent relapse in the future.

Cognitive therapy is based on the hypothesis that depression is the result of faulty perception and cognition. Depressed patients hold negative views about themselves, their worlds, and their futures. Unarticulated rules influence their emotional, behavioral, and thinking patterns. Logical errors—perhaps better rephrased as errors of logic—are exemplified when a depressed person draws conclusions not supported by data, generalizes from isolated incidents, or exaggerates or diminishes the importance of some events.

Therapy attacks these false concepts. Once rapport has been established, the therapist uses questioning to encourage the patient to test the objectivity or validity of specific thoughts or ideas. The rationale for treatment is emphasized to organize the patient's approach to it. The patient is encouraged to monitor himself in a variety of stress-provoking situations, reexamine his premises, gain distance from automatic assumptions and the adverse emotions accompanying them, and to view his perceptions as hypotheses subject to testing. The usual course of therapy consists of two individual sessions a week for ten weeks. Patients who respond best are not usually diagnosed as endogenously depressed; they are more likely to show a normal dexamethasone suppression test.

Why cognitive therapy works remains unclear. Is it a way to restore morale? Is the effort to undermine misleading conceptions central to its effect? Perhaps offering the helpless, confused, out-of-control depressed patient a systematic structure to restore command over himself and his environment is one key factor.

Introduction

Cognitive therapy is a short-term psychosocial intervention designed to ameliorate the symptoms of nonpsychotic, nonbipolar depression (i.e., it is designed for symptom reduction) and to decrease the probability that depression will recur (i.e., it is designed for prophylaxis). This lesson describes briefly the cognitive model of depression, the typical course of cognitive therapy, and its evidence for effectiveness.

The Cognitive Model

The premise of the cognitive model: The premise of the cognitive model is that cognitions (images and thoughts) influence emotions and behaviors. This premise is grounded in a phenomenological approach to psychology, a perspective which assumes that behavior is influenced by the individual's perception of himself and the world. According to the cognitive model, the central feature of depression is distorted cognitions. Therefore, within the cognitive model, other symptoms typical of depression, e.g., motivational deficits, suicidal impulses, and sadness, are augmented by distorted thinking patterns.

Cognitive therapy's unit of focus — distorted cognitions: Rush[1] has defined cognitions as images and thoughts or "what a person thinks to himself in a situation." According to the cognitive model, cognitions are important because they are related to the feelings and behavior which occur in the situation. Beck[2] maintained that the cognitions associated with depression are automatic, involuntary, plausible, persistent, and often contain a theme of loss. Beck distinguished between socially accepted or objective definitions of particular events (e.g., loss) and private meanings of events (i.e., the significance of the event to the individual). He stressed that it is the private interpretation of events that is critical to the emotional responses that follow these events. The emphasis on the private meanings of events reflects the roots of cognitive therapy in phenomenological conceptualization of psychopathology. However, it is also the disparity between private and public meanings of events which result in discrimination between "distorted" and "rational" cognitions (automatic thoughts).

In describing and theorizing about depression, Beck[3-5] identified three elements deemed essential to the psychopathology of depression. These are the cognitive triad, silent assumptions, and logical errors.

Cognitive triad: The cognitive triad consists of the negative views held by depressives about themselves, their world, and their future (Table 1). Gener-

TABLE 1
Examples of Cognitions from the
Automatic Thoughts Questionnaire

I feel like I'm up against the world.
I'm no good.
Why can't I ever succeed?
No one understands me.
I've let people down.
I don't think I can go on.
I wish I were a better person.
I'm so weak.
My life's not going the way I want it to.
I'm so disappointed in myself.
Nothing feels good anymore.
I can't stand this anymore.
I can't get started.

From Hollon SD, Kendall PC: Cognitive self-statements in depression: Development of an automatic thoughts questionnaire, *Cognitive Therapy Research* 4:383–395, 1980.

ally, the depressive assumes that he, his world, and his future lack some feature(s) that are a prerequisite for happiness. For example, the depressive may view himself as unworthy, inadequate, or incompetent. He may view his environment as continually demanding and unsupporting. He may describe the future as hopeless and predict that his deficits and current pain will continue indefinitely. These negative views, the cognitive triad, account for, maintain, or contribute to other symptoms commonly found in the depressive syndrome. That is, if the depressive thinks that "today will be just as miserable as yesterday," then he will feel and behave as if this thought were literally true or valid; for example, he will feel sad and stay in bed. These negative views are called automatic thoughts and they are found in the stream of consciousness of the depressive in specific situations.

Silent assumptions: The second element found in the psychopathology of depression consists of silent assumptions or rules. These are unarticulated rules that influence the depressive's emotional, behavioral, and thinking patterns (Table 2). Silent assumptions are psychological constructs and the patient bases his emotional and behavioral responses on them. For example, the depressive may believe, "If I am not loved by everyone, I'm unworthy." These stable beliefs develop from early experience and subsequently influence the individual's responses to events. According to the cognitive model, these silent assumptions give rise to automatic thoughts. Silent assumptions are typically stated as "if-then" premises that can be identified by examining patterns within a group of automatic thoughts or behavioral responses.

Depressive assumptions are typically inferred by examining the situation, emotions, and themes associated with the array of negative automatic thoughts. For example, a depressed person may report sadness when her spouse does not compliment her on her appearance. She may report thinking, "He is not attracted to me anymore because I am ugly." She may also report feeling dysphoric when a friend talks to her for only five minutes in the grocery store. She may report thinking, "She would want to spend more time with me if I weren't so dull." Through repeated examples and verbal exchange, the therapist and patient may infer the silent assumption, "If others don't attend to me, it's (a) something to be disturbed about and (b) because of a deficit I have."

The cognitive model posits that these inappropriate assumptions are activated more frequently than appropriate (undistorted) assumptions when a person is depressed. It is assumed that as the depression becomes more severe, the individual's thinking becomes more disparate despite logical or objective evidence to the contrary.

Logical errors: The third element essential to this cognitive model are the logical errors spawned by the negative automatic thoughts made by the depressive. Logical errors are identified by examining logical relationships

TABLE 2
Sample Items from Dysfunctional Attitudes Scale

It is difficult to be happy unless one is good-looking, intelligent, rich, and creative.

Happiness is more a matter of my attitude toward myself than the way other people feel about me.

People will probably think less of me if I make a mistake.

If I do not do well all the time, people will not respect me.

Taking even a small risk is foolish because the loss is likely to be a disaster.

It is possible to gain another person's respect without being especially talented at anything.

I cannot be happy unless most people I know admire me.

If a person asks for help, it is a sign of weakness.

From Weissman AW: The Dysfunctional Attitudes Scale: A validation study, (Doctoral dissertation, University of Pennsylvania), *Dissertation Abstracts International* 40:1389–1390B, 1979.

between a specific event and the associated negative automatic thought. Some examples of logical errors include arbitrary inference, selective attention, overgeneralization, magnification or minimization, and personalization. Arbitrary inference occurs when the depressed person draws conclusions that are not supported by logical or environmental data. Selective attention refers to emphasizing certain details and ignoring others. Overgeneralization includes drawing conclusions about one's ability, performance, or worth based on a single incident. Magnification or minimization refers to exaggerating or diminishing, respectively, the importance of an event. Personalization involves associating events with oneself when logic or data would prohibit such associations.

The vulnerability for and maintenance of depression: According to Beck,[5] the existence of silent assumptions increases an individual's vulnerability or predisposition to depression. These assumptions may develop through interactions with significant others. In particular, depressive assumptions are learned in the context of "an unfavorable life situation," e.g., the loss of a parent or chronic rejection by peers. Later in life, when the individual is exposed to a situation analogous to the original unfavorable life situation, he or she employs the previously learned assumptions.

Once activated, these schemata or assumptions are applied to an ever-widening array of stimulus situations, thereby leading to more negative automatic thinking. For example, a person who is overly concerned with approval from others may view normal day-to-day transactions as if they meant he or she is not liked by anyone, e.g., the stewardess on the airplane didn't smile—that means "no one likes me."

The typical emotional, motivational, behavioral, and vegetative depressive symptoms (e.g., hopelessness, apathy, agitation and sleep disturbance) are made worse by this negative automatic thinking. As depressive symptoms worsen, the distorted thinking increases. Beck has termed the relationship between depressive symptoms and thoughts a "vicious cycle," a "circular feedback model," and the "downward spiral of depression."

The Typical Course of Cognitive Therapy

Establishing a therapeutic alliance and rationale: One of the first steps in cognitive therapy involves developing rapport with the patient and establishing a "collaborative alliance." The therapist's role in this alliance is to guide the patient. For example, each session begins with the therapist and patient listing and prioritizing items on the "agenda" to be covered. The competent cognitive therapist not only has refined general psychotherapeutic skills (i.e., he or she is perceived as warm, genuine, empathic, and able to understand and reflect the patient's thinking), but also can remain objective and logical about the automatic thoughts and emotional responses which are identified. The therapist usually phrases most comments as questions, to be answered by the patient, rather than as statements. The cognitive therapist typically avoids attempting to "persuade" the patient that his or her thoughts are dysfunctional. Instead, the therapist encourages the patient to test the objectivity or validity of specific thoughts or ideas by examining their inherent logic and/or by seeking supportive or disconfirming data within the patient's daily life. Such an alliance has been labeled "collaborative empiricism."[7]

The therapeutic alliance is of special importance when working with depressives, who characteristically overpersonalize and are likely to respond negatively to neutral or even positive interpersonal interactions. When problems occur within the therapeutic context (e.g., relationship difficulties, missed appointments), these problems are conceptualized within the cognitive model. That is, corresponding thoughts and emotions are identified and problem-solving strategies are implemented. For example, a depressive may report missing a therapy session after thinking, "I've been depressed before and received therapy. I'm depressed again so this won't work either." The therapist can consider the report of these thoughts as an opportunity to review the (a) similarities and dissimilarities of past and current therapies, (b) evidence supporting or refuting the notion that cognitive therapy will not work, (c) advantages and disadvantages of cognitive therapy to date, and (d) changes that may need to be made in the therapy.

To foster a collaborative alliance, much time is devoted to providing a rationale for treatment. The verbal rationale may be supplemented by asking the patient to read a pamphlet entitled Coping With Depression.[6] This pamphlet aids in "socializing" the patient to cognitive therapy by (a) describing many of the depressive symptoms from which the patient may suffer, (b) illustrating dysfunctional thinking, (c) focusing on the relationship between dysfunctional thinking and depression, and (d) encouraging the patient that his or her problems can be alleviated by learning to recognize negative thoughts, testing the validity of the thoughts, and problem-solving.

Processes and Techniques of Cognitive Therapy

Self-monitoring: Self-monitoring is used to aid the patient in identifying thoughts which accompany uncomfortable emotions and difficult situations. By completing the Daily Record of Dysfunctional Thoughts (Table 3) and through dialogue, the patient begins to distinguish and to note the

TABLE 3

Daily Record of Dysfunctional Thoughts

Date	*Situation* Describe: 1. Actual event leading up to unpleasant emotion, or 2. Stream of thoughts, daydream, or recollection, leading to unpleasant emotion.	*Emotion(s)* 1. Specify sad/ anxious/angry, etc. 2. Rate degree of emotion, 1-100.	*Automatic Thought(s)* 1. Write automatic thought(s) that preceded emotion(s). 2. Rate belief in automatic thought(s), 0-100%.	*Rational Response* 1. Write rational response to automatic thought(s). 2. Rate belief in rational response, 0-100%.	*Outcome* 1. Rerate belief in automatic thought(s), 0-100%. 2. Specify and rate subsequent emotions, 0-100%.

Explanation: When you experience an unpleasant emotion, note the situation that seemed to stimulate the emotion. (If the emotion occurred while you were thinking, daydreaming, etc., please note this.) Then note the automatic thought associated with the emotion. Record the degree to which you believe this thought: 0% = not at all; 100% = completely. In rating degree of emotion: 1 = trace; 100 = the most intense possible.

From Beck AT et al.: *Cognitive Therapy of Depression*, Guilford Press, New York, 1979.

relationship between thoughts, events, emotions, and other behaviors. For example, the patient may note that (a) she feels sad (i.e., the emotion), (b) when a coworker does not say, "Good morning" (i.e., the situation), and (c) she thinks, "Nobody likes me here enough to say hello" (i.e., the automatic thought). After noticing the covariation between this situation, emotion, and thought, it is understandable that this patient now avoids the office coffee break, i.e., she assumes nobody likes her.

After the patient has learned self-monitoring, she is taught to identify themes, ideas which recur across situations, by reviewing past records and sessions (e.g., fearing rejection, seeking approval). By identifying and discussing these pervasive themes, the patient and therapist infer the patient's general rules or silent assumptions.

Evaluating the validity of cognitions: Subsequently, the patient learns to determine the extent to which his or her cognitions (i.e., automatic thoughts and silent assumptions) correspond to an objective appraisal of his or her situation. When the thoughts or assumptions do not match the "evidence," the patient is taught to revise these cognitions with more accurate ones and to carry out responses that are consistent with this modified view.

The general process of evaluating the validity of automatic thoughts or silent assumptions is accomplished through a variety of techniques (Tables 4 and 5). When evaluating the validity of cognitions, the first basic goal is to

TABLE 4
Behavioral Techniques

Activity Scheduling
Mastery and Pleasure Ratings
Graded Task Assignment
Cognitive Rehearsal
Assertive Training/Role Playing
Mood Graph

From Rush AJ: Cognitive therapy of depression. Rationale, techniques and efficacy. *Psychiatric Clinics of North America*, 6:105-127, 1983.

TABLE 5
Cognitive Techniques

Recording Automatic Thoughts (Cognitions)
Reattribution Techniques
Responding to Negative Cognitions
Counting Automatic Thoughts
Identifying Assumptions
Modifying Shoulds
Pro-Con Refutation of Assumptions
Homework to Test Old Assumptions
Homework to Test New Assumptions

From Rush AJ: Cognitive therapy of depression. Rationale, techniques and efficacy. *Psychiatric Clinics of North America*, 6:105-127, 1983.

teach the patient to recognize that thoughts and beliefs are inferences about the world rather than facts. When the patient can conceptualize thoughts as assumptions or hypotheses rather than as facts, he or she can develop some "distance" from the emotions accompanying the thoughts. Hence, the patient learns to scrutinize his or her thoughts by asking questions such as: What part of my situation is a fact and what part is my belief? What evidence is there to support or to refute my thoughts? What are some alternative explanations for my thoughts? How would a nondepressed person view my situation? And even if my thoughts match the facts, is it truly as bad as it seems? Through this type of questioning, the patient learns to recognize and to correct logical errors.

In addition to learning to evaluate his or her thoughts logically, the patient learns to view these thoughts as hypotheses that can be tested. The patient learns to (a) state his cognition in a testable form (i.e., make a prediction), (b) arrange and implement a test of the prediction, (c) record the results, (d) compare the results to the prediction, and (e) query whether additional experiments are necessary to test the validity of the thought.

For example, a depressed lawyer reported, "I'm so disorganized and distracted, I'll never complete my work." Such a prediction is especially suited to a common technique used in cognitive therapy called graded task assignment. Through graded task assignment, the patient was taught to operationalize work, e.g., a legal report, and to break it down into small, specific, realistic tasks to be completed over time. Within the experiment, the lawyer predicted she could not even complete the first step of gathering the related legal books and moving all other distracting materials from the desk. Such thoughts which might interfere with the task (e.g., "I'm too incompetent to complete the first step") were identified and the therapist emphasized partial successes. Each component of completing the legal report was specified, and accomplishing the tasks was viewed as an experiment. Throughout the experiment, the lawyer recorded her progress and compared these results to her initial prediction. At the end of the experiment, she concluded that she was, in fact, able to make some progress on her legal report, and had made overly pessimistic predictions which interfered with her working effectively.

Homework: One of the most important aspects of cognitive therapy is the "homework" assignment which is completed outside of the therapy session. Homework is tailored to address the automatic thoughts, silent assumptions, or particular symptom targets chosen by the patient and therapist. Each session includes a review of the homework. Noncompliance with homework assignments is dealt with using a cognitive model, as is any difficult behavior (e.g., what thoughts and emotions occurred when you had difficulty beginning the homework?).

Frequency, length, and modality of treatment: To date, there are few studies designed to determine what, if any, relationship exists between the frequency or length of treatment and response to cognitive therapy. One preliminary report suggests that moderately to severely depressed patients evidence fewer dropouts and greater reduction in symptoms when treated twice a week than when treated once a week.[7] In research protocols, cognitive therapy typically occurs twice a week for ten weeks, i.e., 20 sessions. Experienced cognitive therapists recommend that the frequency of the sessions be determined by the severity of the depression; as severity increases frequency increases.

No studies to date have adequately examined the effect of maintenance or "booster" sessions on therapeutic response. In practice, it is common for patients to participate in booster sessions (once or twice a month) for six to twelve months after routine cognitive therapy.

The typical modality in which cognitive therapy occurs is individual sessions. Rush and Watkins[8], as well as Wierzbicki and Bartlett[9] have compared cognitive therapy administered in an individual and group modality, and found an advantage for the individual modality. Clinical experience suggests that cognitive therapy can also be used with couples, as well as with individuals and researchers are beginning to evaluate the prospect of doing so.[10]

The Effectiveness of Cognitive Therapy

The outcome data from individual and group cognitive therapy, involving clinic patients, community volunteers, and college students, have been detailed elsewhere.[1,11] A few studies have compared the effects of cognitive therapy and other forms of psychotherapy. For example, cognitive therapy has been associated with greater reductions in depressive symptoms than (a) waiting list controls[12-19]; (b) nondirective therapy[13]; or (c) insight-oriented therapy.[12,16,20] Shaw[13] found a preferential effect for cognitive therapy over "behavior therapy," although Taylor and Marshall[21], Besyner[15], Wilson et al.[18], and Thompson and Gallagher[19] found that the two approaches were equally effective.

Much of the outcome data on cognitive therapy has included comparisons with antidepressant medications. To date, no study has demonstrated that the effects of antidepressant medication exceed those of cognitive therapy. The typical findings are that at the end of treatment the two methods produce equivalent effects[8,22] or that the effects of cognitive therapy exceed those of antidepressant medication.[23-25]

Presently, the question of whether greater symptom reduction or prophylaxis occurs when cognitive therapy and pharmacotherapy are combined cannot be answered definitively. Blackburn et al.[23] found that for psychiatric clinic outpatients a combination of cognitive therapy plus antidepressants reduced symptoms more than either cognitive therapy alone or antidepressants alone. Murphy et al.[22] found the effects of cognitive therapy alone equaled a combination of cognitive therapy plus drugs as well as a combination of placebo and cognitive therapy. In conclusion, it appears that patients who receive cognitive therapy can be divided into two groups: those who show a good response to cognitive therapy alone and those who show a better response when cognitive therapy and antidepressant medication are combined.

The prophylactic effect of cognitive therapy must be demonstrated in order for cognitive therapy to be recognized as a cost-effective treatment for depression. Although more investigation is necessary, the results of several studies suggest that cognitive therapy reduced the rate of relapse more than antidepressant medication.[20,26-27]

Predicting response to cognitive therapy: Researchers are only recently beginning to ask for which patients is cognitive therapy indicated or contraindicated. At present, there are no definitive predictors of response to cognitive therapy. Beck et al.[7] state that patients with hallucinations, delusions, organic brain syndrome, borderline personality disorder, and schizoaffective disorders may not respond to cognitive therapy at all or may not respond when cognitive therapy is conducted in its typical time-limited format. Failure in treating depression with cognitive therapy has been the subject of a review by Rush and Shaw.[28] Keller[29] demonstrated that subjects with low Dysfunctional Attitudes Scale scores (few dysfunctional beliefs) were more likely to respond to cognitive therapy than those with high scores. Similarly, Simons et al.[27] demonstrated that subjects with high scores on the Self-Control Scale[30], a measure of learned resourcefulness, were more likely to respond to cognitive therapy; whereas, those with low scores were more likely to respond to medication.

Clinical experience suggests that responders typically show a 50% symptom reduction (e.g., as shown on the Beck Depression Inventory or Hamilton Rating Scale) by approximately the twelfth to fourteenth session, i.e., assuming sessions occur twice a week for five to seven weeks. Rush hypothesized that endogenous depressions, which are associated with dexamethasone nonsuppression, may show a poor response to cognitive therapy and that biological tests (e.g., the dexamethasone suppression test and the EEG taken during sleep) may be useful in predicting response to cognitive therapy.[31]

Conclusion

Cognitive therapy is an effective approach for treating a subset of nonpsychotic, nonbipolar depressives. To date, the literature suggests that cognitive therapy both reduces depressive symptoms and decreases the probability of relapse in a subgroup who respond initially. Theoretically, it is unclear through what mechanisms cognitive therapy produces its effects or to what extent the cognitive model accurately describes the development and maintenance of a depression. Practical issues involving the conditions under which cognitive therapy is maximally effective are yet to be resolved. These questions include when to combine cognitive therapy with antidepressant medication, what are the most effective and efficient modalities for delivering cognitive therapy, and which patients are most likely to respond to this treatment.

References

1. Rush AJ: Cognitive therapy of depression: Rationale, techniques and efficacy. In Akiskal H (ed): *Psychiatr. Clin. North Am.* 6:105–127, 1983.

2. Beck AT: Thinking and depression: I. Idiosyncratic content and cognitive distortion. *Arch. Gen. Psychiatry* 9:324–333, 1963.

3. Beck AT: *Depression: Clinical, Experimental and Theoretical Aspects*, Harper & Row, New York, 1967.

4. Beck AT: *Depression: Causes and Treatment*, University of Pennsylvania Press, Philadelphia, 1972.

5. Beck AT: *Cognitive Therapy and the Emotional Disorders*, International Universities Press, New York, 1976.

6. Beck AT, Greenberg R: *Coping with Depression*, Center for Cognitive Therapy, Philadelphia, Pa., 1976.

7. Beck AT et al.: *Cognitive Therapy of Depression*, Guilford Press, New York, 1979.

8. Rush AJ, Watkins JT: Group versus individual cognitive therapy: A pilot study. *Cognit. Ther. Res.* 5:95–103, 1981.

9. Wierzbicki M, Bartlett TS: The efficacy of group and individual cognitive therapy for mild depression. *Cognit. Ther. Res.* 11:337–342, 1987.

10. Rush AJ, Shaw BF, Khatami M: Cognitive therapy of depression: Utilizing the couples system. *Cognit. Ther. Res.* 4:103–113, 1980.

11. Jarrett, RJ, Rush AJ: Psychotherapeutic approaches for depression. In Cavenar JO (ed) *Psychiatry*. Vol. 1, Chapter 65. Lippincott, Philadelphia, 1986, pp. 1–35.

12. Morris NE: *A group self-instruction method for the treatment of depressed*

outpatients. National Library of Canada, Canadian Theses Division, No. 35272, 1975.

13. Shaw BF: Comparison of cognitive therapy and behavior therapy in the treatment of depression. *J. Consult. Clin. Psychol.* 45:543–551, 1977.

14. Magers BD: Cognitive-behavioral short-term group therapy with depressed women. (California School of Professional Psychology), *Dissertation Abstracts International*, 38:4468B (University Microfilm No. 78-01687), 1978.

15. Besyner JK: The comparative efficacy of cognitive and behavioral treatments of depression: A multiassessment approach. *Dissertation Abstracts International*, 39:4568B (University Microfilms No. 79-04956), 1979.

16. Carrington CH: A comparison of cognitive and analytically oriented brief treatment approaches to depression in black women. University of Maryland. *Dissertation Abstracts International*, 40:2829-B (University Microfilms No. 79-26513), 1979.

17. Comas-Diaz, L: Effects of cognitive and behavioral group treatment on the depressive symptomatology of Puerto Rican women. *J. Consult. Clin. Psychol.* 49:627–632, 1981.

18. Wilson PH, Goldin JC, Charbonneau-Powis M: Comparative effects of behavioral and cognitive treatments for depression. *Cognit. Ther. Res.* 7:111–124, 1983.

19. Thompson LW, Gallagher D: Efficacy of psychotherapy in the treatment of late-life depression. *Adv. Behav. Res. Ther.* 7:127–139, 1984.

20. Covi L, Lipman RS: Cognitive behavioral group psychotherapy combined with imipramine in major depression: A pilot study. *Psychopharmacol. Bull.* 23:173–176, 1987.

21. Taylor FG, Marshall WL: Experimental analysis of a cognitive-behavioral therapy for depression. *Cognit. Ther. Res.* 1:59–72, 1977.

22. Murphy GE et al.: Cognitive therapy and pharmacotherapy: Singly and together in the treatment of depression. *Arch. Gen. Psychiatry* 41:33–41, 1984.

23. Blackburn et al.: The efficacy of cognitive therapy in depression. A treatment trial using cognitive therapy and pharmacotherapy, each alone and in combination. *Br. J. Psych.* 139:181–189, 1981.

24. McLean PD, Hakstian AR: Clinical depression: Comparative efficacy of outpatient treatments. *J. Consult. Clin. Psychol.* 47:818–836, 1979.

25. Rush AJ et al.: Comparative efficacy of cognitive therapy and pharmacotherapy in the treatment of depressed outpatients. *Cognit. Ther. Res.* 1:17–37, 1977.

26. Kovacs M et al.: Depressed outpatients treated with cognitive therapy or pharmacotherapy: A one-year follow-up. *Arch. Gen. Psychiatry* 38:33–39, 1981.

27. Simons AD et al.: Predicting response to cognitive therapy: The role of learned resourcefulness. *Cognit. Ther. Res.* 9:79–90, 1985.

28. Rush AJ, Shaw BF: Failures in treating depression by cognitive behavior therapy. In Foa EB, Emmelkamp PMG (eds): *Failures in Behavior Therapy*, Wiley, New York, 1983, pp. 213–224.

29. Keller KE: Dysfunctional attitudes and cognitive therapy for depression. *Cognit. Ther. Res.* 7:437–444, 1983.

30. Rosenbaum M: A schedule for assessing self-control behaviors: Preliminary findings. *Behav. Ther.* 11:109–121, 1980.

31. Rush AJ: Clinical and etiologic implications of biologic derangements in major depression. In Maas J, Davis J (eds): *Affective Disorders*, American Psychiatric Press, Washington, D.C., 1983, pp. 53–72.

12

Family and Marital Therapy in the Treatment of Depression

Henry I. Spitz

EDITOR'S NOTE

Depression is very much a family affair. Not only does the presence of a depressed member have a serious impact on the family, but the interactions within a family can significantly provoke and perpetuate a state of depression in one or more of its members. The so-called "suicidal" family has certain characteristics, including intolerance to separation, lack of empathy, crisis intolerance, role disturbance and social maladaptation. It is impossible to fully evaluate the nature of any patient's depression without due consideration to family dynamics.

It has been noted that when a family member is depressed a general reduction in expressions of affection occurs; there is also increased criticism, a power struggle in which one partner tends to control the other, and recurrent episodes of guilt induction. The marriage partners communicate unevenly and in a negative cast. There is little humor and often a serious lack of support. Sexual dysfunctions are, of course, common.

Certain behavior patterns are often seen, such as the use of depression to seek out caring, polarization in which each partner views the other as the cause of disharmony, and the tendency for triadic relationships to develop, such as finding a scapegoat or engaging in extramarital affairs.

All of these various patterns must be considered and dealt with as they occur in the treatment of depressed patients. The therapist should act to stabilize the disturbed family system as quickly as possible, even as he proceeds to treat the depressed patient. Later he may decide whether more active family therapy is indicated if the family disruption is as much a cause of the depression as a consequence.

Introduction

The family has traditionally been a central area of interest in the mental health field. Originally, attention was focused on the family and its role in the genesis and maintenance of psychopathology. In more recent years, the family has been explored as another avenue for the treatment of psychiatric problems. A survey of the relevant literature in the field reflects this trend.

When one considers the specific issue of family and marital therapy as applied to the management of depression, the major lines of study fall into the following broad categories, which are useful for discussion purposes: etiological factors, evaluation and diagnosis, phenomenology and behavioral patterns, and psychotherapeutic approaches.

Etiological Factors

The role of the family as one of the variables in the origins of depression is described primarily in the instance of manic-depressive illness. The emphasis here is weighted largely toward hereditogenetic rather than interpersonal familial influences.

Descriptive studies of family factors in the cause of depression are relatively rare. Richman and Rosenbaum's work[1] represents an effort to outline a family constellation that predisposes to suicide. In their view, the "suicidal family" is characterized by intolerance to separation, preoccupation with themes of death, symbiosis lacking in empathy, crisis intolerance, and role disturbance or failure in most major areas of personal and social function.

In the marital therapy literature, depression is cited as both a cause and a consequence of divorce. Spouses with histories of depression have an increased likelihood of divorce, as well as a greater chance of having depressive episodes following actual dissolution of the marriage. Divorce is also well-known to increase the potential for suicide.

In essence, depression is currently viewed as a complex biopsychosocial phenomenon without clear-cut etiological patterns related to family life, although familial and marital factors appear to influence the form and course of many depressions.

Evaluation and Diagnostic Issues

From a clinical standpoint, comprehensive assessment of the depressed patient is essential. Important information may be gleaned from an examination of the family from a current and a historical perspective. It should be noted that this is in addition to, not a substitute for, other standard methods of examining depressed patients.

The family is the most important and immediate element in the interpersonal field of the depressed patient and, as such, can be employed instructively in both diagnostic and treatment-planning phases of the therapeutic process. How the clinician obtains information about the family varies with his own theoretical orientation. Consensus exists, however, that there are representative family and marital functions that should be reviewed in order for an informed choice to be made regarding the appropriateness (or lack of it) of family and marital forms of intervention.

Since depression, in addition to being a diagnosis, is also an interpersonal process and a style of relatedness, its effects can be observed not only as an individual phenomenon but also as a dyadic experience in marriage and an interactional experience in the family.

Depression-related data may be obtained from families by the taking of a careful family history, with particular emphasis on the generational history regarding depression and suicide. As a corollary to this, the family medical history should be examined, and biological factors, medical illnesses, prior psychiatric treatment, pharmacotherapy, and other somatic treatments should be noted. This can yield data reflective of genetic and familial factors, as in the case of manic-depressive illness.

A good reason for starting with traditional history is in trying to ascertain and address the primary problem first. It may be difficult to assess depression within the family context unless one has a clear conceptual scheme in mind. A common diagnostic question is whether the depression in one spouse is a cause or an effect of a disturbed marital relationship.

In family and marital therapy, common sense must prevail and override issues of technique or the psychotherapeutic "school" of the therapist. Depression is a potential psychiatric emergency and must be carefully considered as such. Involvement of the family in appropriate ways serves to help determine the locus of urgency (individual or interpersonal) more rapidly and accurately.

Various authors have described practical plans for examining families. Minuchin[2] proposed a method that is easily adapted to the assessment of a family with a depressed member. His format is an interactional diagnostic system that measures several classes of information concerning critical aspects of family function. These include (1) observation of family structure and preferred transactional patterns, (2) determination of flexibility or rigidity in response to change, (3) resonance of the system (sensitivity to individual members' actions along a spectrum ranging from enmeshment to disengagement), (4) family life context (sources of support and stress in the environment), (5) the family's developmental stage and the performance of stage-appropriate tasks, and (6) ways in which the identified patient's symptoms are used for maintenance of the family's preferred transactional patterns.

Stuart[3] has advocated the inclusion of a direct measure of mood in each spouse before the start of marital therapy. His technique employs the cheerfulness versus depressed mood subscale of the U.S. Public Health Service's General Well-Being Schedule as the vehicle for obtaining the level of depression in marital partners. He considers mood assessment in spouses as perhaps "the most critical 'internal' measure in the armamentarium of marriage therapists." Depression can interfere with a spouse's motivation to enter into or follow through with therapeutic interventions and can also be a "sign of therapeutic failure when it follows changes that were expected to yield positive affective changes."

To date, no single model encompasses measures of the complex intrapsychic, interpersonal, sociocultural, ideological, and biological vectors at play in depression and the family. Clearly, however, the trend in diagnostic assessment is more cross-sectional than with the older, more factionalistic models. This trend in diagnosis is paralleled in the therapeutic approaches to the management of depression in the family setting.

Phenomenology and Behavioral Observations

One major result of the varied attempts at assessment has been a wealth of direct observational data about marriage and families in which a member shows clinical signs of depression. A general theme that emerges is that there is a general reduction of affective involvement between marital partners. Reduced expressions of affection, increased criticism, and a tendency for one partner to control the other are associated findings. This struggle for interpersonal control, often through guilt induction or provocation, is considered characteristic in these marriages.

Hinchcliffe and colleagues[4] have focused on communication patterns in pairs in which one partner is depressed. Their data revealed that communication was generally uneven, negatively cast, overly protective, and lacking in the tension release, humor, and support elements present in nondepressed couples.

Collaborative ability in marriage and family life is impaired in cases of depression. In couples this is most readily seen in difficulty with parenting, problems with leisure-time activities, and diminished capacity for task execution inside and outside the home.

Sexual dysfunctions are manifest when significant depression exists. Diminished sexual desire, potency problems, and difficulty reaching orgasm are the common conditions requiring attention.

Several authors have conducted more ambitious studies aimed at eluci-
dating specific characteristics evident in depressive dyadic and triadic relationships. The work of Rubenstein and Timmins[5] is noteworthy in this
regard.

The systems nature of relationship function can be seen in the attitudes
assumed by partners in order to maintain the homeostasis of the dyadic or
triadic relationship. The problem presented by depressive dyads and triads is
that these attitudes are rigid, repetitive, and non-growth-promoting. The
behaviors tend to reinforce the status quo of the dysfunctional system.

In depression, this manifests itself in discrete clinical patterns:

Search for a caretaker: The depressed partner's efforts to engage a significant family member in ongoing interaction using depression as the basis for
exchange is an initial phenomenon. Family members often comply by taking
the role of "caretaker." Verbally, the form of communication is hesitant and
low-pitched and contains a small number of verbalizations. The partner
usually responds in kind. Nonverbally, the spouses' body positions are mir-
ror images of one another. The communications initiated by the depressed
partner are fundamentally self-centered. Silences are very common, and
direct eye contact is rare.

Polarization of the relationship: Each partner becomes more firmly en-
trenched in his/her position, and each views the other as the locus of disharmony. Consequently, both partners have opposing views of what (or who)
needs to be changed in order to improve the relationship.

A struggle for control or to be taken care of is the most frequent outcome. In time, both partners tend to develop angry, nongiving stances, and
the behavioral sequences recycle rather than change.

These dyadic interactions are static, nonmaturational, and notoriously
resistant to change. Problem-solving abilities are at a minimum, and often
the relationship itself comes to be viewed as the cause of the problem. Crisis
situations where separation or divorce is seen as the only solution may
readily develop in the process.

Development of triadic relationships: An alternative course that may be
taken in dysfunctional dyadic relationships is the expansion into a three-
person system. When the viability of the relationship is in jeopardy, differences between the partners appear to be insoluble, and the intensity of
negative feelings between spouses is profound, there is a good possibility of
defusing the situation by involving another family member or an outsider.

The role taken by the third person is either to be helpful or to be the
scapegoat for the difficulties in the original dyad. Bowen's notion of
"triangulation" in families and Minuchin's idea[2] of "detouring" through the

use of a sick child in psychosomatic families afford analogous examples of this process in family constellations in which depression is not the chief complaint.

Two major ways in which depressed couples employ third-party participation are extramarital affairs or the use of the couple's child. Relationships with persons outside the marriage serve to drain off or displace intolerable affect from a dyadic system under excessive strain. Lovers function as interpersonal buffers that allow the spouses to titrate themselves against a level of discomfort with the closeness of an intimate relationship.

The use of a child occurs mainly in two ways: as family scapegoat or as a socially acceptable channel for the investment of the spouses' energies in a vector outside the marriage itself. Depressed couples who use children in this way increase the probability of deleterious consequences in the development of the child. Children from families in which they took on caretaking roles for a depressed parent or those made to feel that if not for them the parents would have divorced emerge with a host of psychological problems. Excessive feelings of guilt, an exaggerated sense of responsibility and difficulties with role definition and generational boundary issues are future problems.

Before leaving the subject of behavioral patterns of depressed family members, it is important to mention some data relating to differential diagnosis. Greene and associates[6] point out two striking clinical features in couples in which one spouse had a manic-depressive illness: a "stubborn reluctance on the part of the spouses of these marriages to get divorced" and an intermittent kind of incompatibility, as compared to the more durable kind of incompatibility present in couples who request marital therapy for other reasons.

The first idea has its roots in the partner selection process, wherein it is felt that manic-depressive persons seek spouses who have qualities that will be helpful in coping with severe mood swings. This is similar to the pattern present in other relationships, such as those in which obsessive persons seek out histrionic mates. The spouse chosen by the manic-depressive person is often described as overcontrolling, and the relationship that forms is close-knit and enmeshed. It serves strong needs in both partners and thus results in a bond that is not easily broken.

The periodicity of manic-depressive illness provides the basis for the second observation about intermittent incompatibility. It has been suggested that marriages in which one spouse has a bipolar affective disorder are "healthier" during periods between depressive or manic episodes than are comparable marriages in which one spouse has a unipolar depressive illness. The "bipolar relationship" may be stressed beyond its adaptive capacity during manic episodes, resulting in domestic chaos, physical threats, and other marital crises. Once the manic phase is under control, the relationship very often resumes on a rather congenial basis.

Clarity in diagnosis is directly related to the choice of intervention indicated in a given situation. Marital crisis provides a good example. The relationship in which the husband is in a hypomanic phase and becomes abusive and threatening results in a crisis requiring temporary separation and "cooling off." In contrast, the unipolar couple in crisis stemming from midlife fears of abandonment and separation should be encouraged to remain together in order to face these anxiety-laden issues more directly. Temporary separation would be contraindicated in this case.

Psychotherapeutic Approaches

The ultimate objective in working with families with depressed members is to synthesize the available data to formulate a therapeutic plan with two key goals: resolution of depression and restoration or creation of adaptive family function.

Generally speaking, the field of family and marital therapy has been densely populated by practitioners of varied approaches. The major methods of treatment currently in use may be conceptualized along a spectrum that includes the psychoanalytic, behavioral, social learning, and family systems points of view. The interrelationship of these schools is described in detail in a text edited by Paolino and McCrady.[7]

Technical eclecticism is emerging as a model that is particularly useful in the treatment of depression in families. The key elements combined in this model include crisis-intervention techniques; judicious use of psychotropic medication (primarily tricyclic antidepressants, MAO inhibitors, and lithium); and family systems constructs that emphasize behavioral, educational, and self-awareness components.

This section will be divided in two parts, the first addressing basic goals and assumptions about management of depression in the family context and the second being a review of problems commonly encountered in the course of family and marital therapy.

The goal that is most often agreed upon when serious depression exists in a family is to stabilize the family system as rapidly as possible. In order to do this, the therapist is charged with a task that differs from that in the individual or dyadic therapy of the depressed patient. The family members have a preexisting history with each other and a preexisting set of response patterns of which the therapist is not a part. The initial problem for the therapist is one of entry into the established family system. It is roughly analogous to jumping onto a carousel in motion.

If the family is compared to the structural model of a chemical compound, the therapist must find a place on that molecule that is open for bonding and join the system. Once engaged with the family, the therapist must find a way of taking charge in a manner appropriate to the role of leader in order to help the family reconstitute itself.

This initial phase of treatment requires therapist activity in the form of making a diagnostic assessment, giving advice and direct information when necessary, deciding about medication, and surveying the extended family system to help decide which members will be needed for the ongoing work of psychotherapy.

The therapist offers advice about the problem to the family in a form that should represent the most constructive way of viewing the circumstances. Very often the therapist's conceptualization of the problem differs markedly from the family's initial identification of it. The therapist may have to reframe the initial complaints of a family member in order to enlist the participation of another and to guard against premature therapy dropout. A common maneuver to accomplish this in couples therapy is to suggest that "the relationship is the patient." This joint focus tends to counter mutual blaming and guilt induction and helps create a therapy model rather than a "courtroom" model.

Historical material may be elicited during this first phase. Particular emphasis in depression of an acute or recent nature is devoted to shifts or changes in the family system. This can include addition or loss of family members, social or vocational network changes, and other influences that might be expected to have significant emotional repercussions in the family or in the marriage. An appreciation of the developmental stage in the family life cycle may provide useful information about the cause of current exacerbations of depression.

In cases of recurrent depression, it is helpful to gather information about shared relationship resources used for managing similar episodes in the past. This should encompass a survey of the kin and nonkin networks around the family for future use in planning constructive environmental changes.

Under ordinary circumstances, the initial phase of therapy—including system stabilization, institution of biological therapies if indicated, and reduction of the initial crisis—usually takes a relatively short time to accomplish. Ten sessions are usually the most required for an initial phase as described.

While the initial stage of treatment most closely resembles one of crisis intervention, the later stages of therapy are more varied. Following successful crisis intervention, many couples or families "seal over" and reject the possibility of entering longer-term psychotherapeutic contracts. Others, however, exhibit curiosity and interest in increasing their knowledge about themselves, doing preventive work to lessen the likelihood of recurrence, and learning and practicing alternative ways of relating through their in-session experiences. The form of the therapy must be flexible enough so that the therapist can tailor it in the service of finding a productive way of working with each family and its unique properties.

In the second stage of treatment, the duration of therapy and the session-to-session format are a function of two factors: how ambitious the goals of treatment are and the therapist's orientation. In this respect, the later stages of family and marital therapy for depression do not differ markedly from those found in approaches used for treatment of other family problems.

The behavioral and skills-training models aim at symptom removal, are quite structured and specific in design, and are shorter-term methods that rely heavily on teaching tangible relationship skills for future use. In general, the more psychodynamically oriented approaches are longer-term, more open-ended treatment models that strive for the acquisition of insight, the use of interpretation as a mode of intervention, and the analysis of transference and resistance, and permit a greater discussion of individual issues in the family-therapy setting.

Outcome studies[8] on the results of marital therapy note that most methods rely on some form of structured communication training as a cornerstone of the therapeutic process. In addition, the trend toward using out-of-session tasks or "homework" assignments has gained popularity.

A noteworthy finding in marital-therapy research is the data suggesting that the relationship skills of the therapist, regardless of his orientation, have a considerable effect on the outcome of the treatment.

The areas of agreement among therapists of diverse persuasions are considerable when one is addressing the topic of longer-range goals in family and marital therapy. A representative list[7] includes (1) the specification of problems; (2) the clarification of each spouse's individual needs and desires in the relationship; (3) redefining the nature of the couple's difficulties; (4) encouraging each partner's recognition of his/her mutual contribution to the marital discord; (5) the recognition and modification of communication patterns, "rules" and interactional patterns; (6) increasing reciprocity; (7) decreasing the use of coercion and blaming; (8) increasing cooperative problem solving; (9) establishing a positive working relationship between couple and therapist; and (10) increasing each partner's ability to express his/her feelings clearly and directly and to "hear" his/her mate accurately.

Commonly Encountered Problems in Psychotherapy

In attempting to realize these goals, the therapist may encounter several potential obstacles that occur with regularity.

Leadership problems: The role of the therapist is to set a climate in treatment that helps harness the energy in a family so that it can be used to promote positive growth. The therapist helps contain the disruptive and irrational elements present in the family and maximizes the use of individual and collective strengths.

To do so, the therapist has to be clear about the definition of the problem and set goals that are realistic for the specific family. Setting effective limits for family members is central to this endeavor.

Therapists can encounter difficulty by failing to be active enough in the initial stages of treatment or by abdicating their leadership position through inappropriate self-disclosure in response to the pressure induced by the family system.

The therapist strives to be "in charge" of the family therapy in a fair but firm fashion in order to guide the family through difficult periods and to retain a helpful vantage point as an outsider observing the family in action.

Leadership failures invariably result in treatment failures, many of which are avoidable through careful attention to the aforementioned aspects of the therapist's role.

Management of the resistant spouse: The family systems orientation has demonstrated the importance of involving the entire family in order to gain comprehensive understanding of the assets and liabilities present in a given case. Often family members are made anxious by the prospect of change through family therapy and reflect this concretely by a reluctance or outright refusal to come to sessions. This creates a top-priority situation in family and marital therapy.

The therapist may decide to use existing family ties by suggesting that one member encourage another to come to the next meeting. In marital therapy it is common for one spouse, usually the husband, to resist coming in. In such a case, the therapist can work with the wife to arrive at a plan for enlisting the husband's participation. When encouraging a spouse to bring in the partner, the therapist has to monitor the communication process to ensure that clear, noncontradictory, and direct messages are transmitted to the hesitant partner. This can be rehearsed or role-played in session if necessary.

In the event that this strategy fails, the therapist must be prepared to approach the resistant spouse directly. This is particularly important in cases of depression, because of the potential gravity of the situation. The therapist may feel free to telephone the spouse, to suggest that he come in to present "his side of the story," and to enlist his aid in dealing with a difficult family situation that affects his life directly.

Therapist neutrality: One of the traditional pitfalls in family therapy centers around the therapist's ability to retain a balanced view of the family while being engaged in an ongoing small-group process that necessitates active interaction with them. The situation is made more complex when one family member is overtly symptomatic, as is always the case with depressive illness.

The therapist must be careful not to enter into an unbalanced or collusive alliance with the apparently better-functioning spouse. Although there are times when the depressed partner may be the main focus of therapy sessions, as in the initial phase, the therapist is well advised to clarify certain issues at the outset of therapy. Taking a shared relationship focus with a "priorities" approach allows the therapist to explain to couples that the emphasis of treatment will vary depending on what or who is "stuck" at a given time. The notion of mutual responsibility and focusing the treatment to deal with the emotional urgency in the "here and now" will help to engage rather than alienate a family member who might be sensitive to being singled out as "the sick one."

Combined treatment approaches: Because of the complex nature of depression, the treatment of the family may be one part of an overall program that includes other therapists. A central concern here is that the treatment efforts be collaborative and synergistic and not competitive.

When more than one therapist is involved or when medication is managed by someone who is not the family therapist, one must monitor the possible negative effects of such therapy formats. The problems that arise between cotherapists have been outlined elsewhere.[9] When two therapists work separately but simultaneously, they must arrange to have periodic communication. This helps coordinate their efforts and safeguards against the problem of anxious family members' defensively dealing with their discomfort by trying to split the two therapists or playing one off against the other in the hope of sabotaging the therapy.

Countertransference problems: This broad category encompasses emotional issues that are tapped in the therapist who works with the depressed member of a family. The range of responses generated in family therapists is great, at times causing the therapist to function counterproductively.

The readily identifiable examples of areas in the therapist's past and current life that may come into play include the activation of feelings of identification with a particular family member, difficulty in forming the requisite feelings of empathy or in establishing a therapeutic alliance with one or more family members, a clash with the personal value system of the therapist, and the presence of depressive feelings in him.

Any or all of these factors may render the therapist ineffective until they are recognized and resolved. These countertransference phenomena are best viewed as occupational hazards of being a family therapist, rather than as signs of inherent deficits in the model of family therapy as a choice of therapy for depression. Active and alert management of these therapist variables allows the family therapy to proceed. The personal feelings of the therapist provide an added dimension of understanding about the family in treatment and its methods of operating under interpersonal stress.

Summary

Recent research in the treatment of depression suggests that the combination of pharmacotherapy and psychotherapy holds promise for patients suffering from major depressions.[10] The utilization of family and marital therapies as forms of psychotherapeutic intervention is an area that has much to offer the clinician seeking new resources to deal with this common psychiatric problem.

References

1. Richman J, Rosenbaum M: The family doctor and the suicidal family. *Psychiatry in Medicine* 1:27–35, 1974.

2. Minuchin S: *Families and Family Therapy*, Harvard University Press, Cambridge, MA, 1974, pp. 130–131.

3. Stuart R: *Helping Couples Change*, Guilford, New York, 1980, pp. 107–110.

4. Hinchcliffe MK, Hopper D, Roberts FJ: *Depression in Marriage and Psychosocial Approach to Therapy*, Wiley, New York, 1978.

5. Rubenstein D, Timmins J: Depressive dyadic and triadic relationships. *J. Marriage Fam. Counseling* 4:13–25, 1978.

6. Greene BL, Lee RR, Lustig N: Treatment of marital disharmony where one spouse has a primary affective disorder (manic-depressive illness). *J. Marriage and Family Counseling*, 1:39–50, 1975.

7. Paolino TJ, McCrady BS: *Marriage and Marital Therapy: Psychoanalytic, Behavioral and Systems Theory Perspectives*, Brunner/Mazel, New York, 1978, pp. 542–544.

8. Gurman AS, Rice DG: *Couples in Conflict*, Aronson, New York, 1975, pp. 383–430.

9. Spitz HI, Spitz ST: Cotherapy in the management of marital problems. *Psychiatr. Ann.* 10:160–168, 1980.

10. Weissman MM: The psychological treatment of depression: Evidence for the efficacy of psychotherapy alone, in comparison with, and in combination with pharmacotherapy. *Arch. Gen Psychiatry* 36:1261–1269, 1979.

13

Clinical Applicability of Antidepressant Plasma Levels

John M. Davis, Joseph E. Comaty, and Philip G. Janicak

EDITOR'S NOTE

About 30% of depressed patients treated with tricyclic antidepressants either are refractory to treatment or gain only partial benefit. Determining plasma levels of tricyclics appears to be especially useful in such cases. If the plasma level is low and the presumed dosage intake adequate or high, one may hypothesize either that the patient is not being compliant with the drug regimen or that he is metabolizing the drug too quickly. If, on the other hand, very small doses produce substantial blood levels, then the required effective dose may be somewhat less than average; the patient may be metabolizing the drug very slowly, a genetically determined phenomenon that is seen in the extreme in about 2% of the general population.

The relationship between clinical response and the blood level may be directly linear, sigmoidal, or curvilinear. The so-called "therapeutic window"—a range of plasma levels within which most patients clinically improve but below and above which they tend not to—is associated with the curvilinear type of relationship; nortriptyline is the most thoroughly studied tricyclic that follows this pattern, although the studies are not entirely consistent. With other drugs such as imipramine, a more linear relationship exists—the higher the plasma level, the more likely a successful clinical response, with toxicity appearing at very high plasma levels.

140

Introduction

This chapter will cover the clinical applicability of antidepressant plasma levels which thus far has primarily involved the tricyclic group of drugs. The need for an effective treatment for depression is based on an estimated 4% risk of the general population for severe depressive illness. In addition, 30% to 50% of those patients who have had a major depression will experience a subsequent similar episode. Twenty-five percent of all admissions to psychiatric hospitals, as well as 30% of psychiatric admissions to general hospitals, are for depression; and approximately 15% of these patients will die by suicide.

Since their introduction in the 1950s, the tricyclics have been an effective mainstay of treatment for depression, benefiting approximately 70% of those affected. However, an estimated 30% of those treated with these agents either are refractory to treatment or gain only partial benefit. It is in these 30% that plasma levels may be useful. Admittedly, a certain percentage of these "nonresponders" may in fact respond more favorably to monoamine oxidase inhibitors or second generation antidepressants. However, others may not respond as a result of pharmacological factors, i.e., too little or too much drug reaching the brain. Since patients have large interindividual differences in their tricyclic plasma levels, one questions whether the lack of response can be attributed to an abnormality in the metabolic rate of the tricyclic drug. Certain individuals quickly metabolize the drug, thus failing to build up a sufficient blood level, while other patients slowly metabolize the drug, leading to high plasma and brain levels. Patients may therefore fail to improve clinically because brain levels are too low, because the drug may lose its efficacy at increased levels, or because the level is in the toxic range. Though it has been 20 years since the 20- to 40-fold interindividual variability of steady-state tricyclic antidepressant plasma levels was first recognized, we still do not know the relationship between steady-state plasma levels and clinical response for most antidepressants.

Plasma Levels and Therapeutic Window

The steady-state plasma level of a drug refers to the concentration of that drug after equilibrium between its distribution phase and its metabolism/excretion phase has occurred. At any given daily dose of a medication, the steady-state level is achieved after a period of time equal to five metabolism/excretion half-lives of that drug. As the oral dose of a drug is increased, its steady-state plasma level will also increase; however, the relationship between a given plasma level and clinical response may take one of several forms. If there is a direct linear relationship, as the plasma level increases there should be a corresponding increase in clinical response at any given level of the drug. If the relationship is more sigmoidal, clinical response would initially be linearly related to the plasma level but as the plasma level continues to increase there would be little further change. Finally, if the relationship is curvilinear, at a low plasma level there would be little clinical response; with an increasing plasma level there would be good clinical response; and if the plasma level continued to increase the clinical response would paradoxically decrease. The curvilinear relationship between plasma level and clinical response establishes a "therapeutic window," that is, a range of plasma levels within which most patients will clinically improve. However, if the plasma level falls above or below this range, most patients will not respond as well.

The Empirical Studies

Nortriptyline is the most thoroughly studied tricyclic in regard to the relationship between the plasma level and clinical response. Asberg et al.[1] first examined associations between plasma nortriptyline concentrations and therapeutic response. They found that some patients who failed to respond had noticeably reduced or relatively higher levels of blood nortriptyline. They predicted a possible lower limit to the therapeutic window with this agent. In other words, if an inadequate dose were given, an insufficient quantity of the drug would be available to the receptor site to produce a therapeutic response. They reported that the lower level of the therapeutic window was approximately 50ng/ml, based on five patients who had levels below this and had failed to respond. It is of interest that the precise location of the "low window" is based principally on the data from these five patients. Further, they reported that patients who had plasma levels that exceeded 140 ng/ml also tended to display an unfavorable clinical response. This did not appear to be secondary to CNS toxicity; rather, the drug seemed to lose its therapeutic effectiveness when plasma levels were elevated.

In view of the tremendous theoretical interest generated by the apparent paradoxical property of nortriptyline (i.e., it seemed to diminish in efficacy at higher plasma levels), it was studied closely by several other investigators. Kragh-Sorenson et al.[2-4] and Montgomery et al.[5] both confirmed this result, noting poor responses with plasma levels above 175 ng/ml and 200 ng/ml, respectively. Montgomery et al.[5] reported 16 patients with high plasma levels, 12 of whom improved within one week after their clinical dose was reduced. Kragh-Sorenson et al.[2,3] studied patients whose doses had been adjusted either above 180 ng/ml or below 150 ng/ml, finding that a disproportionate number of subjects in the first group showed a poor clinical response. In a second phase a randomly chosen subgroup of the high plasma level patients (+ 180 ng/ml) had their dose lowered to the therapeutic range. All five of these patients improved, but the six patients with high plasma levels who served as controls had a poor clinical response.

One problem is that the upper end of the therapeutic window varies substantially from study to study. When we examined the pooled data, we could not precisely define an upper limit. In fact, we found that the 140 ng/ml upper limit, so widely quoted in secondary sources, is actually well within the range of the therapeutic window in most studies (see figure 1).

Using a fixed-dose schedule, two other studies failed to find a significant relationship between nortriptyline plasma levels and clinical response. Burrows and his coworkers[6,7] treated patients with a fixed dose of nortriptyline for four weeks. Using the criterion of a 50% decrease on the Hamilton Rating Scale at four weeks for a responder, he found 16 responders and 16 nonresponders. There were six patients with plasma levels below 50 ng/ml at either two or four weeks. Five of these were found to be nonresponders. Of the 26 with levels above 50 ng/ml at both two and four weeks, 11 were nonresponders (p value equals .09 on the Fisher Exact Test, one-tailed).

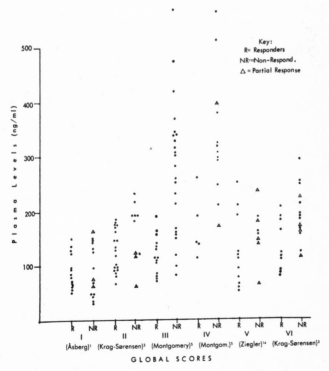

Figure 1.   Nortriptyline plasma levels and clinical response (Hamilton scores). Cubic regression model.

Davies, Burrows, and Scoggins[8] made an interesting clinical observation in another study of patients with a history of good response to tricyclics. Each patient underwent dosage reduction with consequent decrease in plasma level and each patient deteriorated. The patients improved when dose and plasma levels were raised again. The doctor rating the depression was blind to the dose change. Although the plasma levels associated with this deterioration differed widely, it seemed that there was a critical plasma level for each patient below which there was clinical deterioration.

Burrows et al.[9] did a subsequent study treating patients with a moderate dose of nortriptyline for two weeks. They then randomly assigned the patients to receive either a low dose (50 mg/day) or a high dose (200 mg/day) during the third week. At week four, patients who received the low dose in week three crossed over to the high dose and vice-versa. Patients with an increase of three or more points on the Hamilton Rating Scale during the week they received the low dose were classified as worse. Of the six patients classified as worse, three showed plasma levels at or below 50 ng/ml; conversely, only three out of 16 patients whose plasma levels were above 50 ng/ml during the trial's low-dose segment were classified as worse (p value on Fisher Exact Test equaled 0.18, one-tailed). Burrows and his coworkers showed no evidence for an upper end of the therapeutic window.

In summary, most studies agree on a relationship between clinical response and plasma levels for nortriptyline. This relationship seems to be curvilinear, with the optimal plasma level range falling between 50 and 150 ng/ml. However, some studies failed to find evidence for an upper end of the therapeutic window.

Although not as thoroughly studied as nortriptyline, a number of other tricyclic drugs have been investigated. Whyte et al.[10] reported several nonresponders with high protriptyline plasma levels and two nonresponders who had low plasma levels; Biggs and Ziegler[11] found nonresponders had low plasma protriptyline levels (see Table 1). What is particularly striking is that Whyte's patients overall had higher plasma levels than Biggs'. Whyte further reported an inverted U-shaped relationship, with the lower limit to the thera-

TABLE 1
Protriptyline Plasma Levels and Clinical Response

Plasma levels (ng/ml)	Biggs		Whyte	
	Responders	Nonresponders	Responders	Nonresponders
0-100	10	8	0	0
100-200	3	0	5	3
200-300	0	0	7	1
300-400	0	0	2	7
400-500	0	0	0	1

peutic window below 140 ng/ml and the upper limit above 260 ng/ml, using a 40 mg dose. Biggs, using a 20 mg dose, found poor responses in patients whose plasma levels were under 70 ng/ml. Interestingly, while using a 50% lower dose than Whyte, he observed disproportionately lower plasma levels. Therefore, it may be incorrect to state the location of the limits of the therapeutic window for protriptyline, as these studies disagree with each other as to absolute plasma levels. Determinations of plasma levels on patients at a steady-state dose using a specific laboratory method should prove identical from study to study and, in that sense, provide an absolute level. It should further be noted that since protriptyline has an unusually long half-life, levels obtained from patients in the first two weeks of protriptyline studies may not necessarily reflect their final steady state.

Several studies of amitriptyline (Braithwaite et al.,[12] Kupfer et al.,[13] and Ziegler et al.[14]) find a lower limit to the therapeutic window but disagree as to where it is (i.e., at 90 ng/ml or 75 ng/ml, respectively). Rickels and his coworkers[15] reported that all four good responders had plasma levels above 100 ng/ml and that four out of five nonresponders had plasma levels below this. Overall, findings from ten amitriptyline studies show that patients with low plasma levels are divided equally among responders, partial responders, and nonresponders (Figure 2).

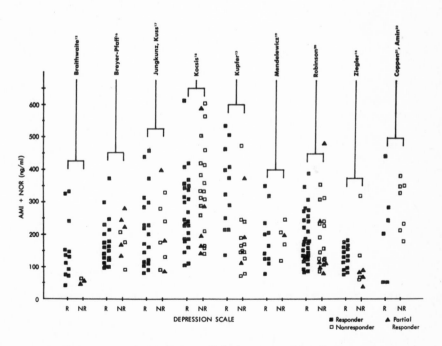

Figure 2.   Amitriptyline vs. clinical response (Hamilton scores).

A potentially important confounding variable to consider in the amitriptyline studies is the efficacious role of its major active metabolite, nortriptyline. That is, when amitriptyline is used it may be more precise to correlate clinical response with the plasma level of both amitriptyline and nortriptyline rather than either alone.

There are three earlier studies (Table 2) using desipramine, and summation of the data indicates that the percent clinically improved is low when plasma levels are below 115 ng/ml. Several subsequent studies have arrived at a similar conclusion. However, one recent study that measured desipramine blood levels in 26 depressed outpatients found evidence for a curvilinear relationship between plasma levels and clinical response. Coryell et al.[28] seem to indicate that a range of plasma levels from 100 ng/ml to 150 ng/ml produced the greatest degree of clinical response after six weeks of treatment. Thus, strong evidence for a curvilinear relationship with desipramine is lacking but the growing data base may soon clarify the picture with this antidepressant.[29]

In well-controlled studies, Glassman et al.[30] and Reisby et al.[31] gave patients a fixed dose of imipramine yielding plasma levels from 50 ng/ml to 1,000 ng/ml. These workers plus others reported poor clinical responses with low plasma levels (under 180 ng/ml or under 240 ng/ml respectively). In addition, these workers did not find an upper limit for the therapeutic

TABLE 2
Desipramine Plasma Level and Clinical Response

		Plasma level ng/ml		
		0-92	82-115	115+
Amin et al.[22]	R	0	0	2
	NR	1	0	2
Hrdina, Lapierre[23]	R	0	0	3
	NR	3	0	1
Nelson et al.[24]	R	2	1	8
	NR	13	5	1
Brunswick et al.[25]	R	1	1	5
	NR	0	1	7
Simpson et al.[26]	R	4	5	14
	NR	1	3	3
Nelson, Jatlow, Mazure[27]	R	1	1	4
	NR	6	5	1
Total	R	8	8	36
	NR	24	14	15

R-Responder
NR-Nonresponder

TABLE 3
Plasma Levels vs. Clinical Response in Patients Treated with Imipramine

| | | Plasma Levels ng/ml | | |
		0-180	180-240	240+
Glassman et al[30]	R	8	22[a]	
Perel et al.[32]	NR	21	8[a]	
Matuzas et al.[33]	R	1	1	0
	NR	6	2	0
Matuzas et al.[34]	R	5	1	2
	NR	5	2	1
Reisby et al.[31b]	R	11	4	18
	NR	23	5	5
Olivier-Martin et al.[35b]	R	0	2	4
	NR	3	1	4
Simpson et al.[36]	R	8	3	7
	NR	6	1	2
Total	R	33	11	53
	NR	64	11	20

Key: R = Responder; NR = Nonresponder
a = Author gave plasma levels only as below or above 180; for the total, the numbers were added to the +240 column
b = Endogenous + Nonendogenous

window because they did not find a loss in the efficacy of the drug effect with high plasma levels. They did find toxicity associated with very high plasma levels, but this defines a different type of upper limit to the therapeutic window. When the data were summated, patients with plasma levels below 180 ng/ml responded at a rate of 30% (which is about the placebo response rate), and about 70% of those above 240 ng/ml responded, giving an indeterminant therapeutic range of 180–240 ng/ml (Table 3).

Conclusion and Clinical Applicability

Most review articles place absolute values on the upper and lower limits for the therapeutic window of tricyclic antidepressants. We feel that there is something misleading about thinking of a therapeutic window as being "written in stone." For example, if the limit of the therapeutic window is from 100 to 200 ng/ml, then a patient with 99 ng/ml is technically below and a patient with 201 is technically above the window. A change in drug dose should also be taken in the context of the patient's clinical status (i.e., response and side effects). Furthermore, patients within the therapeutic window in one study may be clearly below the therapeutic window in another study. For example, many review articles give the upper limit of the nortriptyline therapeutic window as 140 ng/ml; yet many responders have levels above 140 ng/ml.

With this comment in mind, we still think that plasma concentrations of tricyclic antidepressants can be useful in many circumstances. One example is the patient who has failed to respond to apparently adequate doses. Plasma concentrations can indicate when levels are too low, thereby suggesting further increases in dose, or when levels are too high, indicating that treatment resistance is not explained by insufficient plasma levels and suggesting the need to try a different medication. A second example is the patient who experiences intolerable side effects at relatively low doses but has high plasma levels. This suggests the patient is a slow metabolizer who may do well with low doses or need a change in medication. In theory, there should always be a lower end of the therapeutic window.

In summary, while we do not recommend the use of absolute values to establish therapeutic limits of tricyclics, we do suggest that the use of these values in a relative way can assist the clinician. He/she can use these values as indices to guide decisions related to dose and/or medication changes in cases of nonresponse, partial response, and serious side effects.

References

1. Asberg M et al.: Relationship between plasma levels and therapeutic effect of nortriptyline. *Br. Med. J.* 3:331, 1971.

2. Kragh-Sorenson P, Asberg M, Eggert-Hansen C: Plasma nortriptyline levels in endogenous depression. *Lancet* I:113, 1973.

3. Kragh-Sorensen P, Hansen LE, Asberg M: Plasma levels of nortriptyline in the treatment of endogenous depression. *Acta Psychiatr. Scand.* 49:445-456, 1973.

4. Kragh-Sorensen P et al.: Self-inhibiting action of nortriptyline antidepressive effect at high plasma levels. *Psychopharmacologia* 45:305-312, 1976.

5. Montgomery S et al.: High plasma nortriptyline levels in the treatment of depression. *J. Clin. Pharmcol. Ther.* 23:309-314, 1978.

6. Burrows GD, Davies B, Scoggins BA: Plasma concentration of nortriptyline and clinical response in depressive illness. *Lancet* I:619-623, Sept. 23, 1972.

7. Burrows GC et al.: A sequential trial comparing plasma levels of nortriptyline. *Aust. N.Z. J. Psychiatry* 8:21-23, 1974.

8. Davies B, Burrows GD, Scoggins B: Plasma nortriptyline and clinical response. *Aust. N.Z. J. Psychiatry* 9:249-253, 1975.

9. Burrows GD, Maguire KP, Scoggins BA: Plasma nortriptyline and clinical response—a study using changing plasma levels. *Psychiatr. Med.* 7:87-91, 1977.

10. Whyte SF et al.: Plasma concentration of protriptyline and clinical effects in depressed women. *Br. J. Psychiatry* 128:384-390, 1976.

11. Biggs JT, Zeigler VE: Protriptyline plasma levels and antidepressant response. *Clin. Pharmacol. Ther.* 22:269–273, 1978.

12. Braithewaite RA et al.: Plasma concentration of amitriptyline and clinical response. *Lancet* I:1297–1300, 1972.

13. Kupfer DJ et al.: Amitriptyline plasma levels and clinical response in primary depression. *Clin. Pharmacol. Ther.* 22:904–911, 1977.

14. Ziegler VE, Clayton PJ, Biggs JT: A comparison study of amitriptyline and nortriptyline with plasma levels. *Arch. Gen. Psychiatry* 34:607–612, 1977.

15. Rickels K et al.: Tricyclic plasma levels in depressed outpatients treated with amitriptyline. *Psychopharmacology* 80:14–18, 1983.

16. Breyer-Pfaff U et al.: Antidepressive effect and pharmacokinetics of amitriptyline with consideration of unbound drug and 10-hydroxynortriptyline plasma levels. *Psychopharmacology* 76:240–244, 1982.

17. Jungkunz G, Kuss HJ: On the relationship of nortriptyline: Amitriptyline ratio of clinical improvement of amitriptyline treated depressive patients. *Pharmakopsychiatrie Neuropsychopharmakologie* 13:111–116, 1980.

18. Kocsis J et al.: Tricyclic plasma levels and clinical response. *Syllabus and Scientific Proceedings of the American Psychiatric Association* 136:128, 1983.

19. Mendlewicz J et al.: A double-blind comparison of dothiepin and amitriptyline in patients with primary affective disorder: Serum levels and clinical response. *Br. J. Psychiatry* 136:154–160, 1980.

20. Robinson DS et al.: Plasma tricyclic drug levels in amitriptyline-treated depressed patients. *Psychopharmacology (Berlin)* 63:223–231, 1979.

21. Coppen A et al.: Amitryptyline plasma-concentration and clinical effect: A World Health Organization collaborative study. *Lancet* I:63–66, 1978.

22. Amin M et al.: A comparison of desipramine and amitriptyline plasma levels and therapeutic response. *Psychopharmacol. Bull.* 14:45–46, 1978.

23. Hrdina P, Lapierre Y: Clinical response, plasma levels and pharmacokinetics of desipramine in depressed patients. *Prog. Neuro-Psychopharmacol.* 4:591–600, 1981.

24. Nelson JC et al.: Desipramine plasma concentration and antidepressant response. *Arch. Gen. Psychiatry* 39:1419–1422, 1982.

25. Brunswick DJ, Amsterdam JD, Potter L, Croff S and Rickels K: Relationship between tricyclic antidepressant plasma levels and clinical response in patients treated with desipramine or doxepin. *Acta Psychiatr. Scand.* 67:371–377, 1983.

26. Simpson GM et al.: Relationship between plasma desipramine levels and clinical outcome of RDC major depressive inpatients. *Psychopharmacology* 80:240–242, 1983.

27. Nelson JC, Jatlow PI, Mazure C: Desipramine plasma levels and response in elderly melancholic patients. *J. Clin. Psychopharm.* 5(4):217–220, 1985.

28. Coryell W, Turner RD, Sherman A: Desipramine plasma levels and clinical response: Evidence for a curvilinear relationship. *J. Clin. Psychopharm.* 7(3):138–142, 1987.

29. Glassman AH et al.: Tricyclic antidepressants: Blood level measurements and clinical response. In Berger PA, Brodie HKH (eds): *American Handbook of Psychiatry (Vol. 8): Biological Psychiatry*, Basic Books, New York, 1986.

30. Glassman AH et al.: Clinical implications of imipramine plasma levels for depressive illness. *Arch. Gen. Psychiatry* 34:197–204, 1977.

31. Reisby N et al.: Imipramine: Clinical effects and pharmacokinetic variability. *Psychopharmacology* 54:263–272, 1977.

32. Perel J, Stiller R, Glassman AH: Studies on plasma levels/effects relationships in imipramine theory. *Commun. Psychopharmacology* 2:429–439, 1978.

33. Matuzas W et al.: Plasma concentrations of imipramine and clinical response among depressed outpatients. *J. Clin. Psychopharmacology* 2:140–142, 1982.

34. Matuzas W et al.: Plasma and red blood cell concentration of imipramine and clinical response among depressed outpatients. Paper presented at Annual Meeting of the American Psychiatric Association, 1983.

35. Olivier-Martin R et al.: Concentrations plasmatiques de l'imipramine et de la desmethylimipramine et effect antidepresseur au cours d'un traitement controle. *Psychopharmacology* 41:187–195, 1975.

36. Simpson G et al.: Relationship between plasma antidepressant levels and clinical outcome for inpatients receiving imipramine. *Am. J. Psychiatry* 139(3):358–360, 1982.

Further Reading

Andreasen N: *The Broken Brain*, Harper and Row, New York, 1984.

Bernstein JG: *Handbook of Drug Therapy in Psychiatry*, John Wright-PSG, Boston, 1983.

Boyer WF, Friedel RO: Antidepressant and antipsychotic plasma levels. *PCNA* 7:601, 1984.

Cole JO, Orsveak P: Tricyclic antidepressant blood levels. In Cole JO (ed): *Psychopharmacology Update*, Collamare Press, Lexington, MA, 1980.

Davis JH, Javaid JI, Matuzas W: Plasma concentration monitoring of antipsychotic and tricyclic antidepressant treatment. In Hall RCW (ed): *Handbook of Diagnostic Procedures* (Vol. 1), Spectrum, New York, 1984.

14

Lithium Update
Ralph A. O'Connell

EDITOR'S NOTE

Since lithium has been in use for the treatment of affective disorders for some years now, a review of its effectiveness and possible side effects is in order. Its mechanism of action is still unknown, although lithium probably influences membrane excitability and conductivity and interferes with cyclic AMP metabolism to change neuroendocrine response in receptor functions. Lithium is excreted almost entirely via the kidney. Cerebral levels are perhaps best reflected in red blood cell/lithium plasma ratios.

Acute manic episodes continue to be the primary indications for lithium therapy. Because of the difficulty in making an accurate diagnosis in a number of patients, it should be considered in any acute psychosis not of organic origin in which an affective component is significant.

In some depressed patients who have not responded to heterocyclic antidepressants alone, the addition of lithium can facilitate improvement rather quickly, usually within 48 hours.

Lithium is now widely used to prevent recurrences in patients with bipolar affective disorders. Its use on such a long-term basis is determined by a number of considerations, such as the frequency and seriousness of the psychopathologic episodes. Some studies indicate that lithium can also be used to prevent recurrences in strictly depressive disorders, but such cases may really belong in the bipolar diagnostic group.

Depression in thyroid function, weight gain, perhaps malformations during pregnancy, dermatologic changes, and leukocytosis are among the complications of lithium treatment. Renal toxicity has received special attention, and the consensus is that long-term lithium use can cause renal impairment, although chronic renal failure has not been reported.

The author emphasizes that the risks of treatment must always be weighed against the risks of no treatment and that, as with all pharmacologic approaches to therapy, lithium treatment should be part of an overall psychosocial program of rehabilitation guided by the needs of each patient.

Introduction

Lithium was approved for use in the United States in 1970. Since the initial report by John Cade from Australia in 1949, there has been a wealth of accumulated experience with lithium treatment in Europe and in America. Over the past 30 years, we have been able to refine thinking on indications for its use, study the basic biology of the lithium ion, and formulate hypotheses on mechanisms of action. Side effects not initially obvious have become apparent, and these have modified clinical practice. As with any new therapeutic modality, there is usually a pendular swing from initial enthusiasm, to alarm about adverse effects, and finally to a moderate concept of clinical practice. This chapter will review the current thinking on lithium in psychiatry as it applies in 1988 and speculate on some future directions that should be explored.

Mechanism of Action

Lithium is a substance easily found in minerals, although it is normally found only in traces in the human body. It is a member of the alkali group of metals, closely related to sodium, potassium, rubidium, and cesium. Its atomic weight is 6.940, making it the third-lightest element (after hydrogen and helium). Lithium forms salts as a chloride or, more commonly, as a citrate or carbonate, among others. The mechanism of action of lithium is essentially unknown. However, its similarity to sodium and potassium undoubtedly accounts for many of its biological properties in affecting very basic systems of cellular metabolism. Two general areas seem most important: one, substitution with sodium and potassium in intra- and extracellular fluids (thus changing properties of membrane excitability and conductivity) and, two, interference with cyclic AMP metabolism and consequently changing neuroendocrine response in the basic "second messenger" receptor functions. Both of these actions could account for the various effects of lithium, both therapeutic and adverse. The exact mechanism of lithium's therapeutic action in the affective disorders is unknown. Actually, lithium has stimulated much research in areas other than psychiatry, including basic membrane properties in hypertension, thyroid disease, and hematological disorders. The effects of lithium research extend far beyond psychiatry.

Pharmacokinetics

Lithium is radically different from other psychotropic drugs in that it is not bound to serum proteins and not metabolized to degraded by-products and, therefore, has no first-pass effect through the liver. It is excreted almost entirely through the kidney. Lithium is readily absorbed through the gastrointestinal tract. Peak serum levels are reached within a few hours. Lithium passes readily into tissues, and across the blood-brain barrier, to its site of action in the central nervous system. Red blood cell/lithium plasma ratios probably reflect cerebral levels better than serum lithium levels alone. It was hoped that these ratios would provide clues to diagnostic subgroups or predict lithium response, but this has not proved to be consistently so. The RBC/plasma ratio is about 0.5 in adequate maintenance treatment. Thus, if the serum level is 0.8 mEq/L, the intraerythrocytic level should be about 0.4. As there is a lag between the serum level and the intracellular level, the index may provide a practical measure of compliance. We have often felt that many patients who are generally very lax in taking lithium take it more religiously on the day they expect a lithium level to be drawn. Because of the lag in reaching equilibrium, even if the serum level is adequate, a low intraerythrocytic level may signify noncompliance.

Lithium is rapidly excreted from the body. The serum level of lithium will be reduced approximately 50% per 24 hours after lithium intake is stopped. Often, toxic effects will persist in the face of low serum levels. An RBC/plasma ratio is often found to be high in these cases. This may reflect a lag in reaching equilibrium in the opposite direction, and may explain persistent CNS toxicity in the face of low serum lithium levels.

High serum levels account for some side effects, and have been related to the long-term renal effects to be discussed later. The use of slow-release preparations of lithium can moderate some of the peaks and valleys in the serum lithium curves and still maintain a therapeutic range.

Psychiatric Indications

Indications for lithium must be considered under acute and long-term categories. Acute manic episodes are among the primary indications for lithium. The problem here is the diagnosis. In the past ten years, we have become increasingly aware that a manic episode does not necessarily appear classically manic but often has elements more reminiscent of schizophrenia. Manic patients are not always elated; often they are irritable and agitated. They may be deluded and hallucinate as well. Kraepelin was aware of this, but we have had to relearn the lesson, partly because of the availability of lithium. The possibility of lithium should be considered in any acute psychosis not of organic origin, with a large affective component. This is especially true if there is a history of affective illness in the patient or his family, or if the patient's previous functioning and personality are more indicative of an affective than a schizophrenic disorder. Likewise, lithium should be considered in an acute agitated psychosis not responding to neuroleptics.

It is often necessary to use antipsychotic medications, along with lithium, in the first week of treatment of the acute mania, because there is a delay of several days before the therapeutic effect of lithium is reached. There were initial reports of neurotoxicity on combining lithium and haloperidol, but this has not been substantiated. Lithium doses in acute mania should be high enough — about 1800 or 2400 mg/day in divided doses — to reach the desired serum levels of 0.8 to about 1.5 mEq/L. Many clinicians do not realize that higher serum levels are required for the acute phase of treatment than for the long-term preventive phase. The dosage and levels can be reduced after the manic episode has subsided.

Lithium alone is not a potent antidepressant, although it has been shown to have this effect in some patients. The available tricyclic or tetracyclic antidepressants are indicated for major depressive disorders. However, lithium has been found to be very helpful when added to tricyclic antidepressants in some patients previously unresponsive to adequate trials of the latter. Many clinicians do consider using lithium in the treatment of heterocyclic resistant depression; if there is an effect, it is often seen within 48 hours at lithium dosage of 900 mg/day. The mechanism of this effect is not known.

Lithium therapy should be discontinued in any patient who is to undergo electroconvulsive treatment. Lithium potentiates the depolarizing effect of succinylcholine and can prolong the period of apnea.

The most common long-term indication for lithium is the prevention of recurrent bipolar affective disorder. Many well-controlled double-blind studies have confirmed this. The best indication for long-term treatment is a classic history of mania and/or depressive episodes, a previous response to lithium, or a family history of either. Again, the problem is one of diagnostic definition. Long-term lithium therapy has benefited many patients with atypical recurrent psychoses. These have been variously termed "cycloid psychoses," "schizoaffective psychoses," and "periodic psychoses." The common denominator seems to be recurrent or periodic psychosis with a large affective component. Patients whose illnesses have these characteristics should be considered for long-term lithium therapy. Because of the natural history of the illness, a trial of a year or more is often required to determine efficacy.

The more difficult question is when to recommend long-term lithium for a patient. This decision relies on some combination of the severity and frequency of the patient's episodes. A mild or moderately severe episode every eight to ten years probably does not warrant long-term therapy, especially if the patient or his family can recognize the episode early enough to initiate therapy. Because of increasing awareness of side effects, the practice of many clinicians is to treat the acute episode for about six months, during which a good doctor-patient relationship can be founded and the patient and family educated about his illness and the prodrome of an episode. Fortunately, most patients have similar symptoms in their episodes. Thus a patient can be restarted on the appropriate treatment without the need for years of lithium treatment. On the other hand, episodes that are severe and cause serious personal and social morbidity, or occur frequently, indicate the need for routine long-term lithium treatment. The risk-reward ratio here is in favor of lithium treatment.

The question of long-term lithium treatment for patients with recurrent unipolar diseases is still open, but there is increasing evidence of the efficacy of lithium in these disorders. Several studies have shown lithium to be as effective as tricyclics in the long-term preventive treatment of recurrent depression. Often, what is initially diagnosed as a unipolar recurrent depressive disorder turns out, after several years, to be a bipolar disorder. Either the manic or hypomanic episode occurs late in the natural history of the illness or hypomanic episodes were not recognized. Many patients do not seek treatment for hypomanic epidoses. On the contrary, they feel exceptionally well. Many clinicians are prescribing long-term lithium to prevent recurrent depressions, with excellent results. However, whereas the effects on mania or hypomania are seen soon after treatment is initiated, it often takes six months to a year for the preventive effects on depression to be seen.

Besides the above, there are reports of lithium's effectiveness against various other psychiatric and medical disorders. These include recurrent aggressive behavior, premenstrual tension, epilepsy, and cluster headaches. The common denominator seems to be the recurring, periodic nature of the conditions. These indications are still experimental, but research in these areas may supply valuable information on the mechanism of lithium's action.

Side Effects

In the past decade, we have become more aware of the long-term side effects of lithium. This has probably been accelerated by our concern in psychiatry about tardive dyskinesia and our consequent caution about side effects associated with any long-term treatment. Although this thinking is commendable, it is also important to consider the long-term risks of morbidity and mortality associated with the nontreatment of affective psychoses.

Lithium usually produces some transient decrease in thyroid function, compensated for by an increase in thyroid-stimulating hormone. In a small percentage of cases, hypothyroidism and/or goiter may occur. This happens in patients who were probably in borderline thyroid compensation before lithium treatment. There is no reason to stop treatment. A thyroid preparation, usually T$_3$, can be added to the regimen and the lithium continued. Lithium has been used successfully for hyperthyroidism in some patients.

Most patients taking lithium report weight gains of about 10 pounds in the first year. This reflects an increase in tissue mass and not fluid retention. The mechanism is unknown, but most likely reflects an imbalance of caloric intake in the face of a reduced metabolic rate caused by lithium. A reduction of calories is the obvious answer. However, this is easily recommended but not always attained. The problem of weight gain can pose real problems of compliance, especially with women patients.

Lithium should be avoided during pregnancy. Lithium easily crosses the placenta and can theoretically affect cellular metabolism in the developing fetus. A high rate of cardiovascular malformations, including several rare Ebstein anomalies, has been reported in a register of lithium babies, but the statistical significance of the observations has not been demonstrated. The real dilemma is met when one is treating a severe manic-depressive patient desirous of having a baby. The risk of stopping lithium may be significant. The risk to the fetus, especially during the first trimester, has not been established but must be seriously considered. The same holds for antipsychotics. If possible, the best course is to take the patient off lithium and observe closely. Treatment may have to be initiated if symptoms recur.

Dermatological side effects can be a problem with lithium treatment. They usually appear as a maculopapular rash which will diminish with reduction of dosage or discontinuation of treatment. Acneiform reactions may occur. Some patients have reported an exacerbation of psoriasis. These effects may be secondary to changes in steroid metabolism induced by lithium.

An interesting aspect of lithium therapy has been the report of leukocytosis in almost all patients. The leukocytosis is neutrophilic and appears to be benign, with counts usually ranging between 10,000 and 20,000. The lithium appears to enhance colony-stimulating activity in vivo by inhibiting cyclic AMP metabolism. These observations have led hematologists to use lithium in patients with congenital neutropenia and Felty's syndrome, and in conjunction with cytotoxic drugs used in cancer chemotherapy.

The most alarming reports of the past few years are those of renal toxicity associated with long-term use. Increased thirst and urination, as well as polydipsia and polyuria, were reported in as many as 50–70% of patients in early lithium studies. This could become problematic in certain patients, in whom 24-hour urine volume may reach 5 liters. Urine-concentrating ability was decreased as measured by urine osmolality during a water-deprivation test. A small number of patients showed lowered glomerular filtration rates. Renal biopsies done in Scandinavian studies showed morphologic changes. These changes were related to the degree of concentrating disability and elevated serum lithium levels. The concentrating defect tended to return to normal when lithium was discontinued. The consensus is that long-term lithium use, especially with high serum levels, does cause some renal impairment. However, chronic renal failure has not been found after 20 years of worldwide experience. Yet caution is in order. Many centers routinely test urinary function, including serum creatinine and urinary volume and concentrating ability, before the start of lithium therapy and periodically thereafter.

Although the practicality and return on these tests are questionable, many renal experts doubt the validity and interpretation of outpatient renal function tests. One recent study showed no difference in several parameters of renal function between lithium patients and other affective-disorder patients who had never taken lithium. The renal abnormalities could be related to affective disorder and not to lithium.

Lithium and Psychotherapy

Although lithium has been very effective in preventing recurrent affective episodes, many patients fail to respond to the drug. There may be undiscovered biological properties that differentiate these nonresponders, but it is highly probable that psychological and social stresses interact to affect outcome. The importance of these psychosocial factors in psychiatric illness is well-known. Recent studies have shown the interaction of tricyclic antidepressants and psychotherapy in the treatment of depression. The same is probably true in manic-depressive disease, although adequate studies have not been done.

Psychosocial factors can precipitate or aggravate episodes in affective disorders, but the reverse is also true: affective disorders cause psychosocial stress. Studies have shown reduction in stress as measured by life-events tables following lithium treatment. The families and children of manic-depressives are also subjected to severe stress during episodes of illness.

Lithium should not be given in a vacuum apart from the psychological and social factors that may aggravate the clinical condition. A broad biopsychosocial perspective should be applied to all patients in an effort to understand the complex interaction of factors as they affect the illness and the place for psychotherapy, family therapy, or social intervention in the treatment plan. Individual psychotherapy should be considered when dynamic conflicts are evident. Any patient on a lithium regimen needs support in developing the ability to discuss his illness, with its implications and prognosis. He or she needs the chance to discuss side effects and other concerns. Compliance can be easily improved. Group therapy has proved very helpful for lithium patients. They gain mutual support, discuss common problems, and help each other with the stigma of mental illness and the need to take a psychotropic drug. It is very helpful for new patients to meet treatment success. Family therapy is also extremely useful for supportive and educational reasons. Families can spot early symptoms, help with compliance, and act as real therapeutic allies.

No lithium program can be successful without a major psychosocial component. Nor can this be completely delegated to the nonpsychiatrist members of the treatment team. The psychiatrist diagnoses and prescribes the treatment and must take a major role in its implementation.

Conclusion

Lithium has demonstrated its value over the past two decades. It is extremely effective, with a minimum of side effects. However, many patients do not respond, and more research is necessary in this area.

The original scare about renal damages seems to have abated, although the evidence is that there are some changes in lithium patients. Care should be taken, but in general the rewards far outweigh the risks.

Lithium should never be given alone for manic-depressive illness, but always in conjunction with appropriate psychotherapies and with brief supportive, explorative group or family therapy. The broad approach not only is more logical but also will prove more successful.

Several areas in long-term lithium maintenance need to be studied. There are probably several conditions that respond to lithium. If the basic mechanisms were known, the identification of these conditions would be easier. Many researchers think that lithium affects basic biological circadian rhythms. There is a great deal of evidence that this may be so. Other conditions that have a periodicity may respond to lithium — for example, certain types of headaches, behavior disorders, and seizure-like disorders. Extension of this knowledge would be intriguing.

Another area to be studied is affective disorders in childhood and adolescence. We are now more aware of childhood depression. Often, the clinical presentation is not primarily depression, but school and behavioral problems. Classic bipolar manic-depression does not occur until after adolescence, but recent studies have shown significant psychopathology in the children of bipolar manic-depressives. Work needs to be done on treatment concepts for these children.

Lithium has generated many new hypotheses and insights in psychiatry, including refinement of diagnosis, thinking about periodic illness, and reinterest in the biology of affective disorders. More should develop over the next decade.

Additional Readings

The current status of lithium therapy: Report of the APA Task Force. *Am. J. Psychiatry* 132:997–1001, 1975.

Cade, JF: Lithium salts in the treatment of psychotic excitement. *Med. J. Aust.* 2:349–352, 1949.

Coppen A et al.: Renal function in lithium and non-lithium treated patients with affective disorders. *Acta Psychiatr. Scand.* 62:343–355, 1980.

DeMontigny C et al.: Lithium induces rapid relief of depression in tricyclic antidepressant drug non-responders. *Br. J. Psychiatry* 138:252–256, 1981.

Lithium in haematology. *Lancet* 2(8195):626–627, 1980.

O'Connell RA, Mayo JA: Lithium: A biopsychosocial perspective. *Compr. Psychiatry* 22:87–93, 1981.

Vestegaard P et al.: Lithium treatment and kidney function. *Acta Psychiatr. Scand.* 60:504–520, 1979.

15

Pharmacotherapy of the Depressed Alcoholic

Steven M. Mirin and Burns Woodward

EDITOR'S NOTE

In patients who combine alcoholism with depression it is often difficult to determine whether the depression is a result of the alcoholism and its destructive life consequences or a more basic, underlying disorder on which the alcohol problem has been superimposed. The clinician should attempt to make such a distinction. Hence, it is often desirable to observe the depressed alcoholic patient carefully for at least two weeks in a drug-free state before drawing any diagnostic conclusions as to the presence or absence of coexisting affective disorder.

Family history can be revealing. If the patient's relatives manifest a history of alcoholism but an absence of affective disorder, the chances are that the vegetative signs of depression observed in the patient during alcohol withdrawal will resolve once the patient is detoxified. On the other hand, a high genetic loading for affective disorder in the patient's family increases the chances that the observed depressive symptoms will continue after withdrawal and are part of a basic affective disorder.

The dexamethasone suppression test can be useful, a positive finding pointing toward a biologically based affective disorder.

In spite of the commonly held opinion that no psychoactive medications should be given to alcoholics who are struggling to achieve sobriety, the antidepressants should be given serious consideration in those patients who reveal a basic depressive affective disorder and who have achieved a sufficient degree of control over drinking that they will not present the significant risk inherent in combining alcohol with antidepressants. In patients whose alcoholism appears superimposed on a manic-depressive or bipolar disorder, the use of lithium can greatly improve the prognosis for both disorders. While benzodiazepines are useful during the management of acute alcohol withdrawal, they should never be given on a regular basis, since suicide attempts and the formation of mixed alcohol-drug dependence can occur.

Introduction

Patients presenting for alcoholism treatment frequently report depressed mood, accompanied by sleep and appetite disturbance, lethargy, and inability to concentrate. Feelings of guilt, helplessness, hopelessness, worthlessness, and suicidal ideation are also common findings. The prevalence of these signs and symptoms among alcoholics ranges from 20% to 90%, depending on the method of screening employed, the population studied, and the setting in which the data are gathered.[1-4] Moreover, for each patient the expression of depressive symptoms is influenced not only by physiologic variables but also by the adequacy of underlying ego defenses and the availability of external supports.

Although it is generally agreed that depressive symptoms are common in alcoholic patients, it is notoriously difficult to determine their causes. Depression may result from the pharmacologic effects of alcohol, from alcohol withdrawal, from alcohol-induced brain damage, from brain impairment due to other medical sequelae of alcoholism (e.g. cirrhosis), from interpersonal and social losses due to alcoholism, from concurrent drug abuse, from an underlying affective disorder,[5,6] or from a psychiatric disorder other than affective disorder (e.g. personality disorder). For the clinician, the ability to make these distinctions is not only essential for accurate diagnosis but also allows one to develop specific therapies for each discrete clinical problem.

History and Clinical Observation

In the majority of cases, depressive symptoms clear without specific pharmacologic treatment during the first few weeks of abstinence from alcohol.[7-9] For this reason, alcoholic patients with depressed mood should be observed for at least two weeks in a drug-free state before any diagnostic conclusions are made as to the presence or absence of coexisting affective disorder. During this period, careful psychiatric history supplemented by ongoing clinical observation can help to solidify one's diagnostic impression.

History-taking should focus on predrinking patterns of adjustment, the psychosocial context in which the drinking problem developed, its subsequent course, and the consequences of excessive alcohol use. In patients with both alcoholism and depression, an attempt should be made to separate the two disorders with regard to their chronologic development and the etiologic contribution of one to the other. Furthermore, in patients with underlying affective disorder, it is important to distinguish unipolar depression from bipolar (i.e. manic-depressive) disorders [10] where manic or hypomanic periods alternate with episodes of depression. Unfortunately, in patients who drink to intoxication, it is often difficult to distinguish endogenous from exogenous (i.e. alcohol related) alterations in mood.

During and after alcohol withdrawal, weekly administration of psychiatric rating scales, like the Beck Depression Inventory (BDI)[11] and the Hamilton Depression Rating Scale (HDRS),[12] may also be useful in assessing the degree of depression in alcoholic patients. Though the majority of alcoholics entering treatment achieve scores indicative of moderate to severe depression on these and other rating scales, most improve dramatically (i.e. 60% decrease from baseline) over the first 4 weeks of treatment. Approximately 20%–30%, however, continue to manifest substantial depressive symptomatology and sustain high scores on rating scales like the BDI and the HDRS. It is in this group of patients that one finds the preponderance of individuals with concurrent affective disorder.

Family History Data

Yet another aid in diagnosing affective illness in alcoholics is the use of family history data. There is substantial evidence that alcoholism runs in families.[13-15] In male alcoholics, a role for one or more genetic factors is suggested by the finding that the risk for alcoholism in male adoptees appears to be more closely correlated with the presence or absence of alcoholism in their biological relatives, than with the drinking habits of their adoptive parents.[16,17]

Twin studies also support the existence of a genetic factor in alcoholism in that monozygotic twins, who share the same genetic heritage, have a significantly higher concordance for heavy drinking when compared to dizygotic twins.[18] Finally, alcoholics with a family history of alcoholism tend to have earlier onset of symptoms and develop more severe dependence than alcoholics without such a history.[17]

Family pedigree studies initially suggested that depression was an extremely common finding in the families of alcoholics and that alcoholics were overrepresented in the families of depressives.[19,20] These findings led some investigators to suggest that both disorders were part of a depressive spectrum, manifest as alcoholism in males and depression in females.[19] However data from family, pedigree, adoption and genetic-marker studies suggest a separate mode of inheritance for these disorders.[21-24] Thus, the concurrence of these disorders in the same individual is due not only to a confluence of separate genetic factors but also a host of cultural, psychosocial, and environmental factors which enhance the risk of alcoholism and depression developing in the same individual.[25] Studies currently in progress may help to define (1) who within the alcoholic population is at increased risk for developing other forms of psychopathology and (2) which patients with affective disorder are at increased risk for developing alcoholism.

In evaluating the alcoholic patient with depression, family history data obtained from both the patient and his or her first degree relatives can be extremely helpful. A history of primary alcoholism in the absence of affective disorder in the patient's relatives suggests a high probability that the vegetative signs of depression observed during alcohol withdrawal will resolve once the patient is detoxified and some of the accompanying psychosocial problems are addressed. On the other hand the finding of high genetic loading for affective disorder in the patient's family increases one's index of suspicion that the observed depressive symptomatology may be a manifestation of both alcohol withdrawal and underlying affective disorder.

Laboratory Studies

Laboratory tests may also be of some use in evaluating the alcoholic patient with presumptive affective disorder. Also, in patients with concurrent depression biological measures may be useful in selecting a pharmacologic treatment and in monitoring response to that treatment. Though none of these tests are sufficiently specific to warrant routine clinical use in depressed alcoholics, they can provide additional data to consider in equivocal cases. For example, the dexamethasone suppression test (DST) may be helpful in confirming the diagnosis of major depression in alcoholic patients,[26,27] but false positive results occur frequently unless the patient has been alcohol- and drug-free for at least two weeks.[28-31] Given an appropriate (but yet to be defined) waiting period, depressed alcoholics who fail to suppress cortisol output in response to dexamethasone may be good candidates for antidepressant treatment; moreover, in such patients failure of an initially positive DST to normalize during pharmacologic treatment appears to predict relapse to depression and is associated with increased suicidal risk.[32]

Another laboratory measure that has received considerable attention is measurement of the 24-hour urinary excretion of 3-methoxy-4-hydroxy-phenyglycol (MHPG), the major metabolite of norepinephrine originating in the brain.[33] Levels have been used to define depressive subtypes and in predicting response to specific therapy. Low MHPG has been reported in bipolar depressed patients who respond preferentially to antidepressants that increase the availability of norepinephrine at central postsynaptic receptors.[34] The significance of midrange or high levels of MHPG in depressed patients is less clear. Since urinary MHPG levels increase during alcohol withdrawal, testing should be delayed until the patient is alcohol- and drug-free for at least two weeks[35] and perhaps longer.

Aspects of Differential Diagnosis

In assessing the alcoholic patient who presents with depressed mood, it is important to remember that chronic alcohol abuse may lead to the development of substantial central nervous system pathology and that these syndromes may be accompanied by signs and symptoms that may mimic those seen in primary affective disorder. For example, Wernicke's disease (alcohol-induced ophthalmoplegia) is often accompanied by a "quiet delirium" characterized by apathy, lassitude, disorientation, and drowsiness, which may resemble a retarded depression. The concurrent findings of ataxia, nystagmus, bilateral sixth cranial nerve palsy, and paralysis of conjugate gaze helps confirm a diagnosis of Wernicke's. Administration of thiamine usually results in prompt amelioration of the ocular pathology and ataxia, but the delirium recedes more gradually.

Frequently accompanying Wernicke's disease is Korsakoff's psychosis (alcohol-induced amnestic disorder). Patients with Korsakoff's syndrome manifest profound anterograde and retrograde amnesia but are otherwise alert. They also confabulate and are thus, at times, misdiagnosed as manic or schizophrenic.

More subtle neuropsychological deficits are common in recovering alcoholics and may also be mistaken for primary depression. These include impairments in memory, abstraction, and problem solving which may be associated with computerized axial tomographic evidence of increased brain: ventricle ratio.[36] These problems are often at least partially reversible during the first year of sobriety.[37-40] In some cases, alcohol withdrawal symptoms may continue for weeks or even months. Protracted alcohol withdrawal may be accompanied by tremulousness, restlessness, anxiety, depressed mood, and sleep disturbance,[41] which may be misdiagnosed as anxiety disorder or agitated depression.

Chronic alcohol consumption may also damage a number of other organ systems and it is important to remember that some of these alcohol-induced conditions may be accompanied by profound disturbance or mood and/or behavior. Such conditions include hepatic or renal failure, profound malnutrition, some vitamin deficiency states, and anemia.

Finally, both alcoholism and depression may exist concurrently with other psychiatric disorders. Indeed, substance abuse and antisocial personality disorder are more common than primary affective disorder in many alcoholic populations, particularly in males.[35,42] Such patients require more intensive psychosocial rehabilitation and have worse prognoses.[43] Anxiety and panic disorder are also quite common in alcoholics and may require specific psychotherapeutic and pharmacologic approaches.[44] Attention-deficit disorder (residual type) and complex partial seizure disorder may also facilitate the concurrent development of both alcoholism and affective symptomatology.

Alcohol and Suicide

The relatively high prevalence of depression in alcoholic patients has naturally led to consideration of the role of alcohol abuse in patients who attempt or complete suicide. Indeed, alcohol intoxication is implicated in 25–50% of suicide attempts, and many of those who eventually commit suicide are alcoholics.[45,46] From a psychodynamic perspective, alcoholism may be viewed as a form of chronic suicidal behavior.

At least one study has shown that alcoholics who are depressed when they enter treatment are more likely to commit suicide at some later date compared to alcoholics without depressive symptoms.[47] Suicide attempts are often preceded by the loss of a close interpersonal relationship,[48] after which the individual is likely to resume drinking. The disinhibiting effects of alcohol, coupled with the underlying depression, enhance the risk of impulsive self-destructive behavior. In such patients antidepressants and/or benzodiazepines may be combined with alcohol in an overdose attempt. Alcohol intoxication also plays an important role in single car accidents, some of which are masked suicide attempts.

In the alcoholic patient with depression the risk of suicide is particularly high. The clinician must continually monitor the patient's vulnerability, especially at times of interpersonal loss or resumption of drinking. Limiting supplies of prescribed medication, though not a substitute for careful monitoring, is an expression of concern and can add a measure of safety in impulsive overdose attempts.

Pharmacologic Treatment of the Alcoholic with Unipolar Depression

The pharmacologic management of alcohol withdrawal is well described in several recent publications.[49] In this and the next section we will focus on issues specific to the treatment of the alcoholic patient with underlying mood disorder.

Several studies have explored the efficacy of antidepressant drugs in the treatment of alcoholic patients with depression.[49-50] Methodologic problems make the results of these studies somewhat difficult to interpret. Most have employed fixed doses of tricyclic antidepressants administered without benefit of plasma-level monitoring. Moreover, patients who failed to respond to one drug were rarely switched to another, a routine procedure in clinical practice. The criteria for a diagnosis of depression also varied considerably across studies.

Despite these methodologic difficulties, studies to date suggest that, in general, tricyclic antidepressants are superior to benzodiazepines or placebo in ameliorating depressive symptoms in detoxified alcoholics. Not surprisingly, tricyclics appear to be more useful in patients suffering from severe, rather than mild, depression. On the other hand, patients with long-standing "characterologic" depressions have a poor response to antidepressant drugs. In our view, antidepressants should only be used to treat clear-cut affective disorder in alcoholic patients. Following alcohol withdrawal, depressed mood, accompanied by the sustained presence of other signs of depression (e.g., anorexia, loss of pleasure, and hopelessness), suggests consideration of antidepressant therapy, particularly in patients with a history of prior depressive symptoms while drug-free. A family history of affective illness also adds to one's level of diagnostic confidence.[6]

The use of tricyclic antidepressants in the treatment of the recovering alcoholic is not without risk. At plasma levels near the therapeutic range, tricyclic antidepressants increase cerebral capillary permeability to a variety of substances, including ethanol.[51] Consequently, patients receiving tricyclic drugs may become profoundly intoxicated after ingesting relatively low doses of alcohol. Indeed, the combination of tricyclic antidepressants and alcohol is a common cause of drug-induced coma in alcoholics who make suicide attempts.

At least one study[52] has shown that the clearance of imipramine is enhanced in alcoholic patients without significant liver disease, compared with a nonalcoholic control group. Consequently, at comparable doses, imipramine plasma levels were generally lower in these patients. Since tricyclic plasma levels are clearly correlated with clinical response,[53] this finding may explain the failure of some studies to demonstrate a significant advantage for tricyclic treatment in alcoholics with concurrent major depression. Even in alcoholics who remain abstinent, treatment with tricyclic antidepressants requires careful monitoring. In those patients with severely impaired liver function, the metabolic breakdown and kidney clearance of antidepressants and their metabolites may be delayed. Subsequent accumulation of these compounds may, in turn, lead to high plasma tricyclic levels and severe toxicity. Thus, from a practical standpoint, the vagaries of antidepressant kinetics in alcoholic patients require that use of tricyclics include careful monitoring of plasma levels in these patients. In addition, patients should be warned about the potentiating effects of tricyclic antidepressants on alcohol intoxication and the enhancement, by alcohol, of the anticholinergic side-effects of antidepressants.

Some alcoholics with coexisting depression fail to respond to tricyclic antidepressants but do respond clinically when treated with monoamine oxidase inhibitors (MAOIs) like phenelzine or tranylcypromine. Tricyclic antidepressants should be discontinued for a minimum of 5 days before initiating MAOI therapy. In patients who fail to respond to the usual doses of phenelzine (e.g. 60 mg daily), measurement of the degree of suppression of platelet MAO activity may be helpful. In general, suppression of platelet MAO activity to levels to 0.5 units or less appears to be correlated with clinical response.[54] Platelet MAO levels are less helpful in patients receiving tranylcypromine since this drug may dramatically reduce platelet MAO activity even at subtherapeutic doses.

As in the case of tricyclic antidepressants, treatment of alcoholic patients with MAOIs carries some degree of risk. The combination of MAOIs with other drugs, particularly sympathomimetic amines and/or tricyclic antidepressants, may result in an acute hypertensive reaction. MAOIs impair the body's ability to metabolize tyramine, an amino acid found in some red wines (e.g. chianti), beer, and certain foods (e.g. aged cheese). In patients who are impulse-ridden or suicidal, ingestion of prohibited foods or chemicals may precipitate a tyramine-mediated hypertensive crisis with potentially disastrous consequences (e.g. stroke).

Finally, there is evidence that zimelidine and citalopram, two antidepressants which inhibit brain serotonin reuptake (not currently available in the United States) have some effect in reducing drinking in nondepressed alcoholics.[55] Thus, trazodone, another antidepressant that also inhibits serotonin reuptake, is of theoretical interest in the treatment of depressed alcoholics. Unfortunately, trazodone administration is sometimes associated with priapism, even at low doses, and the drug should be used with caution in male patients.[56]

Pharmacologic Treatment of the Alcoholic with Bipolar Illness

Alcohol abuse is also a frequent complication in patients with manic-depressive disease,[57-58] and bipolar patients who drink excessively have worse prognoses than those who do not.[59] The acute euphoria produced by alcohol intoxication is valued by some bipolar patients in their attempts to treat episodic depression or to augment ego-syntonic mania. Conversely, the sedative effect of alcohol may bring temporary relief to the manic or hypomanic patients experiencing agitation, racing thoughts, and hyperactivity. In such patients, alternating periods of alcohol-induced euphoria and depression may obscure the diagnosis of manic-depressive disease. As in the case of the alcoholic with depression, observation of the patient during alcohol-free periods is essential for accurate diagnosis.

In the alcoholic patient with manic-depressive disease, treatment with lithium can greatly improve the prognosis for both disorders. In addition to lithium's mood-stabilizing effects, there are data to suggest that the drug may block the euphorigenic effects of alcohol itself. For example, rats trained to enjoy alcohol consistently drink less during lithium treatment.[60] There is also some experimental evidence to suggest that lithium may exert a direct suppressant effect on alcohol-induced euphoria in man.[61,62] In clinical practice, some alcoholics with bipolar illness report decreased craving for alcohol, and even alcohol aversion, during lithium treatment.

Manic-depressive patients who do not respond or who experience unacceptable side effects with lithium treatment may benefit from treatment with carbamazepine. This anticonvulsant has a mood-stabilizing effect on bipolar individuals similar to, but less potent than, that of lithium.[63] The combination of lithium and carbamazepine can also be helpful in some patients who do not respond to lithium alone. Similarly, there is emerging evidence that another anticonvulsant, sodium valproate, is effective in some patients with bipolar disorder.[64]

In alcoholic patients with underlying bipolar disorder, a trial of a mood stabilizing drug like lithium is clearly indicated, since relapse to alcohol use is extremely common during episodes of mania or depression in these patients. In addition, a number of investigators have explored the efficacy of lithium carbonate in the treatment of alcoholics without manic-depressive disease.[65-68] The results suggest that in some patients lithium may enhance the maintenance of sobriety.[65] In practice, this possibility must be weighed against the risk of lithium intoxication or overdose in impulsive patients.[49]

Anxiolytics

Benzodiazepines are the medications most commonly prescribed to alcoholic patients. Their use in the treatment of alcohol withdrawal has done much to reduce the morbidity and mortality associated with this condition. However, chronic use of these agents is fraught with hazard. Alcoholics quickly learn that benzodiazepines, as well as other central nervous system (CNS) depressants, will reduce the irritability associated with alcohol withdrawal. Unfortunately, chronic administration of benzodiazepines may result in the development of mixed alcohol-benzodiazepine dependence, which greatly complicates the treatment of alcohol withdrawal. Acute administration of benzodiazepines, particularly in high doses, may produce a brief euphoria, followed by CNS depression. In patients with affective disorder (e.g. major depression) this may exacerbate depressive symptoms. Though alprazolam appears to have some antidepressant activity,[69] and both alprazolam and clonazepam are enjoying some popularity in the treatment of panic disorder, we know of no data supporting the efficacy of these agents in the treatment of depression in alcoholics. On the other hand, suicide attempts involving the combination of alcohol and benzodiazepines are relatively common among alcoholic patients with depression. For this reason, benzodiazepines should be reserved for patients who have failed treatment with other agents (e.g. antidepressants) and in whom the expected benefit clearly outweighs the risk.

Finally, buspirone, an anxiolytic with a mechanism of action apparently different from the benzodiazepines, does not suppress symptoms of benzodiazepine withdrawal[70] and does not appear to have any antidepressant effects. To our knowledge its use in alcoholic populations has not been investigated.

The Maintenance of Sobriety: Disulfiram

The alcoholic has developed a lifestyle in which there is a preoccupation with alcohol and loss of control over its consumption. As tolerance develops, there is a tendency to increase the dose. With the development of physical dependence, drinking to prevent or relieve abstinence symptoms becomes an additional motivation for alcohol use. In the detoxified alcoholic with affective disorder, episodes of depression or mania may be accompanied by relapse to heavy drinking. By the same token, resumption of drinking may exacerbate underlying affective symptoms, even in patients maintained on antidepressants or lithium.

Some alcoholic patients, with or without affective disorder, may benefit from maintenance on disulfiram (Antabuse), a drug that interferes with the metabolic breakdown of acetaldehyde, an intermediate product in alcohol metabolism. Patients maintained on disulfiram who subsequently ingest alcohol experience a characteristic set of symptoms, including a sensation of heat in the face and neck, throbbing headache, flushing, a feeling of constriction in the throat, and a profound sense of anxiety. Nausea and vomiting, hypotension, chest pain, coughing, and labored breathing may also occur. Symptoms begin shortly after alcohol ingestion and peak 30 minutes to several hours later.

The severity of the "Antabuse reaction" is usually correlated with the dose of disulfiram the patient has been taking and the amount of alcohol ingested. Patients with preexisting heart disease, cirrhosis, diabetes, or any debilitating medical disorder are particularly at risk for untoward and dangerous complications, including seizures, respiratory depression, cardiac arrhythmias, myocardial infarction, acute heart failure, and death. In such patients the decision to take disulfiram should be carefully weighted and low doses (e.g. 125 mgs qd) should be used. Disulfiram can also increase plasma levels of tricyclic antidepressants[71] so that patients taking antidepressants who begin disulfiram treatment may require a reduction in antidepressant dosage. There have also been reports of adverse drug interactions between MAOIs and disulfiram.

Disulfiram is probably most useful in older, well-motivated patients whose drinking is triggered largely by recurrent psychological stress or by environmental cues conducive to drinking (e.g. cocktail parties). The drug should be taken each morning when the investment in sobriety is usually highest. Patients with poor impulse control, schizophrenia, or depression with suicidal ideation are at considerable risk for drinking while on disulfiram and should be carefully evaluated before treatment is initiated.

There are several case reports of major psychiatric complications of disulfiram treatment.[72] These have usually involved doses higher than those now used in the treatment of alcoholism (i.e. greater than 500 mgs/day). A recent prospective study found no increased risk of psychiatric symptoms in patients with no previous psychiatric history taking 250 mgs per day.[73] While the risk appears quite low, the possibility that disulfiram may exacerbate psychiatric symptoms in alcoholics with affective disorder must be kept in mind.

Conclusions

In treating the alcoholic with affective disorder it is well to remember that both are chronic, relapsing illnesses. With respect to alcoholism, periods of stable abstinence may be interrupted by occasional relapse and abstinence alone should not be the sole criterion of successful rehabilitation. Psychological and social recovery in these patients requires the integration of various approaches into a comprehensive treatment program. In addition to appropriate pharmacotherapy, regular attendance at meetings of Alcoholics Anonymous; individual group, couple and family therapy; and behavior therapy may also be needed. As in other areas of medicine, accurate diagnosis and careful treatment of each disorder greatly improves prognosis.

References

1. Weissman MM, Pottenger M, Kleber H, Ruben HL, Williams D, Thompson WD: Symptom patterns in primary and secondary depression. *Arch Gen Psychiat* 34:852–862, 1977.

2. Akiskal HS, McKinney WT: Overview of recent research in depression. *Arch Gen Psychiat* 32:285–305, 1975.

3. Cardoret R, Winokur G: Depression in alcoholism. *Ann N.Y. Acad Sci* 233:1–77, 1974.

4. Weissman MM, Meyers JK: Clinical depression in alcoholism. *Am J Psychiatry* 137:372–373, 1980.

5. Jaffe JH, Ciraulo D: Drugs used in the treatment of alcoholism. In Mendelson JH, Mello NK (eds): *The Diagnosis and Treatment of Alcoholism*, 2nd ed., New York: McGraw-Hill, pp 355–389, 1985.

6. Schuckit MA: Genetic and clinical implications of alcoholism and affective disorder. *Am J Psychiatry* 143:140–147, 1986.

7. Schuckit M: Alcoholic patients with secondary depression. *Am J Psychiatry* 140:711–714, 1983.

8. Overall JE, Reilly EL, Kelley JT, Hollister LE: Persistence of depression in detoxified alcoholics. *Alc Clin Exp Res* 9:331–333, 1985.

9. Nakamura MM, Overall JE, Hollister LE, Radcliffe E: Factors affecting outcome of depressive symptoms in alcoholics. *Alc Clin Exp Res* 7:188–193, 1983.

10. *Diagnostic and Statistical Manual of Mental Disorders* (3rd ed—revised). Washington, DC: American Psychiatric Association, 1987.

11. Beck AT, Ward CH, Mendelson M, et al.: An inventory for measuring depression. *Arch Gen Psychiat* 4:561–571, 1961.

12. Hamilton M: A rating scale for depression. *J Neurol Neurosurg Psychiatry* 23:56–62, 1960.

13. Goodwin DW: Is alcoholism hereditary? A review and critique. *Arch Gen Psychiat* 25:545–549, 1971.

14. Wolin SJ, Bennett LA, Noonan DL: Family rituals and the recurrence of alcoholism over generations. *Am J Psychiat* 136:589–602, 1979.

15. Franks DD, Thacker BT: Assessing familial factors in alcoholism from MMPI profiles. *Am J Psychiat* 136:1084–1086, 1979.

16. Cadoret RJ, Cain CA, Grove WM: Development of alcoholism in adoptees raised apart from alcoholic biological relatives. *Arch Gen Psychiat* 37:561–563, 1980.

17. Goodwin DW: Alcoholism and genetics. *Arch Gen Psychiat* 42:171–174, 1985.

18. Partanan J, Bruun K, Markkanen T: *Inheritance of drinking behavior*. New Brunswick: Rutgers University Center of Alcohol Studies, 1966.

19. Winokur G: Alcoholism and depression in the same family. In Goodwin DW, Erickson CK (eds): *Alcoholism and Affective Disorders*, New York: SP Medical and Scientific Books, 49–56, 1979.

20. Cloninger CR, Reich T, Wetzel R: Alcoholism and affective disorders: Familial associations and genetic models. In Goodwin DW, Erickson CK (eds): *Alcohol-*

ism and Affective Disorders, New York: SP Medical and Scientific Books, 57–86, 1979.

21. Merikangas KR, Leckman JF, Prusoff BA, Pauls DL, Weissman MM: Familial transmission of depression and alcoholism. *Arch Gen Psychiat* 42:367–372, 1985.

22. Mirin SM, Weiss RD, Michael J: Family pedigree of psychopathology in substance abusers. In Meyer RE (ed): *Psychopathology and Addictive Disorders*, New York: Guilford Press, 55–77, 1986.

23. Goodwin DW, Schulsinger F, Miller N, Hermansen L, Winokur G, Guze SB: Drinking problems in adopted and nonadopted sons of alcoholics. *Arch Gen Psychiat* 31:164–169, 1974.

24. Camps FE, Dodd BE, Lincoln PJ: Frequencies of secretors and nonsecretors of ABH group substances among 1000 alcoholic patients. *Brit Med J* 4:457–459, 1969.

25. Cloninger CR, Bohman M, Sigvardsson S: Inheritance of alcohol abuse. *Arch Gen Psychiat* 38:861–868, 1981.

26. Khan A, Ciraulo DA, Nelson WH, Becker JT, Nies A, Jaffe JH: Dexamethasone suppression test in recently detoxified alcoholics: clinical implications. *J Clin Psychopharmacol* 4:94–97, 1984.

27. Dackis CA, Stuckey RF, Gold MS, Pottash ALC: Dexamethasone suppression testing of depressed alcoholics. *Alc Clin Exp Res* 10:59–60, 1986.

28. Jubiz W, Meikle AW, Levinson RA, et al: Effect of diphenylhydantoin on the metabolism of dexamethasone. *NEJM* 283:11–14, 1970.

29. Brooks SM, Werk EE, Acherman SJ, et al: Adverse effects of phenobarbital on corticosteroid metabolism in patients with bronchial asthma. *NEJM* 286:1125–1128, 1972.

30. Ravi SD, Dorus W, Park YN, Collins MC, Reid RW, Borge GF: The dexamethasone suppression test and depressive symptoms in early and late withdrawal from alcohol. *Am J Psychiat* 141:1445–1448, 1984.

31. Nelson WH, Sullivan P, Kahn A, Tamragour RN: The effect of age on dexamethasone suppression test results in alcoholic patients. *Am J Psychiat* 143:237–239, 1986.

32. APA Task Force on Laboratory Tests in Psychiatry: The dexamethasone suppression test: an overview of its current status in psychiatry. *Am J Psychiat* 144:1253–1262, 1987.

33. Maas JW, Landis DH: In vivo studies of the metabolism of norepinephrine in the central nervous system. *J Pharmacol Exp Ther* 163: 147–162, 1968.

34. Schildkraut JJ, Orsulak PJ, Schatzberg AF, et al: Toward a biochemical classification of depressive disorders. I. Differences in urinary excretion of MHPG and other catecholamine metabolites in clinically defined subtypes of depression. *Arch Gen Psychiat* 35:1427–1433, 1978.

35. Ogborne AC, Kapur BM: Drug use among a sample of males admitted to an alcohol detoxification center. *Alc Clin Exp Res* 11:183–185, 1987.

36. Hill SY, Mikhael MA: Computerized transaxial tomographic and neuropsychological evaluations in chronic alcoholics and heroin abusers. *Am J Psychiat* 136:598–602, 1979.

37. Grant I, Adams KM, Reed R: Aging, abstinence, and medical risk factors in

the prediction of neuropsychologic deficits among long-term alcoholics. *Arch Gen Psychiat* 41:710–718, 1984.

38. Grant I, Reed R, Adams KM: Diagnosis of intermediate-duration and subacute organic mental disorders in abstinent alcoholics. *J Clin Psychiat* 48:319–323, 1987.

39. Ryan C, Butters N: Cognitive deficits in alcoholics. In Kissin B, Begleiter H (eds): *The Biology of Alcoholism*, vol. 7, New York: Plenum Press, 485–538, 1983.

40. Parsons OA, Leber WR: The relationship between cognitive dysfunction and brain damage in alcoholics: causal, interactive, or epiphenomenal? *Alc Clin Exp Res* 5:326–343, 1981.

41. Kissin B: Biological investigations in alcohol research. *J Stud Alcohol* 40, supp. 8:146–181, 1979.

42. Schuckit MA: The clinical implications of primary diagnostic groups among alcoholics. *Arch Gen Psychiat* 42:1043–1049, 1985.

43. Lewis CE, Rice J, Andreasen N, Endicott J, Rochberg N: The antisocial and the nonantisocial alcoholic: clinical distinctions in men with major unipolar depression. *Alc Clin Exp Res* 11:176–182, 1987.

44. Bowen RC, Cipywnyk D, D'Arcy C, Keegan D: Alcoholism, anxiety disorders, and agoraphobia. *Alc Clin Exp Res* 8:481–550, 1984.

45. Rushing WA: Alcoholism and suicide rates by status set and occupation. *Q J Stud Alcoholism* 29:399–412, 1968.

46. Kessel N, Grossman G: Suicide in alcoholics. *Brit Med J* 2:1671–1672, 1961.

47. Berglund M: Suicide in alcoholism. *Arch Gen Psychiat* 41:888–891, 1984.

48. Murphy GE, Armstrong JW: Suicide and alcoholism. Interpersonal loss confirmed as a predictor. *Arch Gen Psychiat* 36:65–69, 1979.

49. Liskow BI, Goodwin DW: Pharmacological treatment of alcohol intoxication, withdrawal, and dependence. A critical review. *J Stud Alcohol* 48:356–370, 1987.

50. Ciraulo DA, Jaffe JH: Tricyclic antidepressants in the treatment of depression associated with alcoholism. *J Clin Psychopharmacol* 1:146–150, 1981.

51. Kalant H, Rangaraj N, Woo N, Endrenyi L: Effects of ethanol on neuronal membrane transport systems. In Manzo, L et al. (eds): *Progress in Neurotoxicology* (Proc. 1st Internat. Congr. Neurotoxicol., Varese, 1979). Oxford, Pergamon Press, 1979.

52. Ciraulo DA, Alderson LM, Chapron DJ, Jaffe JH, Bollepalli S, Kramer PA: Imipramine disposition in alcoholics. *J Clin Psychopharmacol* 2:2–6, 1982.

53. Amsterdam J, Brunswick D, Mendels J: The clinical application of tricyclic antidepressant pharmacokinetics and plasma levels. *Am J Psychiat* 137:653–661, 1980.

54. Robinson DS, Nies A, Ravaris CL, Ives JO, Bartlett D: Clinical pharmacology of phenelzine. *Arch Gen Psychiat* 35:629–635, 1978.

55. Naranjo CA, Sellers EM, Lawrin MO: Modulation of ethanol intake by serotonin uptake inhibitors. *J Clin Psychiat* 47:16–22, 1986.

56. Warner MD, Peabody CA, Whiteford HA, Hollister LE: Trazodone and priapism. *J Clin Psychiat* 48:244–245, 1987.

57. Dunner DL, Hensel BM, Fieve RR: Bipolar illness: Factors in drinking be-

havior. *Am J Psychiat* 136:583–585, 1979.

58. Morrison JR: Bipolar affective disorder and alcoholism. *Am J Psychiat* 131:1130–1133, 1974.

59. Reich LH, Davies RK, Himmelhoch JM: Excessive alcohol use in manic-depressive illness. *Am J Psychiat* 131:83–86, 1974.

60. Sinclair JD: Lithium-induced suppression of alcohol drinking by rats. *Med Biol* 52:133–136, 1974.

61. Judd LL, Hubbard B, Janowski DS, Huey LY, Abrams AA, Riney WB, Pendery MM: Ethanol-lithium interaction in alcoholics. In Goodwin DW, Erickson CK (eds): *Alcoholism and Affective Disorders*. New York: SP Medical and Scientific Books, 49–56, 1979.

62. Judd LL, Huey LY: Lithium antagonizes ethanol intoxication in alcoholics. *Am J Psychiat* 141:1517–1521, 1984.

63. Lerer B, Moore N, Meyendorff E, Cho S-R, Gershon S: Carbamazepine versus lithium in mania. *J Clin Psychiat* 48:89–93, 1987.

64. McElroy SL, Keck PE, Pope HG: Sodium valproate: its use in primary psychiatric disorders. *J Clin Psychopharmacol* 7:16–24, 1987.

65. Fawcett J, Clark DC, Aagesen CA, Pisani VD, Tilkin HM, Sellers D, McGuire M, Gibbons RD: A double-blind, placebo-controlled trial of lithium carbonate therapy for alcoholism. *Arch Gen Psychiat* 44:248–256, 1987.

66. Merry J, Reynolds CM, Baily J, Coppen A: Prophylactic treatment of alcoholism of lithium carbonate: A controlled study. *Lancet* 7984: 481–482, 1976.

67. Kline NS, Wren JC, Cooper TB, Varga E, Canal O: Evaluation of lithium therapy in chronic and periodic alcoholism. *Amer J Med Sci* 268:15–22, 1974.

68. Reynolds CM, Merry J, Coppen A: Prophylactic treatment of alcoholism by lithium carbonate: An initial report. *Alcoholism Clin Exp Res* 1:109–111, 1977.

69. Rickles K, Chung HR, Csanalosi IB, Hurowitz AM, London J, Wiseman K, Kaplan M, Amsterdam JD: Alprazolam, diazepam, imipramine, and placebo in outpatients with major depression. *Arch Gen Psychiat* 44:862–866, 1987.

70. Lader M, Olajide D: A comparison of buspirone and placebo in relieving benzodiazepine withdrawal symptoms. *J Clin Psychopharmacol* 7:11–15, 1987.

71. Ciraulo DA, Barnhill J, Boxenbaum H: Pharmacokinetic interaction of disulfiram and antidepressants. *Am J Psychiat* 142:1373–1374, 1985.

72. Weddington WW, Marks RC, Verghase JP: Disulfiram encephalopathy as a cause of the catatonia syndrome. *Am J Psychiat* 137:1217–1219, 1980.

73. Branchey L, Davis W, Lee KK, Fuller RK: Psychiatric complications of disulfiram treatment. *Am J Psychiat* 144:1310–1312, 1987.

16

Sleep Deprivation in the Treatment of Depression
Burkhard Pflug

EDITOR'S NOTE

The use of sleep deprivation as an experimental method of treatment for depression is based on the hypothesis that affective disorders may involve dysfunction in circadian rhythms. Three types of deprivation have been employed: total; partial, in which the patient is kept awake either during the first or the last half of the night; and selective, during which there is specific deprivation of REM sleep.

Sleep deprivation — total or partial (during the second half of the night) — appears to relieve endogenous symptoms of depression such as depressive mood, psychomotor retardation, loss of interest, anxiety. Combining sleep deprivation with antidepressant medication is reported to result in a better outcome than either method alone.

Some depressed patients improve considerably after only one night's sleep deprivation and maintain their improvement. For most patients, however, improvement does not sustain itself; after a day or two, symptoms return to a varying degree. If no further improvement occurs, subsequent sleep deprivation experiences can be employed at weekly intervals.

This strategy seems to work best in depressed patients who are younger, who have a shorter history of illness, and when it is used earlier in the course of the condition. It can also be used for other diagnostic groups, if endogenous depressive symptoms are evident.

Introduction

The observation that staying awake for a night can improve the depressive mood was first made by patients themselves. Systematic studies of the phenomenon began in 1968. In 1971 the first comprehensive review of the topic was published.[1] It was shown that improvement in depressive symptoms could be activated by sleep deprivation, and that sleep deprivation could probably be used intentionally in the therapy of depression.

During the following years, the antidepressive effect of sleep deprivation was confirmed in many international studies. At the same time, studies were conducted to understand the mode of action, indications for its use in treatment, modifications in approach, practicability, and the course of illness and recovery after planned sleep deprivation.

Forms of Sleep Deprivation

Approaches to the therapeutic sleep deprivation take three forms: total, partial, and selective.

Total sleep deprivation: In total deprivation procedures, patients stay awake for a day, a night, and the following day. Depression usually improves during the sleepless night and improvement continues the following day. Frequently a dramatic change can be seen in the early morning hours (between 2 a.m. and 6 a.m.). Sleep deprivation under varying conditions has shown no difference in therapeutic results; thus, it is of no relevance if patients stay awake in groups or alone or are involved in some defined activity. In contrast to healthy persons, depressed patients do not find it difficult to undergo sleep deprivation.

Partial sleep deprivation: Partial sleep deprivation means that patients stay awake part of the night only. Studies conducted so far have dealt with the first half of the night (staying awake until 1:30 a.m.) or the second half of the night (staying awake after 1:30 a.m.). It has been shown that patients who undergo sleep deprivation during the second half of the night improve in their symptoms as significantly as when they undergo total sleep deprivation.[2] Sleep deprivation during the first half of the night also has an antidepressive effect, but less so than either total sleep deprivation or partial sleep deprivation during the second half of the night.[3]

Selective sleep deprivation: Selective sleep deprivation consists of the deprivation of selected periods of sleep in the course of a night's sleep. In polygraphic studies the deprivation of REM-sleep (as opposed to non-REM-sleep) over a period of three weeks was accompanied by clinical improvement.[4] The method of REM-sleep deprivation does, however, depend on a great deal of apparatus and is therefore not practical as a widespread method of treatment.

Sleep Deprivation in the Treatment of Endogenous Depression

The use of sleep deprivation as a therapeutic strategy seems to work for a number of diagnostic groups, particularly when endogenous symptoms of depression are prominent. The most desirable patients are those meeting the diagnostic criteria for endogenous depression (ICD Nr. 296.1 and 296.3; *DSM-III*: major depressive disorders).

Total sleep deprivation or partial sleep deprivation during the second half of the night can be used effectively in such patients regardless of the stage of depression and the particular set of symptoms. It can be used early, near the onset of depression as the sole mode of treatment; it can be attempted when treatment with drugs fails to yield satisfactory results and, in general, when depression does not improve at all in spite of reasonable, traditional treatment. All forms of sleep deprivation have produced the best results in the group of patients with symptoms of endogenous depression, whether unipolar or bipolar (see Figure 1). The following symptoms improved most distinctly the day after total sleep deprivation: depressive mood, suicidal tendencies, psychomotor retardation, anxiety and restlessness, and lack of interest. The influence on somatic symptoms was less distinct. Infrequently a hypomanic attack followed sleep deprivation. A number of studies have been able to show that combining antidepressant treatment (e.g., chlorimipramine) with sleep deprivation is more successful than either one of the two treatments on its own.[5,6]

A small number of depressive patients improve considerably after only one night's sleep deprivation and continue to improve in the further course until they are free of symptoms. With most patients, however, improvement does not remain stable for more than one or two days. Frequently, on the second day after sleep deprivation, patients feel worse again to a varying degree. If depression does not reach the extent it had prior to sleep deprivation and if the patient continues to improve slowly, a second sleep deprivation should be postponed. If, however, there is a standstill in the patient's condition or if it deteriorates, a second sleep deprivation is indicated. Occasionally improvement is found on the second day after sleep deprivation and not immediately thereafter. It is therefore always advisable to wait and observe the patient for a few days after sleep deprivation before repeating the procedure.

Intraindividual comparisons made on 60 patients with unipolar depression showed that sleep deprivation tends to shorten depressive episodes. This tendency depends on the time of treatment: The earlier in the course of illness sleep deprivation is used, the shorter the depressive episode. Younger patients react better than older patients.[7]

Studies dealing with partial sleep deprivation during the second half of the night suggest that its therapeutic effect on endogenous depressives is the same as that of total sleep deprivation.

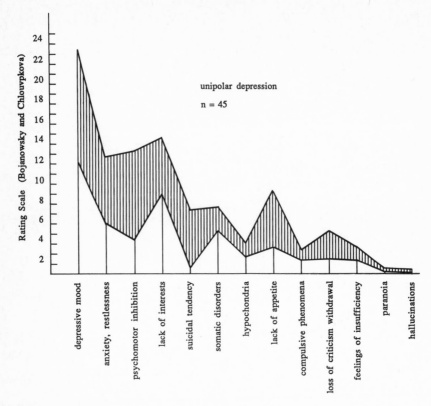

Figure 1.   Profile of depressive symptoms in the group of unipolar depressions.
The effect of sleep deprivation is shown by the shaded area, which
corresponds to the decrease in intensity.

Neurotic Depression (ICD Nr. 330.4)

The therapeutic effect of sleep deprivation in neurotic depressions varies in
degree and is on average less pronounced than in endogenous depressions
(see Figure 2). It seems to depend on the extent of vital symptoms (feelings
of localized anxiety, feelings of oppression, and disturbed feelings in varying
organs with diurnal variation of the symptoms). The more pronounced such
symptoms are, the better the therapeutic results. In one study involving 22
patients, the greatest improvement was seen in those with definite endogenous symptoms of depression.

Different studies indicate that patients in this group are typical so-called
second day responders, i.e. improvement or further improvement is seen on
the second day after sleep deprivation.

Experience with partial sleep deprivation in this group is still too limited to draw any conclusions.

Depression in Schizophrenics

Recent studies on post-psychotic depression in patients basically suffering from schizophrenia indicate that total sleep deprivation may result in improvement similar to that in patients with endogenous depression.[8]

Improvement in depressive mood is distinct the day after sleep deprivation and recedes again the second day after sleep deprivation, i.e., after one night's sleep. However, the depressive mood does not return as severely as prior to sleep deprivation. This procedure is of practical importance as an alternative to antidepressive drugs.

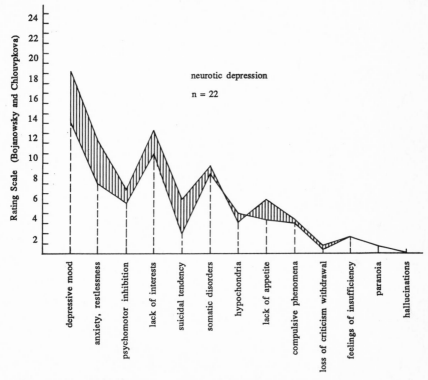

Figure 2.   Profile of depressive symptoms in the group of neurotic depressions. The effect of sleep deprivation is shown by the shaded area, which corresponds to the decrease in intensity.

Practical Suggestions

Sleep deprivation for one night (total sleep deprivation) and partial sleep deprivation during the second half of the night appear to be of practical importance as modes of treatment, particularly in patients who are not responding adequately to usual treatment methods.

Most of the studies on sleep deprivation were conducted on hospitalized patients and, on the whole, these patients suffered from quite severe depression. Nevertheless, treatment with sleep deprivation can be used on less severely depressed outpatients as well. The following rules should be observed:

(1) The primary indication for treatment is depression accompanied by distinct vital symptoms.
(2) The patient should, on at least one occasion, undergo sleep deprivation therapy in hospital.
(3) Combined therapy with an antidepressant drug is recommended in view of the better prognosis.
(4) Family members can be very helpful in assisting the patient to stay awake, especially if partial sleep deprivation is used.
(5) Sleep deprivation should probably be used at weekly intervals, if improvement is not stable or does not continue.

Contraindications

Apart from somatic diseases coinciding with depression, there are few, if any, contraindications. Complications were reported in only one case, consisting of a seizure which occurred after the withdrawal of hypnotics as part of the sleep deprivation procedure.

Theoretical Concepts: The Circadian System in Man

The organization of sleeping and waking and of many related physiological and psychological functions in the human proceeds in a diurnal variation. Under common environmental conditions, man—with his psychological and physical functions—is adjusted to the 24-hour day. If the periodic signals of the environment are excluded (so-called free run), the circadian periodicity of man deviates from 24 hours and amounts to 25.0 ± 0.5 hour.[9] Such a periodicity is endogenous, i.e., it is produced in the organism itself. Exogenous time influences synchronize periodicity to 24 hours. Under certain conditions, the periods of individual body function can proceed at different speeds. This is called internal desynchronization. The manifold endogenous and exogenous processes developing in the 24-hour range constitute the circadian system, and are characterized by their period lengths, amplitudes, phase relations, couplings and range of entrainment.

According to Aschoff,[10] the circadian system has the following two major functions: (1) to coordinate the individual circadian body functions and synchronize them internally; and (2) to entrain the whole organism to the periodically changing environment, i.e., to achieve an external synchronization.

According to Wever,[9] the circadian system of man is a multioscillatory system, composed of different strong and weak oscillators. The weak oscillators (governing the sleep-waking cycle, for example) are coupled to strong oscillators in a stable phase relationship. Such strong oscillators govern the rapid eye movement (REM) sleep propensity, body temperature, and cortisol secretion. Under certain conditions these relations may alter—for example on transmeridianal flights, in isolated conditions in an underground bunker, or in an arctic environment with constant light.

Disturbances in the Circadian System Occurring in Endogenous Depression

Several investigations in the last few years have shown that endogenous depressions correlate with disturbances in the circadian system. In this context the following hypotheses will be discussed (see Figure 3).

Desynchronization[11]: This hypothesis says that during depression different circadian functions of the organism show varying lengths of period. The superimposition of periodic functions (beat) occurring in this context forms the basis of a depressive episode. There are several studies which point out that, in fact, such desynchronization seems to occur during a depressive period and can no longer be found when symptoms of depression have receded.[12]

Phase advance: According to this hypothesis, during depression various functions show an earlier phase relation in their position to the sleep-waking rhythm. Such phase positions are found, for example, for the chronological distribution of REM sleep: the REM latency is shorter, the first REM episodes are longer, and most of the REM sleep takes place during the first third of the night, whereas this normally happens during the last part of the

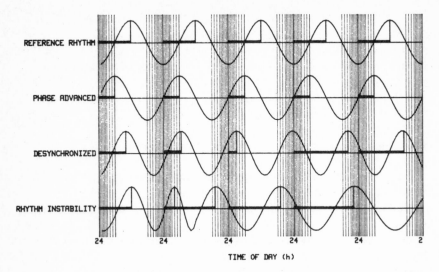

Figure 3.   Schematic presentation of some possibilities for the phase relationship between 24-h Zeitgeber (time cues) and a physiological variable in the weakened synchronizing mechanisms.

night.[13,14] In depressive patients, a similar advance of rhythm was also found in studies on cortisol secretion, body temperature, and MHPG excretion.[15]

A therapeutic experiment was published by Wehr et al.[16] in which an antidepressive effect was achieved in a depressive female patient by advancing the sleep-waking time.

Instability of circadian functions: In long-term studies on the circadian course of body temperature, it has been shown — with the help of the analysis of time series — that during depression and also during manic attacks there is a greater variability of the daily pattern of temperature which is the result of changes in the phase relationship of higher harmonics. Moreover, the dysregulation in the circadian system seems to be linked with the mood of the patient.

Depending on the method of investigations and the parameters investigated, it is possible to come to different conclusions concerning the deviation in the circadian system in depressive patients. We may assume that we are not just dealing with one definite form of rhythm disturbance that is typical for depression as such. Rather, different possibilities of rhythmic peculiarities must be considered, according to different individual circumstances as well as different degrees of severity of depression. The therapeutic experiment derived in each case is the most important criterion for the acceptance or rejection of a causal correlation between certain disturbances of chronobiological functions and depressive illness.

Sleep deprivation and the circadian system: In the literature there are a number of indications that chronobiologically effective substances (e.g. lithium salts) and interference with the 24-hour rhythm (various forms of sleep deprivation) have therapeutic effects which can be explained by a chronobiological mechanism. In bunker experiments with 12 healthy subjects, it was shown that, during a phase of sleep deprivation (63.5 hours awake), the circadian periods of various psychological and physiological parameters were delayed by two to eight hours. The delay in tests of psychological performance amounted to four hours, in self assessment eight hours, in rectal temperature two hours, and in urine excretion (volume, potassium, sodium, calcium) three hours. This delaying effect of sleep deprivation appears to be of significance for the therapeutic sleep deprivation.

Both total sleep deprivation and partial sleep deprivation (in the second half of the night) show two possibilities in the phase-advance model of depression. Either the advancing of waking leads to the "normalizing" of the phase relation with the phase-advanced oscillator, or else a delaying of the phase-advanced oscillator permits such normalization; the latter may be assumed in the case of total sleep deprivation and also in the case of selective sleep deprivation in which a progressive improvement of the depression can be achieved by REM phase deprivation over several weeks.

In the light of the desynchronization hypothesis and also that of the hypothesis of unstable phase relations, the effect of sleep deprivation seems to consist of synchronization due to a delaying of the circadian oscillator. Another hypothesis is based on the normalization of the adjustment to the 24-hour external time cycle made possible by the increased sensitivity of the oscillator.

All of these hypotheses proceed from the assumption of a connection between the circadian rhythm and depression. The important question of whether the relation is a causal one or, rather, symptomatic in nature has not yet been solved, and would appear to involve great methodological difficulties. The model of therapeutic sleep deprivation may be considered similar to an experiment in nature.

Summary

Different forms of sleep deprivation (sleep deprivation during one night or partial sleep deprivation in the second half of the night) deserve consideration as therapeutic measures in depressive illness. The effect of sleep deprivation is most distinct in endogenous depression. In neurotic depression results are good in those cases where vital symptoms occur. Moreover, sleep deprivation is a possible therapeutic method in post-psychotic depressions with patients basically suffering from schizophrenia. In some cases, improvement after sleep deprivation is stable; however, in most cases recurrences occur which require further treatment with sleep deprivation. Consecutive sleep deprivation treatments should probably be spaced at weekly intervals. Treatment with sleep deprivation is possible with outpatients and in the hospital.

The mode of action of sleep deprivation is unknown. Certain peculiarities of the circadian system (desynchronization, phase advance, instability) suggest that the chronobiological activity of sleep deprivation is responsible for its results in the treatment of depressed states.

References

1. Pflug B, Tölle R: Disturbance of the 24-hour rhythm in endogenous depression by sleep deprivation. *Int. Pharmacopsychiatr.* 6:187–196, 1971.

2. Schilgen B, Tölle R: Partial sleep deprivation as therapy for depression. *Arch. Gen. Psychiatr.* 37:267–271, 1980.

3. Goetze U, Tölle R: Antidepressive Wirkung des partiellen Schafentzuges während der ersten Hälfte der Nacht. *Psychiatria Clin.* 14:129–149, 1981.

4. Vogel GW, Thurmond A, Gibbons P et al: REM sleep reduction effects on depression syndromes. *Arch. Gen. Psychiatr.* 32:765–777, 1975.

5. Loosen PT, Merkel U, Amelung U: Kombinierte Schlafentzugs-/clomipraminbehandlung Endogener Depression. *Arzneimittelforsch. (Drug. Res.)* 26:1177–1178, 1976.

6. Elsenga S, van den Hoofdakker RH: Clinical effects of sleep deprivation and clomipramine in endogenous depression. *J. Psychiat. Res.* 17:361–374, 1982/83.

7. Pflug B: The influence of sleep deprivation on the duration of endogenous depressive episodes. *Arch. Psychiatr. Nervenkr.* 225:173–177, 1978.

8. Fähndrich E: Effects of sleep deprivation on depressed patients of different nosological groups. *Psychiatr. Res.* 5:277–285, 1985.

9. Wever R: *The Circadian System of Man*, Springer, New York, Heidelberg, Berlin, 1979.

10. Aschoff J: Das circadiane System. Grundlagen der Tagesperiodik und ihrer Bedeutung für angewandte Physiologie und Klinik. *Verh. dtsch. Ges. innere Med.* 79 Bd., 19–31, J.F. Bergamann, München, 1973.

11. Halberg F: Physiologic considerations underlying rhythmometry. In Ajuriaguerra JD (ed): *Cycles biologiques et psychiatrie*, Masson, Paris, 1968, pp. 73–126.

12. Pflug B, Engelmann W, Gaertner HJ: Circadian course of body temperature and the excretion of MHPG and VMA in a patient with bipolar depression. *J. Neural. Transm.* 53:213–215, 1982.

13. Kupfer DJ: REM latency: A psychobiologic marker for primary depressive disease. *Biol. Psychiatr.* 11:159–174, 1977.

14. Vogel GW, Vogel F, McAbee RS, Thurmond AJ: Improvement of depression

by REM sleep deprivation: New findings and a theory. *Arch. Gen. Psychiatr.* 37:247–253, 1980.

15. Wehr TA, Muscettola G, Goodwin FK: Urinary 3-methoxy-4-hydroxyphenyl-glycol circadian rhythm: Early timing (phase advance) in manic-depressives compared with normal subjects. *Arch. Gen. Psychiatr.* 37:257–263, 1980.

16. Wehr TA, Wirz-Justice A, Duncan W, Gillin JC: Phase advance of the sleep-wake-cycle as antidepressant. *Science* 206:710–713, 1979.

17

Depression and the Immune System

Elinor M. Levy and Richard Krueger

EDITOR'S NOTE

The powerful interactions between mind and body have recently been highlighted by investigations into the connection between stress and the immune system. Psychological stress—or the inability to cope successfully with stress—has been clearly linked to an increase in the incidence or severity of physical disease. The immune system, one of the body's major defenses against toxic and pathogenic substances, including malignant cell bodies, is sensitive to neuroendocrine hormones and neurotransmitters and is probably an important mediator of such an influence.

In this chapter, the author presents a brief sketch of how the immune system operates, describes several methods used to assess immune function, and offers experimental evidence for the effects of glucocorticosteroids, catecholamines, endorphins, and enkephalins on immune function.

Several studies suggest diminished immune function in states of depression. For example, depressed men who had recently experienced a death or serious illness in the family showed an impairment in their ability to respond to mitogens and allogenic cells. In another study depressed patients showed a reduced response to mitogens, and in a third a significant decrease in the proportion of T4 and T11 cells. Whether these changes are directly related to depression, to the hormonal changes and neurotransmitter changes reported to occur in depressed individuals, or to other behavioral features, such as heavy drinking, smoking, sleeplessness, dietary changes, or medications, remains unclear.

If, however, periods of depression are associated with reduced immune competence, then these must be viewed as episodes during which the depressed person may be especially at risk for other physical illnesses. If the depression is not recognized and managed properly, illness, even death, may ensue, as suggested by the increased morbidity and death rates among men during the first year after being widowed or following retirement.

Interactions Between the Brain and the Immune System

There is a common, popular belief that the mind can determine susceptibility to disease. The evidence which exists from clinical studies and animal models to support this concept has recently been reviewed.[1,2] The data indicating a role for the psyche in influencing both the severity and incidence of infectious disease, particularly viral infections, are convincing. There are also intriguing data suggesting associations between the mind and autoimmune diseases, including allergies and cancer. In most of these studies, psychological factors, such as stress or an inability to cope with stress, have been linked to an increase in the incidence or severity of illness. Other studies, however, indicate that stress can be protective under certain circumstances.

In recent years, attention has focused on changes in the immune system as a mechanism by which psychological factors can influence disease processes. The immune system seems a reasonable choice for transforming psychological signals into somatic ones. For one thing, in all the above mentioned diseases, the immune system plays a potentially prominent role. There also is ample evidence that the immune system is sensitive to neuroendocrine hormones and transmitters. Thus, dysregulated immune function can be expected to alter susceptibility to these diseases. Immune reactivity is modified by glucocorticosteroids, ACTH, the endorphins and enkephalins, catecholamines, and acetylcholine. This is a fact largely ignored by immunologists. An article by Marx[3] points out that it is time for immunologists to recognize that the immune system "belongs in the body." There is also a fascinating new body of evidence which shows that the immune system can influence the mind. For example, following antigenic challenge, the neuronal firing rate in the hypothalamus increases and plasma cortisol levels increase as well.[4] This increase in cortisol may be in response to an ACTH-like molecule which activated lymphocytes can produce.[5] Thus, it seems clear that the immune system and the brain can interact, and that this interaction might well influence disease processes.

While theoretically this concept has great appeal, it has been difficult to document in man. Animal models have clearly demonstrated that psychological stress can increase the growth of tumors and susceptibility to infections. Such models also show that the same stressors reduce immune function. While there are many parallels between human and murine immune systems, there are also some important differences. One of these is the different ways the two systems respond to glucocorticosteroids. Therefore, in this area, one has to extrapolate from mouse to man with caution.

In man, work in this area is hampered by natural variability between individuals, the enormous complexity of the immune system, and the formidable complexity of the neuroendocrine system. A promising new approach to this problem has been to focus on individuals with major psychiatric depression. The severity and duration of this condition allow significant differences in immune function to be correlated with alterations in neuroendocrine hormone levels. Results of research in this area are reviewed later in this chapter.

The Immune System: An Overview

The immune system acts to protect us from a large variety of pathogens and toxins. It first recognizes these elements as being foreign, and then uses one of several mechanisms at its disposal to eliminate or inactivate them. Immune responses are divided into those that involve antibody (termed humoral responses) and those that involve cell-mediated immunity. In addition to pathogens, the immune system has the capability to recognize and destroy transformed or cancerous cells. It can, with some cancers, protect against the growth and metastasis of tumor cells. However, the immune system is not fallible, as those of us with allergies or autoimmune disease can attest. The list of diseases classified as autoimmune continues to grow and includes rheumatoid arthritis, myasthenia gravis, and certain forms of diabetes and asthma. To prevent misplaced reactivity and to limit the exuberance of otherwise appropriate immune reactions, the immune system includes a variety of checks and balances. A brief overview of the components of the immune system and how they interact is given below.

The immune system is remarkably complex. Its central players are the lymphocytes which provide specificity and memory. Each lymphocyte can respond to only one or a closely related set of antigenic determinants. Having been stimulated by an appropriate antigen, some lymphocytes differentiate to become memory cells. Memory cells are more sensitive than lymphocytes and respond rapidly to subsequent encounters with antigen. Other lymphocytes differentiate into effector or regulatory cells after an encounter with antigen.

The lymphocytes are divided into B cells, T cells, and null cells. B cells produce antibody, T cells provide specific cell-mediated immunity, and null cells can provide a quick but nonspecific form of cell-mediated immunity.

B cells are, in turn, subdivided according to the type of immunoglobulin they carry on their surface, i.e., IgM, IgD, IgG, IgA, or IgE. The different antibody classes have different functional roles. IgA, for instance, is released into secretory fluids and may be particularly important in preventing respiratory infections. Antibodies, in general, coat pathogens and help inactivate them or target them for destruction by the granulocytes, complement and the reticuloendothelial system.

T cells are subdivided into functional subgroups. There are helper, indu-

TABLE 1
Cells of the Immune System

Cells	Cell Markers	Cell Products	Function
Lymphocytes			
B Cells	IgM, IgD, IgG, IgE, IgA	Antibodies	Antibodies inactivate some viruses and bacteria, and target other pathogens for destruction by other cells of the immune system
T Cells	T3, T11 T4 or Leu 2 (on helper/inducer cells) T8 or Leu 2 (on cytotoxic/suppresor cells)	Lymphokines (e.g., IL-2, interferon, B cell growth fator)	Regulates function of B cells, effector T cells, and macrophage Cytotoxic T cells kill infected host cells and neoplastic cells
NK Cells	HNK-1	Interferon	Kills certain virally infected and neoplastic cells
Macrophages	Mo1, Ia	IL-1, interferon, H_2O_2, prostaglandins	Bactericidal, tumoricidal, accessory role in immune reactions

cer, suppressor, and cytotoxic T cells. These cells are described below. To a large extent T cells can be classified according to certain surface antigens they possess. Helper and inducer cells are generally positive for the T4 antigen; suppressor and cytotoxic cells are generally positive for the T8 antigen.

Null cells are a heterogeneous collection of lymphoid cells which cannot be classified as B or T cells. They include immature T and B cells as well as natural killer cells. Natural killer cells (NK) can kill certain tumor and virally infected cells. In animal models, NK cells can be shown to be important in the early stages of certain viral infections, and in clearing certain tumor cells, particularly from the lungs.

The T cells are the cells which orchestrate the immune response. Let us consider antibody production as an example. Although B cells can recognize antigens directly, they require additional signals, provided by T helper cells, to proliferate and differentiate into memory or antibody-secreting plasma cells. The T helper cells not only stimulate B cells, but also amplify the antibody response by the induction of proliferation and differentiation of other relevant T helper cells. T inducer cells help control the reaction by activating suppressor cells that can then turn off T helper cell activity. T cells produce factors such as immune (gamma) interferon and interleukin-2 (IL-2 or T cell growth factor), called lymphokines. The lymphokines are now recognized as important immunoregulatory molecules.

In other situations other T cells can be activated to become cytotoxic cells. These cells can kill pathogens, host cells infected with viruses or other intracellular pathogens, and transformed cells. T cells can also activate other cells such as macrophages to become bactericidal or tumoricidal.

Monocytes and macrophages are important in the initial stages of an immune response when they act as accessory cells. These cells process antigen, present in a particularly antigenic form to T cells, and produce factors which stimulate B and T cells. One of these factors, interleukin 1 (IL-1), also has wide-ranging systemic effects, including the induction of fever and the modulation of sleep. At other times macrophages which have become activated can act as suppressor cells and inhibit the immune response through the release of suppressive factors such as prostaglandin E.

Thus the immune system includes both effector and regulatory cells which interact to produce humoral and/or cell-mediated responses. Contact with antigen will stimulate a network of reactions. The end result depends on which of these pathways predominate. This in turn depends on the number and type of competent cells available for interaction.

Measurements of Immunocompetence

There are a variety of tests used to try to assess general immunocompetence. One such measure is performed in vivo. It measures the delayed type hypersensitivity reaction to five to seven commonly encountered antigens. It requires antigen recognition, migration, and activation of T helper cells and macrophages.

A commonly used measure of immunocompetence is the in vitro mitogen test. Mitogens are substances, such as the plant-derived phytohemagglutinin (PHA) or concanavalin A (conA), which stimulate lymphocytes to divide. PHA and conA are called T-cell mitogens because they stimulate the majority of T cells. Mitogenesis requires T-cell-macrophage cooperation and the production of many of the same factors needed to produce effective humoral or cell-mediated immunity. One quantitates activation by the amount of radioactive thymidine cells incorporate during DNA synthesis when cultured in the presence of mitogen. Other mitogens such as pokeweed mitogen (PWM) predominantly stimulate B cells to proliferate but require T cells as helpers.

The quantitation of lymphokine production in response to a stimulus is another measure of immunocompetence. IL-2 in culture supernatants, for instance, can be measured by its ability to promote the growth of T-cell lines.

The amount of proliferation is directly related to the concentration of IL-2 (T-cell growth factor).

NK cell activity is measured as the release of an isotope, such as chromium, from labeled sensitive target cells. Most commonly the tumor-cell line arbitrarily called K562 is used as a target cell. The damaged cells release isotope into the culture supernatant, which is then counted in a gamma counter. The percentage of target cells killed is a measure of NK-cell activity.

An additional assessment of immune status can be obtained from the quantitation of the number or proportion of T4 (helper/inducer cells) and T8 cells (suppressor/cytotoxic cells). While moderate changes in the overall T4/T8 ratio may not mean that much, major changes tend to indicate a severely dysregulated immune system. In the acquired immunodeficiency syndrome (AIDS), for instance, a retrovirus infects T4 cells and leads to a gradual reduction in their number. This is felt to be the major event in the pathogenesis of AIDS, which leaves its victims unable to combat infections from opportunistic organisms. Other antigens such as T3 or T11 can be used to measure the total number of T cells present.

Interaction of the Immune System with the Neuroendocrine System

The immune system is responsive to regulation by a number of neuroendocrine hormones. The effects of the glucocorticosteroids have been studied extensively. In certain species, such as rats and mice, corticosteroids actually destroy immature T cells. This, however, is not the case in man.[6] Glucocorticosteroids, however, are generally immunosuppressive in humans when given at high doses. Both lymphocyte migration patterns and lymphocyte and macrophage function are affected. The effect of the glucocorticosteroids depends on the subset examined, the location of the population studied, and the time of addition of steroid relative to antigen. In mice, for instance, the antibody response in the spleen is suppressed at the same time the antibody response in the bone marrow is enhanced after steroid administration in vivo. This is, in part, probably due to the redistribution of competent cells. Glucocorticosteroids suppress secretion of early activation factors by lymphocytes and macrophages. However, once activated, macrophages produce a factor which protects T helper cells from the inhibitory effects of glucocorticosteroids. In certain models, dexamethasone can, in fact, enhance antibody responses because of a differential effect on suppressor cell activity, that is, by inhibiting suppressor cells, the net reaction is augmented. Thus, at moderate doses, the effects of steroids can be rather complicated.

Catecholamines can also influence both the function and distribution of

TABLE 2
The Influence of Neuroendocrine Hormones and
Transmitters on Lymphocyte Function*

Suppressors	*Enhancers*
ACTH	acetylcholine
epinephrine	arginine vasopressin
endorphins	endorphins
glucocorticosteroids	enkephalins
norepinephrine	glucocorticosteroids
serotonin	growth hormone
somatostatin	insulin
	oxytocin
	substance P

*Note: Certain modulators such as the endorphins and gluco-corticosteroids can either enhance or suppress immune function depending on their dose, time of addition, and type of function assayed.

lymphocytes. Catecholamines have been reported to suppress antibody production when added to lymphocyte cultures. In vivo their effect seems to be largely caused by their ability to change the distribution of lymphocytes. Crary et al.[7] reported that the injection of epinephrine into volunteers caused a rapid increase in the total number of lymphocytes in the peripheral blood. There was a relative decrease in the proportion of T4 cells, and a relative increase in the proportion of NK cells. Cells drawn at this time for in vitro testing had a reduced ability to proliferate in response to the T-cell mitogen PHA. However, adding epinephrine to mitogen cultures in vitro or preincubating cells with the catecholamine prior to mitogenic stimulation had no effect. This suggests that the in vivo effect of epinephrine was due to the change in the relative proportion of the lymphocyte subsets in the circulation, rather than to a direct effect of epinephrine on the lymphocytes. The alterations caused by a bolus of epinephrine in vivo were maximal at 30 minutes and had returned to normal by two hours.

Neuropeptides have recently also been shown to have immunomodulatory properties. Both the endorphins and enkephalins can influence immune function; however, the current literature is somewhat contradictory. Beta-endorphin is reported to stimulate or suppress mitogenesis. Alpha-endorphin and the enkephalins reportedly suppress in vitro antibody synthesis. NK-cell activity is also modulated by beta-endorphin. In vitro beta-endorphin can stimulate NK-cell activity, but the effect is not mediated via an opiate receptor. In contrast, in in vivo experiments, electrical shocks given in a particular protocol resulted in reduced NK-cell activity. The effect could be blocked by naloxone, suggesting the effect was mediated by endogenous opiates binding to opiate receptors. (Both lymphocytes and macrophages have opiate receptors.) Additional work also suggests that endogenous opiates may influence immune status in vivo. Injection of leucine enkephalin or methonine enkephalin was shown to cause an increase in thymic and a decrease in splenic weight in mice.

Alterations in the Levels of Neuroendocrine Hormones in Depression

Some depressed patients have abnormally high levels of cortisol in their circulation. The abnormality of resistance to suppression of cortisol production in depressed patients is well known. In one study, 69% of the depressed patients were resistant to the suppressive effects of dexamethasone on cortisol production, as compared to 9% of the healthy controls. It has been suggested that this may be a result of decreased concentrations of serotonin and catecholamines in the hypothalamus in depressed patients. Lymphocytes may also become insensitive to the effects of glucocorticosteroids in depressed patients as the number of receptors/cells reportedly decreases.[8] Recently, other abnormalities in the hypothalamic-pituitary-adrenal axis have been reported in depressed patients. Patients had a reduced ACTH output in response in infused corticotropin-releasing factor (CRF) but nevertheless responded with a slightly greater than normal amount of cortisol secretion.[9] In another study by Nemeroff et al.,[10] the level of CRF-like material in cerebral spinal fluid was elevated in a group of patients with major depression (as classified in *DSM-III*), but not in groups with schizophrenia or senile dementia (as classified in *DSM-III*).

Immune Status in Depressed Patients

There have been several studies of immune status in depressed patients. All agree that immune measures are in some way impaired. Linn[11] reported that men who had a high score on the depression factor of the Hopkins Symptom Checklist were impaired in their ability to respond to mitogens and allogeneic cells. The subjects were men with a recent death or severe illness in the family.

Kronfol et al.[12] studied 26 patients hospitalized for depression who were drug-free for at least two weeks prior to study. Their mean score was 16.3 on the 17-item Hamilton Depression Rating Scale. The group had a reduced proliferative response to both the T-cell mitogens, conA and PHA, as well as to the T-dependent B-cell mitogen PWM. There was a nonsignificant trend for more depressed patients to have lower mitogen responses than less depressed patients. The authors stated that there was no difference in the responses of those patients who had been taking medications prior to the two-week drug-free period preceding the study, and those who had not, i.e., if there was an effect due to medication, two weeks without drugs appeared to be sufficient to eliminate that effect.

Schleifer et al.,[13] in a later study of 18 hospitalized depressed patients, also noted a reduced response to the mitogens conA, PHA, and PWM, as compared to age) and sex-matched controls. These patients were also drug-free for at least two weeks prior to the study. Their mean Hamilton Depression Score was 28. The study also noted a decrease in the absolute numbers of peripheral blood B and T cells, although there did not appear to be a change in the relative proportion of B and T cells. In this study, rosetting techniques were used to enumerate B and T cells. Cortisol levels were significantly elevated in the depressed patients (14.05 μg/dL compared to 8.62 μg/dL for controls). The authors noted that the changes observed appeared to be independent of the length of hospitalization prior to assessment of immune status, suggesting that the acute stress of hospitalization was not responsible for their results. It is known that hospitalized patients in general tend to have elevated cortisol levels.

A follow-up study by Schleifer et al.[14] of ambulatory patients with major depressive disorder did not find any difference between the mitogen responses of patients and healthy controls. The 15 patients in this follow-up study had a mean Hamilton Depression score of 18.9. Control groups of hospitalized schizophrenics and surgical patients also had mitogen responses similar to the healthy control group. This again suggests that hospitalization alone seems unlikely to explain the results of the first study. The authors suggest that the failure to detect immunosuppression in the ambulatory group might be due to their depression being less severe.

Krueger et al.,[15] in a study of six patients hospitalized for depression, examined changes in the lymphocyte subset distributions. The mean Hamilton Depression Score was 26.8. There was a significant decrease in the proportion of T4 (helper/inducer) and T11 (total T cells) as judged by immunofluorescence with monoclonal antibodies. The proportion of B cells, T8 cells (suppressor/cytotoxic), and NK cells was unchanged. These findings could help explain the decreased mitogen responses noted in the other studies, since a decreased proportion of T4 cells would be expected to reduce the mitogen response. However, in a larger study of 28 non-medicated patients hospitalized for depressive illness, there was no difference between patient and control T4 or T8 cell distributions (unpublished observation). Similarly, Kronfol et al.[16] found no significant difference between the number of T4 or T8 cells in depressed patient and control groups. The most likely explanation for the different results in the initial pilot and these later two studies is the medication status of the patients.

Although we were unable to confirm a difference in T4 cell distributions, we did note a substantial, statistically significant decrease in NK activity in the non-medicated depressed patient population.[17] NK activity seems particularly sensitive to certain forms of stress in a number of human and animal studies.

Bartrop[18] and Schleifer[19] also note decreased mitogen responsiveness in their studies of bereaved spouses. In these studies no changes in the levels of cortisol, prolactin, growth hormone or thyroid hormone were found. NK activity was also reported to be lower in bereaved spouses.[20]

Possible Confounding Factors Associated with Depression

Although depression offers an opportunity to study the relationship between psychological status and the immune response, several cautions should be noted. The immune response may be affected by a number of behavioral changes which may be associated with depression. These include heavy drinking, heavy smoking, sleeplessness, dietary changes, and medications.

Drinking can cause decreased NK-cell activity in alcoholics, but these changes are associated with liver damage and nutritional deficiencies.[21] Abnormalities in humoral immunity have also been reported. Acute high levels of blood alcohol would be expected to have a temporary inhibitory effect on immune function in vivo. In studies of the effect of alcohol in immune function in vitro, levels of 0.5–2.0% alcohol depressed NK-cell and cytotoxic function. The effect depended on the continued presence of alcohol, in that cells that were pre-incubated with alcohol and then washed regained normal function.

TABLE 3
Immune Changes in Depressed Patients

Study	Changes
B. Linn[11]	Decreased mitogenesis, decreased proliferation in response to allogenic cells
T. Kronfol et al.[12]	Decreased mitogenesis
S. Schleifer et al.[13]	Decreased mitogenesis, decrease in T and B cell numbers
R. Krueger et al.[15]	Decrease in proportion of T4 cells

In several studies, smoking has been associated with decreased immune status. A habit of heavy smoking was associated with a modest decrease of T4/T8 ratios.[22] This was caused by both a decrease in the proportion of T4 cells and an increase in the proportion of T8 cells. Neither the total number nor the proportion of T cells changed. The T4/T8 ratio returned to normal in heavy smokers who gave up smoking for six weeks. The effects in moderate smokers were not significant. In another study, smoking more than 10 cigarettes a day was associated with decreased NK-cell activity and mitogen responses.[23] Again, there was an improvement in immune function in smokers who were tested after they stopped smoking. The effects reported have been less pronounced than those observed in depression. Thus, it is possible that heavy smoking could contribute to the observed changes in depression. As far as we know this has yet to be examined.

Sleep deprivation can also lead to decreased mitogen responsiveness. In studies by Palmblad et al.,[24] subjects kept awake for 64 hours showed decreased mitogen responsiveness. Their mitogen response returned to normal within five days. The effect of lesser amounts of sleeplessness are not known.

Changes in dietary habits might also influence the immune response, but again effects are difficult to demonstrate except in extreme situations. It is known that protein-calorie malnutrition causes decreases in mitogenesis and decreases the T4/T8 ratio in children. These changes are accompanied by elevated serum cortisol levels. Deficiencies in single elements such as zinc and vitamins A and E can also depress immune function, as can high levels of dietary fats, particularly the polyunsaturated fatty acids.

Medications likely to be used to treat depression and their influence on the immune system are not well studied. Antidepressants which affect catecholamine turnover may very well have some effect on immune function. However, the studies of Kronfol[12] and Schleifer[13] in drug-free patients suggest that, although the use of drugs should be taken into account, there are significant effects in depressed patients which are independent of medication.

Conclusion

Modern technology has, over the past decade, afforded us a heretofore unavailable capacity to study the immune system. Radioimmune assays have also greatly enhanced the ability to measure neuroendocrine mediators. A new and exciting area of research is the exploration of the relationship between psychological, behavioral, and psychobiological factors with the immune system. One way of exploring the relationship is to assess immune function in depressed patients. While such studies are few in number and must take into account the extraordinary number of factors which have been demonstrated to affect immune function, they suggest that depression is associated with immune suppression. Continued study of this association should elucidate one pathway for the transformation of psychological factors into increased morbidity.

References

1. Jemmott J, Locke S: Psychosocial factors, immunological mediation, and human susceptibility to infectious disease: How much do we know? *Psychol. Bull.* 95:78–95, 1984.

2. Solomon G, Amkraut A: Psychoneuroendocrinological effects on the immune response. *Annu. Rev. Microbiol.* 35:155–184, 1981.

3. Marx J: The immune system "belongs in the body." *Science* 227:1190–1192, 1985.

4. Besedovsky H et al.: The immune response evokes changes in brain noradrenergic neurons. *Science* 221:564–565, 1983.

5. Smith E, Blalock J: Human lymphocyte production of corticotropin and endorphin-like substances: Association with leukocyte interferon. *Proc. Natl. Acad. Sci.* 78:7530–7534, 1981.

6. Cupps T, Fauci A: Corticosteroid-mediated immunoregulation in man. *Immunol. Rev.* 65:133–150, 1982.

7. Crary B et al.: Epinephrine-induced changes in the distribution of lymphocyte subsets in peripheral blood of humans. *J. Immunol.* 131:1178–1181, 1983.

8. Whalley L, Borthwick N, Copolov D, Dick H, Christie J, Fink G: Glucocorticoid receptors and depression. *Br. Med. J.* 292:859–861, 1986.

9. Holsboer F et al.: Blunted corticotropin and normal cortisol response to human corticotropin-releasing factor in depression. *N. Engl. J. Med.* 311:1127, 1984.

10. Nemeroff C et al.: Elevated concentrations of CSF corticotropin-releasing factor-like immunoreactivity in depressed patients. *Science* 226:1342–1344, 1984.

11. Linn B: American Psychosomatic Meeting, 1982.

12. Kronfol T et al.: Impaired lymphocyte function in depressive illness. *Life Sci.* 33:241–247, 1983.

13. Schleifer S et al.: Lymphocyte function in major depressive disorder. *Arch. Gen. Psychiatry* 41:484–486, 1984.

14. Schleifer S, Keller S, Siris S, Davis K, Stein M: Depression and immunity. Lymphocyte function in ambulatory depression, hospitalized schizophrenic, and herniorrhaphy patients. *Arch. Gen. Psychiatry* 42:129–133, 1985.

15. Krueger R et al.: Lymphocyte subsets in patients with major depression: Preliminary findings. *Advances* 1:5–9, 1984.

16. Kronfol Z, House J: Depression, cortisol, and immune function. *Lancet* I:1026–1027, 1984.

17. Levy E, Black P: Depression and the immune system. *Clin. Immunol. News.*, 1988.

18. Bartrop RW et al.: Depressed lymphocyte function after bereavement. *Lancet* I:834–836, 1977.

19. Schleifer S et al.: Suppression of lymphocyte stimulation following bereavement. *JAMA* 250:374–377, 1983.

20. Irwin M, Daniels M, Bloom E, Weiner H: Life events, depression, and natural killer activity. *Psychopharm. Bull.* 22:1093–1096, 1986.

21. Charpentier B et al.: Deficient natural killer cell activity in alcoholic cirrhosis. *Clin. Exp. Immunol.* 58:107–115, 1984.

22. Miller L et al.: Reversible alterations in immunoregulatory T cells in smoking. *Chest* 5:526–529, 1982.

23. Hersey P, Prendergast D, Edwards A: Effects of cigarette smoking on the immune system. *Med. J. Aust.* 2:425–429, 1983.

24. Palmblad J et al.: Lymphocyte and granulocyte reactions during sleep deprivation. *Psychosom. Med.* 41:273–277, 1979.

Additional Reading

Ader R: *Psychoneuroimmunology*, Academic Press, New York, 1984.

18

Circadian Rhythms in Human Performance

Timothy H. Monk

EDITOR'S NOTE

Depressive disorders may well be related to malfunctions in the pathways regulating circadian rhythms in man. Current research argues for internal endogenous time-keeping mechanisms that govern the fluctuations seen in a variety of biological parameters during each 24-hour cycle. Two of the more obvious rhythms are body temperature and sleep-waking patterns.

Mental performance seems to follow a diurnal rhythm. The morning time appears to be the best time for strictly mental work, particularly that involving immediate memory. By contrast, the afternoon period seems better for tasks requiring longer term recall.

Some patients with affective disorder reveal significant changes in the subjective activation rhythm — the end of the waking day becomes the period of greatest activation, while the beginning is a time of low activation and poor affect.

The relationships between time of day and more complex mental activities have also been studied, raising interesting speculation on whether the time of day in which psychotherapy is carried out contributes to or impedes the learning process required for insight and recovery.

The Nature of Circadian Rhythms

There is now a wealth of evidence[1] that there are regular, nontrivial fluctuations in almost every physiological measure over the 24-hour period. Because these fluctuations take the form of a rhythm with a period of about a day, the term "circadian rhythms" has been coined to describe them.[2]

One of the most easily measured physiological circadian rhythms is, of course, that in body temperature. Body temperature in the healthy human being varies rhythmically, with a difference of about 0.7 degree centigrade between peak and trough values. The minimum value occurs in the early hours of the morning, with a pronounced rise over the early waking hours and a gentler rise over the remainder of the day, reaching a peak in the early evening (see Figure 1).

The timing of trough (during sleep) and peak (during wakefulness) might suggest that circadian rhythms are merely simple reactions to changes in the person's gross behavior or immediate environment. Such factors are referred to as exogenous factors, and one might hypothesize that circadian rhythms are totally exogenous, being simply the product of processes having a low value during times of sleep and inactivity and high values during wakefulness and exertion. A way to test this is to place the subject in a constant time-free environment, keep him awake, and regulate his activities and diet. If the circadian rhythms persist, one must attribute them to some internal endogenous timekeeper, rather than to the exogenous factors, which in this case have been rigidly controlled. An excellent example of such a study is provided by Froberg et al.[3] who investigated a variety of physiological and psychological circadian rhythms in 29 subjects who experienced 72 hours of sleep deprivation. The gross activity and feeding behavior of these subjects were also kept completely uniform. A typical result is shown in Figure 2, which

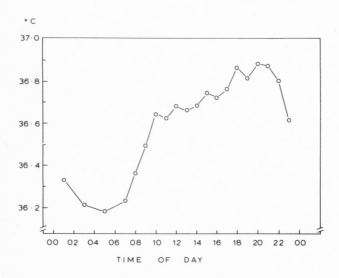

Figure 1.　Oral temperature rhythm collected from a group of 70 young men on a normal day-oriented routine. (After Colquhoun.[16])

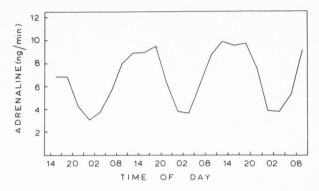

Figure 2.   The average epinephrine excretion rate of 29 subjects experiencing 72 hours of sleep deprivation. (After Froberg et al.[3])

plots the mean level of epinephrine secretion as a function of time. The clear evidence of a circadian rhythm in this variable demonstrates the existence of an endogenous timekeeper.

Longer-term temporal isolation experiments, involving a choice by the subject of sleeping and waking times, give us further insights into the nature of the endogenous circadian system. These experiments are described as "free-running" experiments, and have been carried out mainly by Aschoff and his colleagues in West Germany[4] and by Elliot Weitzman's group in New York.[5] (Both groups are continuing this research, despite Aschoff's retirement and Weitzman's tragic death.) The most striking finding is that under such isolation conditions, the circadian system appears to run "slow," having a period that is usually about 30 to 60 minutes longer than the 24 hours of the world outside. This means that after three or four weeks in temporal isolation, the subject works his way all around the clock, thus effectively "losing" a day. Individual differences occur in the exact value that this "free-running period" (referred to as tau) takes, and it has been hypothesized that certain psychiatric disorders, particularly affective states, may be associated with a shortened tau.[6] This has yet to be verified definitively, however.[7]

A second finding to emerge from these studies is that the temperature rhythm and the sleep/wake cycle can sometimes run at different periods. This split in the two rhythms has suggested a two-oscillator model of the circadian system, with a deep endogenous oscillator indicated by the body temperature rhythm and a more labile one primarily responsible for the cycle of sleep and wakefulness.[8,9]

Not surprisingly, the systematic and wide-ranging differences in physiological makeup that result from the circadian system are reflected in corresponding changes in mood and performance efficiency. These rhythms are not merely the step-function that would result from poor performance at night being compared with better performance during the day, nor are they of trivial magnitude or always peculiar to the individual. They are robust fluctuations of significant magnitude and (for about 80% of the population) predictable in form, given knowledge of the task being tested.[10] Even over the normal waking day, fluctuations in performance efficiency can equal those induced by ingesting the "legal limit" of alcohol or restricting the previous night's sleep to three hours.

Special Research Strategies in Assessing the Influence of Circadian Rhythms on Performance

Before considering the effects of time of day on performance, it is worth considering the methodological and statistical techniques that have been used to study circadian performance rhythms, since they are often very different from those conventionally used by the physiologist. First, performance differs from most physiological measures in that there is nearly always a marked practice effect. This means that subjects will almost invariably tend to perform better on a given trial than they did on the trials preceding it. Unfortunately, such practice effects are extremely hard to eradicate, even when dozens—or hundreds—of trials are given and discarded before the actual experiment. Failure to realize this can result in totally spurious conclusions about the timing of peak performance, since performance will be worse in the morning and better in the evening, simply because the former precedes the latter in the sequence of trials. A technique used to circumvent this problem has been either to have a separate group of unpracticed subjects at each time of day or to have different groups of subjects experiencing the time-of-day conditions in different orders. (Thus, for one group, for example, the 1100 session may be their first, while for another it is their fifth.) By combining groups, one can "balance out" any practice effects and obtain an accurate circadian performance rhythm for the sample as a whole, although no subject in the sample will actually have shown exactly that patterns of results.

Second, performance measurement is almost always intrusive in that subjects are required to interrupt their ongoing activity for performance to be measured. This means (1) that sampling can seldom be more frequent than once every two or three hours at best, and (2) that sampling has to be either reduced or suspended during sleep hours, since otherwise either sleep deprivation effects or "sudden waking" effects might outweigh any truly circadian ones. In practice, this means that performance measurement is very often restricted to comparatively few (e.g., six or under) times during the "normal waking" day.

Third, performance measurement can be notoriously inaccurate, depending on such chance factors as differences in the motivation of the subject, his perception of the task, and whether he is distracted by some nontask event. This means that one cannot, for example, take a single performance reading and feel that one has meaningfully measured performance. The only way in which circadian performance rhythms can be accurately measured is by using a design that employs sufficient replications for such inaccuracies to be evened out. Thus, each trial should contain a large number of measured events (e.g., reactions) and each time of day should be associated with a large number of trials, coming from different subjects, from different days, or, preferably, from both.

An example of the care needed to circumvent all these problems — and several more — is provided by an early study of scholastic performance carried out by Laird.[11] Laird used 112 subjects divided into seven squads, matched for intelligence. Six weeks' experimentation was necessary, with each squad attending at six times of the day, in a design that enabled both time of day and day of week to be studied independently of each other and uncontaminated by either practice effects of the actual material given. At each session a battery of nine different tasks was given, with tasks often being represented by several different instances (e.g., about 50 computations for the "simple additions" task). To avoid contamination due to personal prejudices, the subjects were misled into believing that the experiment was a study of temperature changes. The study was successful in demonstrating reliable day-of-week and time-of-day trends in various cognitive tasks, including a time-of-day effect in immediate memory, which was replicated by Folkard and Monk[12] half a century later.

It is, perhaps, rather chastening to realize that, even in this present age of electronic data analysis and on-line experiment control, the care and elegance of Laird's study have seldom been approached, let alone surpassed. All too often, performance measures, sometimes of the most trivial sort, have simply been "lumped in" as part of a battery of otherwise physiological tests, without their special needs and controls being taken into account.

Early Studies of Circadian Performance Rhythms

Interestingly, studies of circadian performance rhythms predate the study of circadian physiological rhythms in man — and, indeed, the coinage of the term "circadian" — by more than half a century. Thus, in the latter part of the 19th century, Ebbinghaus was aware of time-of-day differences in performance and controlled for them in his pioneering work on memory. Much of the early work was concerned with the applied problem of determining the optimal time of day for the teaching of academic subjects. Although some of the research was poor, much of it was very good (e.g., the study by Laird[11] mentioned above). Because of the educational nature of the research, the tasks given were usually heavily cognitive ones, such as mental arithmetic and memory for prose. Although the results were far from uniform, the general trend was toward a morning superiority. Thus, Gates[13] concluded that "in general, the forenoon is the best time for strictly mental work . . . while the afternoon may best be taken up with school subjects in which motor factors are predominant." The mechanism for these effects was held to be a buildup in "mental fatigue" over the day, thus (in our modern parlance) tying the performance rhythm to the sleep/wake oscillator. As we shall see below, this is in direct contrast to later approaches to the problem, which were concerned more with the relationship between performance and temperature.

The Work of Kleitman and Colquhoun

In contrast to the earlier work, studies carried out in Chicago in the 1930s by Kleitman and reported in his book *Sleep and Wakefulness*,[14] were concerned mainly with simple repetitive tasks, such as card dealing, which had a comparatively small cognitive load. Perhaps because of the tasks chosen, there was strong evidence for a parallelism between the circadian rhythms of body temperature and performance speed. Kleitman felt that there was a causal relationship between the two, even going as far as to assert that one could simply infer the performance rhythm from oral temperatures, thus avoiding the use of "time-consuming performance tests which, in themselves, interfere with, or disrupt, the scheduled activities of the persons studied."[15]

When, in the 1960s, Colquhoun and his coworkers at Cambridge addressed the problem of circadian performance rhythms, the emphasis was still very much on simple repetitive tasks and on a parallelism between temperature and performance rhythms. However, the notion of a causal relationship between the two was carefully avoided, a mechanism involving a rhythm in basal arousal (or the inverse of sleepiness) being invoked instead as a mediating factor.[16]

This arousal rhythm was never specified in any fine detail, but it was held to parallel the temperature rhythm and to mediate changes in performance level through an "inverted U" relationship, whereby rises in arousal level are associated with improvements in performance up to a certain arousal level, after which performance starts to decline. (A good example of superoptimal arousal is the difficulty in unlocking one's car door when a downpour of rain has made speed imperative.) From outside the circadian rhythms area, the Yerkes-Dodson law postulated such a relationship, with the optimal arousal level of a task dependent on its complexity, the more complex tasks having a lower optimal arousal level.

The mechanism of the inverted U was needed because of a finding the Cambridge group frankly regarded as rather anomalous — namely, the decline in performance over much of the waking day that they had observed in the memory task of digit span.[17] By the invoking of the arousal model, this apparent anomaly could be explained by the postulation that digit span had a low optimal arousal, with the time-of-day variation thus occurring on the falling arm of the inverted U. A further advantage was that time of day could then be regarded as just another arousing agent, such as white noise or knowledge of results. A series of experiments involving the combination of these agents could then be carried out, and the various interactions explored in detail.[18] These experiments produced results that were in agreement with the model, but one of the problems of the inverted U concept is one of tautology, so the positive results are perhaps not entirely surprising.

Thus, through the 1960s and early 1970s, the notion was of a single performance rhythm usually parallel to the temperature rhythm, with the exception of memory tasks such as digit span, whose rhythms were explained in terms of superoptimal arousal. As can be seen in Figure 3, for

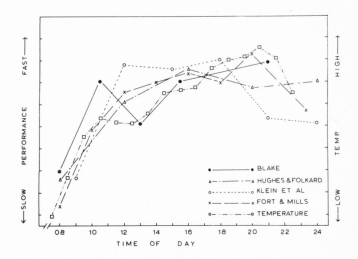

Figure 3.   The time-of-day function for a series of studies involving serial search tasks, plotted together with the time-of-day function in temperature. (After Monk.[19])

some tasks, at least, the parallelism with temperature is quite striking. This notion persisted until the mid-70s when Folkard[20] (who, like the present author at that time, was a member of Colquhoun's group) studied the time-of-day effect in two complex cognitive tasks — namely, logical syllogisms and the Baddeley reasoning test.[21] These tasks represented a dramatic departure in that they involved the subject in fairly complex thought processes, and could not simply be churned through in a routine fashion. The results are shown in Figure 4, which reveals time-of-day curves having a midday peak, unlike either the digit span or simple repetitive-task time-of-day functions. This result heralded a new approach to the study of circadian performance rhythms, with more emphasis on the differences between circadian performance rhythms than on their similarities, and greater theoretical richness in considering the mechanisms by which circadian performance rhythms might occur.

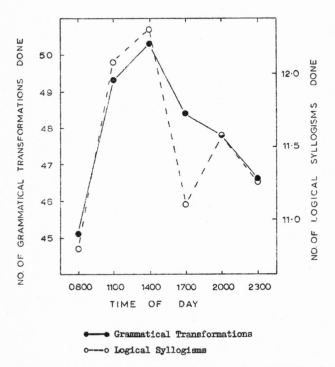

Figure 4.   The time-of-day function for performance in a logical syllogisms (0- - -0) and grammatical transformation (•_____•) tasks. (After Folkard.[20])

Contemporary Research

This section will cover the research carried out from the mid-1970s to mid-1980s. It can be divided into parts concerned with "pure" memory tasks, "working" memory tasks, simple repetitive tasks, subjective activation, and the underlying oscillatory mechanisms.

Pure memory tasks: Even from the early studies, it was clear that the time-of-day function for memory was very different from that for other tasks. Later research, by Baddeley et al.[22] and Hockey et al.,[23] confirmed that for relatively "pure" tasks of immediate memory (i.e., memory tested within a few minutes of presentation), performance was better in the morning than in the afternoon or evening. This result was explained by the arousal model — by the theory that immediate memory was interfered with by high arousal, and that the time-of-day range in arousal coincided with the falling arm of the inverted U. This agreed with evidence from outside the time of day area that arousing manipulations such as anxiety could produce decrements in immediate memory performance.[24] In contrast, a more robust finding from these arousal manipulation studies was that high arousal was actually beneficial to long-term memory for the material. Thus, if one waited a few days rather than a few minutes before testing the memory, the high-arousal presentation condition resulted in superior performance.

These experiments suggested that the time-of-day function for long-term memory might be very different, in terms of time-of-day presentation effects, from that of immediate memory. Thus, the time of day giving an arousal level that was optimal for immediate memory might be associated with a suboptimal arousal level for long-term memory. That prediction was tested by Folkard et al.,[25] who presented a story to groups of schoolchildren at either morning (0900) or afternoon (1500) sessions. Memory for the material was tested either immediately after presentation or after one week's delay. The predictions of the model were perfectly validated. The morning presentation group performed better than the afternoon group on the immediate test but worse than them on the delayed test. (The time of testing for the memory appeared to have no effect.) Interestingly, the magnitudes of the time-of-day effects for immediate and delayed tests were 64% and 44%, respectively, of the difference in performance due to the week's delay. Clearly, even when one is considering differences between 0900 and 1500, time-of-day effects are important and striking. In practical terms, of course, the study has ramifications for the scheduling of school timetables, which had been the focus of the early studies. Thus, for good long-term retention, afternoon teaching might be more efficient.

The schoolchildren study was later validated at more extreme times of day using night nurses, comparing memory for a training film presented at either 0400 or 2030. Again, the conclusions of the arousal model were validated, with a crossover between immediate and delayed memory occurring,[26] and time of recall again proving to be irrelevant. This has ramifications for those who "burn the midnight oil" in study. In the early hours of the morning, when arousal is low, one's good immediate memory might hoodwink one into thinking that the material has been successfully remembered, whereas long-term retention of the material might actually be rather poor.

A time-of-day function for immediately memory was determined by Folkard and Monk.[12] As can be seen in Figure 5 (taken from their article), the observed decline over the waking day coincided very well with that found by Laird[11] more than half a century earlier, and was markedly different from the rise over the day observed in body temperature.

Further detail regarding the mechanisms by which memory performance changed over the day was discovered by Folkard and collaborators in a series of experiments.[27] Essentially, it revealed that subvocal rehearsal is an important mediating factor that is more in evidence in the morning than in the evening, when more semantic based rehearsal strategies tend to predominate. Thus, such manipulations as articulatory suppression, semantic and syntactic confusability, and presentation modality and rate all serve to dramatically affect the observed time-of-day function.

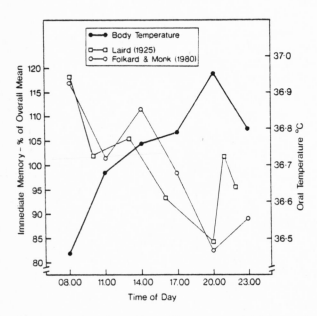

Figure 5.   The time-of-day effect in immediate memory for information presented in prose. (After Folkard and Monk.[12])

Working memory tasks: As is described above, it was the investigation of time-of-day effects in working memory tasks such as verbal reasoning that brought about an "opening up" of research in the circadian performance rhythm area.[20] The dramatic changes in the relationship between temperature and performance rhythms that can be wrought by simply increasing the memory load of the task are illustrated in Figure 6. The good parallelism between temperature and performance rhythms (top panel) is seen to break down (middle panel) and eventually become inverted (bottom panel) as the memory load of the task is increased. Thus, even within the same basic task — in this case, a serial search task — increasing the memory load can totally alter the associated time-of-day function.[28]

In the later study,[29] it was shown that the memory load of a task affects not only the phase of the circadian performance rhythm but also its rate of phase adjustment to a change in routine (e.g., from nightwork). This difference in phase adjustment rate is difficult to account for in terms of the standard arousal model, and will be returned to when the multi-oscillatory nature of circadian performance rhythms is discussed.

Simple repetitive tasks: Through to the late 1970s, the study of circadian performance rhythms in simple repetitive tasks having little or no cognitive or memory component tended to be neglected because of the prevailing belief in a consistent parallelism with temperature. However, when a collection of time-of-day functions for simple repetitive tasks was made,[30] the expected uniformity (and parallelism with temperature) was far from evident. Rather, it appeared that, like memory tasks, simple repetitive tasks have time-of-day functions that are mediated by changes in strategy, rather than by simple changes in the information-processing capacity of the brain. Using a computer analogy, we can say that the changes in performance observed over the day appear to result from a change in the number of program steps used to complete the task, rather than from a change in the rate at which program steps can be executed.

Subjective activation: From the tenets of the arousal theory, one might assume that if one asked a subject how he felt over the day, he would produce a time-of-day function in subjective activation (or the inverse or sleepiness) that was broadly parallel to the temperature rhythm. However, a recent survey of the literature by Folkard[31] and a set of experiments by Monk et al.[36] indicate that this is not the case. Rather, it would appear that the peak in activation occurs toward the end of the morning, about seven hours before the peak in temperature (see Figure 7). Although there is a difference in peak times, when subjects are kept awake through the night the troughs of the two rhythms coincide (at about 0600).[33] Thus, it would appear that subjective alertness is at least partly under the same oscillatory control as the

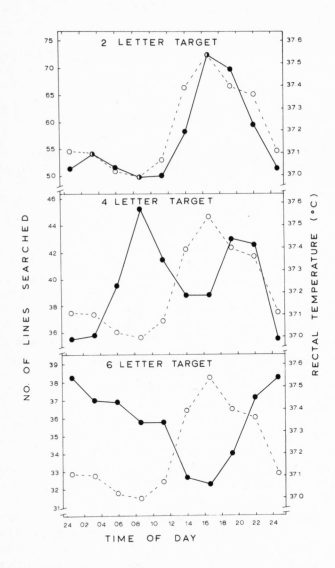

Figure 6.   The time-of-day function for low- (two-letter), medium- (four-letter), and high- (six-letter) memory load versions of a serial search task (•——•), plotted together with rectal temperature rhythm (0- - -0). (After Folkard and Monk.[28])

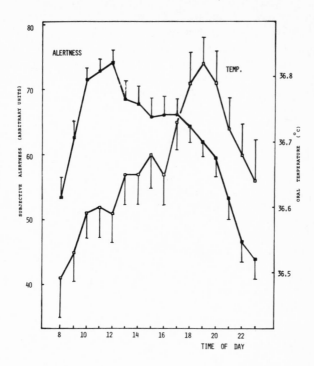

Figure 7. The time-of-day functions for subjective alertness and oral temperature collected from 38 normal subjects over an eight-day period. Each bar represents one standard error. (After Monk et al.[36])

temperature rhythm, but that there are other factors involved too. Recent research in our laboratory has indicated that the subjective activation rhythm is under the control of both the oscillator controlling the temperature rhythm and the oscillator responsible for the cycle of sleep and wakefulness. However, it is not simply a function of body temperature, nor is it simply a learned response to bed timings.

A major interest from a psychiatric point of view is the change in the subjective activation rhythm that occurs in some patients with affective disorders. For many such patients, the end of the waking day is the period of greatest activation, with the beginning of the waking day being a time of low activation and poor affect.[34] A greater understanding of the mechanisms underlying the circadian rhythmicity in activation in both healthy normals and patients with affective disorders is clearly needed if the circadian aspects of psychiatric illness are to be properly understood.

Underlying oscillatory mechanisms: Recent research in circadian performance rhythms has moved inevitably toward the conclusion that there is not one performance rhythm, but many. These different performance rhythms have different peaks and rates of phase adjustment, with memory load (among other aspects) being an important determining factor. The hypothesis naturally arises that the different performance rhythms are under different oscillatory control, much as the physiological rhythms are. This hypothesis has very recently been confirmed by studies in both West Germany[35] and the United States,[32] using experiments in which unusual schedules are enforced in order to split apart the temperature rhythm from the sleep/wake cycle. Thus, it would appear that, depending on the task given, both temperature and sleep/wake cycle oscillators can be active in controlling circadian performance rhythms. This conclusion brings one around full circle, back to the conclusions regarding "mental fatigue" put forward at the beginning of the century.

Conclusions

There is not one single performance rhythm, but many. Different tasks are associated with different time-of-day functions, adjusting at different rates to a change in schedule, and under different oscillatory control. The cognitive complexity or working memory load of a task appears to be an important index of its circadian behavior, although even within the area of memory, there are dramatic differences between short- and long-term retention. The mechanisms underlying these differences in both memory and nonmemory tasks appear to be based primarily upon changes in strategy rather than changes in capacity. As such, they indicate the importance of the affective state and mental stability of the individual in governing his or her rhythmicity in performance efficiency. That relationship, together with the relationships already known to exist between circadian rhythms and psychiatric disorders, makes the future decade of research into circadian performance rhythms a potentially exciting one.

References

1. Conroy RTWL, Mills JN: *Human Circadian Rhythms*, Churchill, London, 1970.
2. Halberg F: Chronobiology. *Annu. Rev. Physiol.* 31:675–725, 1969.
3. Froberg JE, Karlsson CG, Levi L, Lidberg L: Circadian rhythms of catechola-

mine excretion, shooting range performance and self-ratings of fatigue during sleep deprivation. *Biol. Psychol.* 2:175–188, 1975.

4. Wever R: *The Circadian System of Man: Results of Experiments Under Temporal Isolation*, Springer-Verlag, New York, 1979.

5. Weitzman ED, Czeisler CA, Zimmerman JC, Ronda JM, Krauer RS: Chronobiological disorders: Analytic and therapeutic techniques. In Guilleminault C (ed): *Disorders of Sleep and Waking: Indications and Techniques*, Addison-Wesley, Reading, MA, 1982, pp. 297–329.

6. Wehr TA, Wirz-Justice A: Circadian rhythm mechanisms in affective illness and in anti-depressant drug action. *Pharmacopsychiatria* 15:31–39, 1982.

7. Beersma DGM, Hoofdakker RH, Berkestijn HWBM: Circadian rhythms in affective disorders: Body temperature and sleep physiology in endogenous depressives. In Mendlewicz J, van Praag HM (eds): *Biological Rhythms and Behavior*, S. Karger, New York, 1983, pp. 114–127.

8. Wever R: The circadian multi-oscillator system of man. *Int. J. Chronobiol.* 3:19–55, 1975.

9. Kronauer RE, Czeisler CA, Pilato SF, Moore-Ede MC, Weitzman ED: Mathematical model of the human circadian system with two interacting oscillators. *Am. J. Physiol.* 242 (Regulatory Integrative Comp. Physiol. 11):R3–R17, 1982.

10. Folkard S, Monk TH: Circadian rhythms in the human memory. *Br. J. Psychol.* 71:295–307, 1980.

11. Laird DA: Relative performance of college students as conditioned by time of day and day of week. *J. Exp. Psychol.* 8:50–63, 1925.

12. Folkard S, Monk TH: Circadian rhythms in human memory. *Br. J. Psychol.* 71:295–307, 1980.

13. Gates AI: Variations in efficiency during the day, together with practice effects, sex differences, and correlations. *U. Calif. Publ. Psychol.* 2:1–156, 1916.

14. Kleitman N: *Sleep and Wakefulness*, University of Chicago Press, Chicago, 1939, revised 1963.

15. Kleitman N, Jackson DP: Body temperature and performance under different routines. *J. Appl. Psychol.* 3:309–328, 1950.

16. Colquhoun WP: Circadian variations in mental efficiency. In Colquhoun WP (ed): *Biological Rhythms and Human Performance*, Academic Press, London, 1971, pp. 39–107.

17. Blake MJF: Time of day effects on performance in a range of tasks. *Psychon. Sci.* 9:349–350, 1967.

18. Blake MJF: Temperament and time of day. In Colquhoun WP (ed): *Biological Rhythms and Human Performance*, Academic Press, London, 1971, pp. 109–148.

19. Monk TH: Temporal effects in visual search. In Clare JN, Sinclair MA (eds): *Search and the Human Observer*, Taylor & Francis, London, 1979, pp. 30–39.

20. Folkard S: Diurnal variation in logical reasoning. *Br. J. Psychol.* 66:1–8, 1975.

21. Baddeley AD: A three-minute reasoning test based on grammatical transformation. *Psychonomic Sci.* 10:341–342, 1968.

22. Baddeley AD, Hatter JE, Scott D, Snashall A: Memory and time of day. *Q. J. Exp. Psychol.* 22:605–609, 1970.

23. Hockey GRJ, Davies S, Gray MM: Forgetting as a function of sleep at different times of day. *Q. J. Exp. Psychol.* 24:389–393, 1972.

24. Craik FIM, Blankstein KR: Psychophysiology and human memory. In Venables PH, Christie MJ (eds): *Research in Psychophysiology*, Wiley, London, 1975.

25. Folkard S, Monk TH, Bradbury R, Rosenthall J: Time of day effects in school children's immediate and delayed recall of meaningful material. *Br. J. Psychol.* 68:45–50, 1977.

26. Monk TH, Folkard S: Concealed inefficiency of late-night study. *Nature* 273:296–297, 1978.

27. Folkard S: Circadian rhythms and human memory. In Brown FM, Graeber RC (eds): *Rhythmic Aspects of Behavior*, Erlbaum, Hillsdale, NJ, 1982, pp. 241–272.

28. Folkard S, Monk TH: Shiftwork and performance. *Hum. Factors*, 21:483–492, 1979.

29. Monk TH, Knauth P, Folkard S, Rutenfranz J: Memory-based performance measures in studies of shiftwork. *Ergonomics*, 21:819–826, 1978.

30. Monk TH, Leng VC: Time of day effects in simple repetitive tasks: Some possible mechanisms. *Acta Psychol. (Amst.)* 51:207–221, 1982.

31. Folkard S: Diurnal variation in human performance. In Hockey GRJ (ed): *Stress and Fatigue in Human Performance*, Wiley, Chichester, 1983, pp. 245–272.

32. Monk TH, Weitzman ED, Fookson JE, Moline ML, Kronauer RE, Gander PH: Task variables determine which biological clock controls circadian rhythms in human performance. *Nature* 304:543–545, 1983.

33. Monk TH, Embrey DE: A field study of circadian rhythms in actual and interpolated task performance. In Reinberg A, Vieux N, Andlauer P (eds): *Night and Shift Work: Biological and Social Aspects*, Pergamon, Oxford, 1981, pp. 473–480.

34. Wehr TA, Goodwin FK: Biological rhythms and psychiatry. In Arieti S, Brody HKH (eds): *American Handbook of Psychiatry,* Vol. 7, Basic Books, New York, 1981, pp. 46–74.

35. Folkard S, Wever RA, Wildgruber CM: Multi-oscillatory control of circadian rhythms in human performance. *Nature* 305:223–226, 1983.

36. Monk TH, Leng VC, Folkard S, Weitzman ED: Circadian rhythms in subjective alertness and core body temperature. *Chronobiologia* 10:49–55, 1983.

19

Seasonal Affective Disorder and the Use of Light as an Antidepressant

Frederick M. Jacobsen and Norman E. Rosenthal

EDITOR'S NOTE

The authors explore the concept that planned exposure to light can be used in the treatment of depressive disorders with a decidedly seasonal flavor (worse in the fall and winter, during the dark months of the year, and better—even to the point of elation—during the brighter spring and summer months). Such depressive states appear to differ from traditional depression in that they resemble atypical forms of mood disorder, with such features as oversleeping, lethargy, overeating, and weight gain.

The approach to treatment involves regular exposure for anywhere from two to six hours a day to bright light (2500 lux of full spectrum light). In receptive patients, improvement is often seen within a few days; relapse occurs if the program is terminated before natural, seasonal conditions change to provide the patient with more natural light. Some patients with a seasonal component plus the usual signs and symptoms of major depressive disorder may also respond well, but in such instances phototherapy must be considered adjunctive to psychotherapy and/or antidepressant pharmacotherapy.

Why light may work in such a curative or rehabilitative way is not known. Light does activate the metabolism of vitamin D and, in turn, calcium metabolism; shifts in calcium have been associated with depressive states. Although the authors suggest that the effect may be mediated regardless of actual visual perception of light, they do feel that retinal activity is very important; hence their findings raise the question of a possible relationship between light, depression, and the adequacy of visual perceptual systems.

Phototherapy: Historical Background

The biological effects of light are increasingly recognized as playing an important role in modern health care. Phototherapy, the use of light as a treatment, has been successfully used to treat a number of diseases, including hyperbilirubinemia, psoriasis, and rickets. Based on considerable evidence that sunlight plays a critical role in the genesis of circadian and circannual rhythms in lower animals and in man, increasing attention is being paid to the use of phototherapy in diseases influenced by daily and seasonal rhythms.[1]

Phototherapy: Current Perspectives

The first thing to be taken into account when considering the use of phototherapy in psychiatry, as with any treatment in medicine, is the range of disorders for which it may be appropriate. New and innovative medical treatments carry the risk of being initially perceived of as panaceas, and are often subsequently overused or inappropriately used during their introduction to the marketplace. With a drug, this initial phase of misuse is then frequently followed by a period during which the treatment falls out of favor with the medical profession and lay public after the high expectations are unmet or side effects are discovered. A careful matching of the treatment to the patient is warranted, therefore, not only for the health of the patient but also for the broader public health implications of the treatment.

Phototherapy has been demonstrated to have significant effects in the treatment of several disease spectra of interest to psychiatrists, including affective illness and chronobiological disorders. It has also been used with some success in the treatment of psychiatric disorders which have a "seasonal component." In this paper, we will focus on the proven uses of phototherapy in psychiatry, particularly as an antidepressant, explain the theoretical and physiological bases for its use, and provide guidelines for the use of phototherapy by the psychiatrist in a clinical setting.

Light and the Human Central Nervous System

Light has been shown to have a number of physiological effects on the human central nervous system that may be separate from its visual effects. Very bright—but not dim—light is capable of suppressing the production and release of the pineal hormone melatonin[2] and of setting the clock times, within a certain range, for circadian rhythms.[3] Light has also been demonstrated to increase arousal[4-5] in normal subjects.

Light and Seasonal Responses

Seasonal behaviors in animals, such as activity, reproduction, and migration, are triggered by changes in the duration of daily sunlight.[6-8] Humans also show seasonal patterns, for example, in the incidence of menarche, birthrate, the growth rate of children, hemoglobin and hormonal levels, mortality, and suicide.[9] Like circannual rhythms in animals, human seasonal changes may be influenced by the duration of sunshine.[9]

Seasonal Affective Disorder

Seasonal affective disorder (SAD) is a cyclic mood disorder characterized by fall/winter depressions alternating with periods of euthymia or hypomania in the spring and summer.[10] Four-fifths of SAD patients are female, and most are mildly to moderately depressed, with rare suicide attempts and psychosis but with a high degree of work and interpersonal dysfunction. Criteria for SAD are:

(1) A history of depression fulfilling Research Diagnostic Criteria (RDC) for major affective disorders, depressed.[11]
(2) A history of at least two consecutive years of fall/winter depressive episodes remitting in the spring or summer.
(3) The absence of other major (Axis I) psychiatric disorders or psychosocially contributive seasonal variables.[10]

Most SAD patients fit RDC criteria for bipolar II disorder (a history of major depression and hypomania), although a smaller number are bipolar I (major depression and mania) or unipolar. SAD patients often fulfill the DSM-III-R mood disorder subclassification of having a "seasonal pattern."[12]

SAD typically begins in the second or third decade of life, although we

Affective Disorders

have identified several children with the disorder.[13] The majority of SAD patients complain of certain "atypical" depressive symptoms, including hypersomnia, increased appetite, weight gain, and fatigue, which are relatively uncommon in major depression.[14] Moreover, many SAD patients report symptoms (daytime drowsiness, carbohydrate craving) that are not diagnostic of either major or atypical depression but may occur in sleep disorders[15] or eating disorders.[16] SAD women have an increased incidence of the premenstrual syndrome, characterized by "atypical" depressive symptoms, which often worsen during their winter depressive episodes.[17] Table 1 shows the winter symptoms profile of SAD patients studied at the National Institute of Mental Health from 1981 to 1985.

Untreated, SAD depressive episodes typically end in the spring and are frequently succeeded by a constellation of symptoms opposite to those seen in the winter. Summer manifestations usually include mild hypomania with elated or irritable mood, increased libido, socially outgoing behavior, in-

TABLE 1
Self-reported Wintertime SAD Symptoms (N = 156)

		Percentage of patients
Decreased activity:		96
Changes in affect:	Sadness	94
	Irritability	79
	Anxiety	84
Changes in appetite:	Increase	66
	Decrease	19
	Mixed	14
	No change	1
	Carbohydrate craving	67 (N = 123)
Changes in weight:	Increase	72
	Decrease	13
	Mixed	1
	No change	15
Changes in sleep:	Earlier onset	60
	Later wakening	69
	Increased duration	79
	Change in quality	77
	Daytime drowsiness	82 (N = 123)
Decreased libido:		62
Difficulties at work:		88
Interpersonal difficulties:		94
Depression milder nearer equator:		74 (N = 71)
Menstrual difficulties:		61 (N = 116)

TABLE 2
Clinical and Demographic Features of SAD (N = 156)

Age (years): 40.2 ± 10.1

Age of onset (years): 22.8 ± 10.9

Sex ratio (F/M): 127:29 (4:1)

Length of depressions (months): 4.3 ± 1.4

Psychiatric Diagnosis:*	Bipolar II	83%
	Bipolar I	7%
	Unipolar	10%
Family history (at least one affected first-degree relative):	Major Affective Disorder	69%
	SAD	37%
	Alcohol Abuse	19%
Previous treatment history:	No treatment	46%
	Antidepressants	30%
	Lithium	13%
	Thyroid	9%
	Hospitalization	12%
	Electroconvulsive therapy	0%

*by Research Diagnostic Criteria

creased creativity, increased energy, decreased need for sleep, diminished appetite, and loss of winter weight. Not all patients show hypomanic symptoms during the summer. Some (10%) have unipolar winter depressions without summer symptoms, while others (7%) have had episodes of mania (usually in the summer) in addition to their winter depressions (Table 2).

Family history data suggest that SAD may be genetically related to other forms of affective illness since over a third of SAD patients have a first-degree relative with a seasonal affective disorder. Moreover, more than two-thirds of SAD patients have a first-degree relative with a major affective disorder (Table 2). These results are comparable to the results of recent epidemiological studies showing increased rates of depression in first-degree relatives of depressed patients.[18] The following is a typical case of a patient with SAD.

G. R. is a 40-year-old white male who has noted dramatic effects of sunlight and the changing seasons on his mood and behavior since childhood. Although raised in the Northeast, he has spent most of his adult life in the South, which had "relatively mild" winters. Difficulties began several years ago when, due to a job promotion, he was transferred to a windowless office. Prior to that time, G. had always aligned his desk to face his window "to receive the full benefit of the sun," and had arranged his work schedule so that he could be at the desk during the hours of highest light intensity.

Soon after settling into his windowless office in the fall of 1982, G. noted the onset of increased fatigue and daytime sleepiness with actual napping, an incessant craving for chocolate and sweets, slowed thinking with inability to concentrate on his new work, and feelings of despair, depression, and severe anxiety. He stated that he "barely made it through the winter" and kept his door locked at work because of a fear that someone would find him asleep at his desk.

By late winter, G. began to "self-medicate" with sunlight, spending as much time as possible outside on sunny days, even though it was still quite cold outside. His concentration slowly began to improve and by the late spring he found himself "flying high," with vastly increased energy and creativity, and a decreased need for sleep. He then started and completed several major projects within a short period of time, impressing his superiors and leading to another promotion — this time to an office with a window.

G. did well, with only a mild decrement in the winter, until the following year, when he was promoted again and sent to company headquarters in New England. Here the winters were not only more severe, but he was again given a windowless office. As the fall approached, G. became very anxious and increasingly incapable of functioning at work. He subsequently became depressed and was contemplating suicide when a private psychiatric consultation led to his referral to our program.

Within three days of beginning treatment of six hours of daily phototherapy, the patient's depression began lifting. Concentration, sleep, energy and appetite returned to baseline, and G.'s anxiety diminished considerably. Following our recommendation to his employer, G. was given an office with a window. He did considerably better the following year using the lights prophylactically in the fall.

Biology of Seasonal Affective Disorder

We have studied several biological correlates of SAD. Standard laboratory tests and physical examinations have been unremarkable.[10] Functional probes of the adrenocortical axis (serial serum cortisol and overnight dexamethasone suppression test),[10] thyroid axis (T3, T4, and TSH), carbohydrate metabolism (serum glucose and 5-hour glucose tolerance test),[10,17] and pineal (melatonin)[19] have also not revealed significantly abnormal values in SAD patients. However, comparison of hormonal levels of depressed SAD patients and normal controls during the winter has indicated that SAD patients may have higher basal secretory levels of serum cortisol and prolactin than controls.[20] Moreover, there is evidence that depressed SAD patients may have subjective and physiological alterations in serotonergic function associated with their antidepressant response to phototherapy.[21]

Electroencephalographic (EEG) all-night sleep monitoring has confirmed patients' reports of an increase in total sleep time during winter depressive episodes compared with sleep EEGs obtained during summer periods of euthymia/hypomania. There is also a tendency for slow wave sleep to be reduced in SAD patients during their winter depressions compared with levels of this sleep parameter in normals.[22]

Phototherapy of Seasonal Affective Disorder

Our initial conceptualization of SAD and the use of light as a treatment modality was derived from animal models of seasonal rhythms. In some lower mammals, the length of daily sunlight, or photoperiod, has been shown to be an important stimulus for the induction of seasonal patterns of behavior such as hibernation, reproduction, migration, and coat color changes.[8] We hypothesized that if winter depressive symptoms were due to an abnormal physiological response to the short days of winter, then a typical summer clinical picture could be induced in seasonally affected patients by artificially lengthening their daylight hours to approximate those of summertime.

Working from this photoperiodic model, we initially used five to six hours of daily phototherapy given in divided doses at the ends of the day. Recently, however, our group and others have obtained significant antidepressant effects using as little as two hours of daily exposure to bright light,[23-25] and some patients have responded to as little as 15 minutes of daily phototherapy. Obviously, these findings have practical implications as well as raising theoretical questions regarding the mechanism of phototherapy's antidepressant effect. For example, is the timing of light exposure critical to its effect? Lewy and colleagues have argued that only morning light can successfully treat SAD based on the theory that the disorder is due to an abnormal shift of the sleep-wake cycle into the morning hours.[23] This theory appears to be refuted by at least two studies showing that evening light alone has antidepressant effects,[25,26] and also by our recent finding that midday phototherapy is as effective as morning phototherapy.[27] Our current recommendations are to use at least two to four hours of light per day at a time that is convenient for the patient. However, if no response occurs after a week of treatment, it is worth shifting the light treatment to another time of day. As with many pharmacologically active treatments, it is quite possible that light may have different effects at different time points of the human circadian cycle. However, these details remain to be determined.

We have administered light in both outpatient and inpatient settings using a box containing eight bright white full-spectrum fluorescent lamps (Vita-lite® 40W) behind a neutral density plastic diffusing screen. Light intensity measured 90 cm from the light box was approximately 2500 lux. In all of our studies patients have been instructed to sit 90 cm in front of the light box and to glance briefly at the light once or twice a minute while engaged in reading or desk work. Table 3 lists some of the clinical features of phototherapy.

We initially chose 2500 lux as the intensity of light treatment for SAD patients based upon its proven biological activity in humans, particularly its capacity to suppress the secretion of melatonin, which is known to be a crucial endocrine modulator of seasonal rhythms in many lower mammals. In most studies of phototherapy with SAD patients that have compared the effects of bright (2500 lux) light with the intensity of light ordinarily found in the home or office (100–300 lux), bright light has been significantly more effective as an antidepressant. We believe that this antidepressant effect is due to the light's specific biological activity. However, it should be noted that the possibility of a placebo response to light, such as the famous "Hawthorne effect" demonstrated years ago in industrial studies,[29] cannot be completely rejected due to the difficulty of administering light in a double-blind fashion.[30]

Our choice of full-spectrum light for the treatment of SAD was based on the desire to mimic the spectrum of sunlight within the human visual range. While full-spectrum fluorescent light has been demonstrated to have antidepressant effects, other types of light, e.g., incandescent and limited-spectrum fluorescent,[32] may also be effective for the treatment of seasonal mood disorders. However, we are unaware of controlled comparisons of the antidepressant effects of full-spectrum fluorescent versus other types of light

TABLE 3
Clinical Features of Phototherapy

---

position of lights: patient's head should be about 3 feet from lights

light intensity: 2500 lux (eight 40 watt Vitalites® at 3 feet)

light wavelength: full spectrum*

timing: 2–4 hours of light per day given at time convenient to patient (some patients may need up to 6 hours of daily light)

duration of treatment: fall/winter to early spring/summer

latency to response and relapse: 3–7 days

non-responders: will usually respond to standard antidepressants

partial responders: light may be used together with antidepressants

side effects: headache, eye strain — will generally subside, standard analgesics often benefit

irritability, hypomania — may need to decrease the duration of daily light exposure

*incandescent may be effective

and therefore we cannot currently recommend the use of other types of light.

Several strategies may be considered for the use of phototherapy with SAD patients. The physician may employ it acutely for patients once a firm diagnosis of SAD has been established. In patients whose diagnosis has been previously established, phototherapy may also be used prophylactically. For example, phototherapy may be started at a point in the fall or winter prior to the approximate date when the patient began to "slide" into his or her depression in the past. Such a strategy may be particularly useful when the patient's depressive symptoms have had severe effects on his or her job or personal affairs and phototherapy has been successful in alleviating the depression. Most SAD patients manifest a gradual, rather than abrupt, onset of depressive symptoms — often over a period of weeks. It should also be noted that diagnosis of SAD patients is generally reliable based on their reported history of recurrent winter-only depressive episodes with atypical symptoms.

Response to Phototherapy in Seasonal Affective Disorder

In our experience approximately 80% of patients with diagnosed SAD have responded to phototherapy alone when given as detailed above. A much smaller percent have required treatment with antidepressants in addition to the phototherapy. Unlike the response to standard antidepressant medications, response to phototherapy usually occurs within three to five days of initiating treatment. Once patients' depressions have remitted, most will maintain a euthymic state as long as the phototherapy is continued. Some will become hypomanic within the first few days of treatment, a condition which may necessitate decreasing the number of hours of treatment. Clinical judgment is key to titrating the "dose" of light required for treatment, since different patients require different durations of daily exposure to bright light and there is currently no known physiological measure on which to base a dose-response curve of bright lights' antidepressant effect.

SAD patients should generally be maintained on phototherapy until the onset of spring, although some patients will need to use the lights into the beginning of summer. In our experience, withdrawal from lights before the end of winter often leads to a relapse of SAD symptoms. Interestingly, this relapse usually does not occur immediately, but takes about three days, which is approximately the amount of time necessary for the antidepressant response to occur.

Prediction of response to treatment is increasingly being recognized as important to the modern practice of psychiatry. The ability to measure and predict outcomes has not only become necessary for participation in third-party reimbursement plans, but has also become increasingly feasible with the increased emphasis on quantifiable biological interventions. Attention is now being paid to numerous diagnostic subgroups in terms of treatment efficacy.

Because many of the cardinal symptoms of SAD fall within the spectrum of depressions often labeled "atypical," standard rating scales of depression such as the Hamilton Depression Scale (HDS),[33] were found to be inadequate for characterization of the illness. In fact, apparent improvement on some of the typical depression items on these scales, such as an increase in appetite or duration of sleep, actually indicate a worsening of SAD. To address this problem, we added seven supplementary items to the HDS to reflect more adequately the complaints of SAD patients (see Table 4). These supplementary items, which we have validated for SAD[34] may also be of use in evaluating other forms of atypical depression.

In an attempt to predict the outcome of phototherapy in SAD, we recently analyzed the symptoms accounting for significant amounts of variance in SAD patients who responded to phototherapy.[35] We found that several symptoms are particularly important in the antidepressant response to phototherapy, including fatigability, hypersomnia, anxiety, and diurnal variation. We are now investigating the relationship of these symptoms to the mechanism of phototherapeutic action in SAD.

Seasonal Component

We have encountered numerous affectively disturbed patients and some thought disordered patients with fall or winter exacerbations of their illnesses. It has been our experience that many of these patients may be helped during their winter declines by the supplementation of other treatment modalities with phototherapy. This light supplementation has been particularly useful with severely depressed unipolar or bipolar I patients. Use of phototherapy with these patients may be done in much the same manner as described for other SAD patients, giving two to four hours of light per day in divided doses. It should be emphasized, however, that phototherapy in psychiatric patients with a seasonal component to their illness is an adjuvant therapy, and is not intended to be the mainstay of treatment.

Nonseasonally Depressed Patients

Several studies have investigated the effects of bright artificial light in nonseasonally depressed patients. Kripke et al. employed phototherapy in the treatment of major nonseasonal depression using a paradigm of one hour of

TABLE 4
Supplementary HRS Items for SAD

1. Fatigability (or low energy level or feelings of being heavy, leaden, weighed down)
   0. Does not feel more fatigued than usual
   1. Feels more fatigued than usual but this has not impaired function significantly; less frequent than in (2)
   2. More fatigued than usual; at least one hour a day; at least three days a week.
   3. Fatigued much of the time most days.
   4. Fatigued almost all the time.
2. Social Withdrawal
   0. Interacts with other people as usual.
   1. Less interested in socializing with others but continues to do so.
   2. Interacting less with other people in social (optional) situations.
   3. Interacting less with other people in work or family situations (i.e. where this is necessary).
   4. Marked withdrawal from others in family or work situations.
3. Appetite Increase
   0. No increase in appetite.
   1. Wants to eat a little more than usual.
   2. Wants to eat somewhat more than usual.
   3. Wants to eat much more than usual.
4. Increased Eating
   0. Is not eating more than usual.
   1. Is eating a little more than usual.
   2. Is eating somewhat more than usual.
   3. Is eating much more than usual.
5. Carbohydrate Craving
   0. No change in food preference.
   1. Eating more carbohydrates (starches or sugars) than before.
   2. Eating much more carbohydrates than before.
   3. Irresistible craving for sweets or starches.
6. Weight Gain
   0. No weight gain.
   1. Probable weight gain associated with present illness.
   2. Definite weight gain (according to patient).
7. Hypersomnia (Compare sleep length to euthymic and not to hypomanic sleep length. If this cannot be established, use 8 hours)
   0. No increase in sleep length.
   1. At least 1 hour increase in sleep length.
   2. 2+ hour increase in sleep length.
   3. 3+ hour increase in sleep length.
   4. 4+ hour increase in sleep length.
   Was euthymic sleep length used? Yes _____ No _____
   Was 8 hour sleep length used? Yes _____ No _____

bright "warm white" light administration in the early morning.[36] They obtained a small but significant antidepressant effect which could not be ascribed to sleep deprivation. A follow-up study using five days of treatment with two hours of bright light in divided doses failed to demonstrate a significant antidepressant effect.[37] Dietzel et al. obtained a more robust, but transient, antidepressant response when exposing four seasonal and six nonseasonal depressed patients and ten controls of seven hours of bright (>1500 lux) full spectrum light on a single day.[38] Lewy et al. have demonstrated that manic-depressive patients may be supersensitive to light, at least as measured by the suppression of melatonin production,[39] but it is unclear whether this observation has treatment implications. To our knowledge, bright light has not yet been systematically tried in the treatment of other psychiatric conditions. We conclude that it is still too early to tell what role phototherapy may play in the treatment of nonseasonal depression and other major psychiatric disorders.

Chronobiological Disorders

Several investigators have recently reported that bright artificial light may be useful in the treatment of certain disturbances of the sleep/wake cycle which have a circadian or seasonal basis. Lingjaerde et al. described a seasonal insomnia apparently unaccompanied by significant depression that was at least partially treatable with exposure to one hour of bright light in the morning.[40] Several investigators have suggested the treatment of circadian rhythm disturbances, such as jet lag and shift-work fatigue, by exposure to bright light at specific points of the 24-hour cycle.[23,41-42] One of the major problems of these studies for clinicians is that they have involved small number of patients in uncontrolled studies and have not yet been replicated. We are confident that more work will be done in this area and expect to see a greater use of phototherapy in psychiatry in the future.

Side Effects of Phototherapy

Some patients initially complain that the intensity of light used in the treatment of SAD causes eye strain. In our experience, most of these patients acclimate to the light within a few days without ill effects. Moreover, the National Eye Institute found no evidence of physical damage to the eye after two weeks of six hours daily exposure to the Vitalites® we use in the treatment of SAD. To our knowledge, other types of lights have not been tested for retinal toxicity after phototherapy, and we therefore cannot recommend their usage. We should also note that studies of the potential long-term effects of phototherapy have yet to be performed.

A few patients complain of light-induced headaches which, although transient and usually easily controlled by standard analgesics, may necessitate cessation of treatment in particularly bothersome cases. Some patients become excessively activated when using the lights and occasionally frankly hypomanic. In our experience, cases of phototherapy-induced hypomania have been easily managed by decreasing the patients' exposure to the lights by an hour or two. We have not seen any cases of frank mania precipitated by phototherapy in strictly diagnosed SAD patients, nor have we had to use tranquilizers to control symptoms of light-induced hypomania. However, use of the lights too late in the evening may result in an initial insomnia characterized by difficulty falling asleep.

References

1. Wurtman RJ, Baum MJ, Potts JT (eds.): The medical and biological effects of light. *Ann NY Acad Sci* 453, 1985.

2. Lewy AJ et al.: Light suppresses melatonin secretion in humans. *Science* 210:1267–1269, 1980.

3. Wever RA, Polasek J, Wildgruber CM: Bright light affects human circadian rhythms. *Pflugers Arch* 396:85–87, 1983.

4. Chavez ME, Delay ER: Effects of ambient illumination over days in human vigilance performance. *Percept Mot Skills* 55:667–672, 1982.

5. Kallman WM, Isaac W: Altering arousal in humans by varying ambient sensory conditions. *Percept Mot Skills* 44:19–22, 1977.

6. Gwinner E: Circannual systems. In Aschoff J (ed.): *Handbook of Behavioral Neurobiology*, vol. 4, Plenum Press, New York, 1981, pp. 391–410.

7. Gwinner E: Annual rhythms: Perspective. In Aschoff J (ed.): *Handbook of Behavioral Neurobiology*, vol. 4, Plenum Press, New York, 1981, pp. 381–389.

8. Hoffman K: Photoperiodism in vertebrates. In Aschoff J (ed.): *Handbook of Behavioral Neurobiology*, vol. 4, Plenum Press, New York, 1981, pp. 449–473.

9. Aschoff J: Annual rhythms in man. In Aschoff J (ed.): *Handbook of Behavioral Neurobiology*, vol. 4, Plenum Press, New York, 1981, pp. 475–487.

10. Rosenthal NE et al.: Seasonal affective disorder: A description of the syndrome and preliminary findings with light therapy. *Arch Gen Psychiatry* 41:72–80, 1984.

11. Spitzer RL, Endicott J, Robins E: Research diagnostic criteria: Rationale and reliability. *Arch Gen Psychiatry* 35:773–782, 1978.

12. *Diagnostic and Statistical Manual of Mental Disorders Third Edition–Revised (DSM III-R)*, American Psychiatric Association, Washington, DC, 1987.

13. Rosenthal NE et al: Seasonal affective disorder in children and adolescents. *Am J Psychiatry* 143:356–358, 1986.

14. Liebowitz MR et al.: Phenelzine vs. imipramine in atypical depression. *Arch Gen Psychiatry* 41:669–667, 1984.

15. Garvey MJ, Mungas D, Tollefson GD: Hypersomnia in major depressive disorders. *J Affective Disord* 6:283–286, 1984.

16. Dement W, Guilleminault C (eds.): Diagnostic classification of sleep and arousal disorders. *Sleep* 2:1–154, 1979.

17. Jacobsen FM, Wehr TA, Rosenthal NE: The pineal and seasonal reproduction in seasonal affective disorder. In Pancheri P, Zichella L (eds.): *Biorhythms and Stress in the Physiopathology of Reproduction*, Hemisphere Publication Corporation, Washington, DC, in press.

18. Weissman MM et al.: Psychiatric disorders in the relatives of probands with affective disorders. *Arch Gen Psychiatry* 41:13–21, 1985.

19. Rosenthal NE et al.: The role of melatonin in seasonal affective disorder (SAD) and phototherapy. In Wurtman RJ, Waldhauser F (eds.): *Melatonin in Humans*, Center for Brain Sciences and Metabolism Charitable Trust, Cambridge, Mass., 1985.

20. Jacobsen FM et al: Neuroendocrine responses to 5-hydroxytryptophan in seasonal affective disorder (SAD). *Arch Gen Psychiatry* 44(12):1086–1091, 1987.

21. Jacobsen FM et al: Subjective and physiological responses of patients with seasonal affective disorder and controls to intravenous m-CPP. *Abstr 42nd Ann Mtg Soc Biol Psychiatry*, p. 236, 1987.

22. Rosenthal NE et al.: Seasonal affective disorder and phototherapy. In Wurtman RJ, Baum JT (eds.): The Medical and Biological Effects of Light. *Ann NY Acad Sci* 453:260–269, 1985.

23. Lewy AJ, Sack RL, Singer CM: Treating phase typed chronobiologic sleep and mood disorders using appropriately timed bright artificial light. *Psychopharmacol Bull* 21(3):368–372, 1985.

24. Wirz-Justice A et al.: Light treatment of seasonal affective disorder in Switzerland. *Acta Psychiatr Scand*, in press.

25. Hellekson CJ, Kline JA, Rosenthal NE: Phototherapy of winter depression in Alaska. *Proceedings, IV World Cong. Biol. Psychiatry*, Philadelphia, 1985.

26. James SP et al.: Treatment of seasonal affective disorder with evening light. *Brit J Psychiatry* 147:424–428, 1985.

27. Jacobsen FM et al: Morning- versus midday- phototherapy of seasonal affective disorder. *Am J Psychiatry* 144(7):1301–1305, 1987.

28. Lewy AJ et al.: The use of bright light in treatment of chronobiologic sleep and mood disorders: The phase-response curve. *Psychopharmacol Bull* 19:523–525, 1983.

29. Roethlisberger FJ, Dickson WJ: *Management and the Worker*, Harvard University Press, Cambridge, MA, 1939.

30. Rosenthal NE et al.: Phototherapy for seasonal affective disorder: Dealing with the placebo effect when an intervention cannot be administered "blind." Abstract of the Annual Meeting, American College of Neuropsychopharmacology, Vanderbilt Univ., Nashville, 1985.

31. Yerevanian BI et al: Effects of bright incandescent lights on seasonal and nonseasonal major depressive disorder. *Psychiatry Research* 18:355–364, 1986.

32. Rosenthal NE et al: Phototherapy for seasonal affective disorder. *J Biol Rhythms*, in press.

33. Hamilton M: Development of a rating scale for primary depressive illness. *Brit J Soc Clin Psychol* 6:278–296, 1967.

34. Rosenthal NE, Heffernan MM: Bulimia, carbohydrate craving, and depression: a central connection? In Wurtman RJ, Wurtman JJ (eds.): *Nutrition and the Brain*, vol 7. Raven Press, New York: 1986, pp. 139–166.

35. Jacobsen FM et al.: Predictors of response to phototherapy in seasonal affective disorder. Submitted for publication.

36. Kripke DF, Risch SC, Janowsky D: Bright white light alleviates depression. *Psychiatry Res* 10:105–112, 1983.

37. Kripke DF: Therapeutic effects of bright light in depression. In Wurtman RJ, Baum MJ, Potts JT (eds.): The medical and biological effects of light. *Ann NY Acad Sci* 453:270–281, 1985.

38. Dietzel M, Saletu B, Lesch OM: Bright light treatment of depressive illness; polysomnographic data-analysis. *J Interdiscip Cycle Res* 16(2):165–166, 1985.

39. Lewy AJ et al.: Supersensitivity to light: Possible trait marker for manic-depressive illness. *Am J Psychiatry* 142(6):725–727, 1985.

40. Lingjaerde O, Bratlid T, Hansen T: Insomnia during the "dark period" in Northern Norway. An explorative, controlled trial with light treatment. *Acta Psychiatr Scan* 71(5):506–512, 1985.

41. Wever RA: Use of light to treat jet lag: Differential effects of normal and bright artificial light on human circadian rhythms. In Wurtman RJ, Baum MT, Potts JT (eds.): The Medical and Biological Effects of Light. *Ann NY Acad Sci* 453:282–304, 1985.

42. Lewy AJ et al: Antidepressant and circadian phase-shifting effects of light. *Science* 235:325–324, 1987.

Index